CONTENTS

DAILY
DISCIPLESHIP

A DEVOTIONAL

LEROY EIMS

NAVPRESS

BRINGING TRUTH TO LIFE

NavPress Publishing Group

P.O. Box 35001, Colorado Springs, Colorado 80935

The Navigators is an international Christian organization. Our mission is to reach, disciple, and equip people to know Christ and to make Him known through successive generations. We envision multitudes of diverse people in the United States and every other nation who have a passionate love for Christ, live a lifestyle of sharing Christ's love, and multiply spiritual laborers among those without Christ.

NavPress is the publishing ministry of The Navigators. NavPress publications help believers learn biblical truth and apply what they learn to their lives and ministries. Our mission is to stimulate spiritual formation among our readers.

ISBN 1-57683-097-7

Cover photo by Avenue Des Champs Elysees-Paris by Ron Chapple/FPG International

Some of the anecdotal illustrations in this book are true to life and are included with the permission of the persons involved. All other illustrations are composites of real situations, and any resemblance to people living or dead is coincidental.

Printed in the United States of America

1 2 3 4 5 6 7 8 9 10 11 12 13 14 15 / 05 04 03 02 01 00 99 98

INTRODUCTION

Daily Discipleship presents 312 practical devotional readings dedicated to the classic themes of discipleship and spiritual growth.

The readings—adapted from material written by long-time Navigator LeRoy Eims and originally delivered as radio messages—will take you through one year. These daily thoughts focus on a variety of themes that influence many aspects of every believer's life: God, the Word, faith, prayer, basic Christian beliefs, sin, holiness, spiritual growth, vision, calling, the kingdom, leadership, and witness.

These daily devotions reflect on a disciple's growth, from the foundational knowledge of God and the Word . . . to the heart changes that result in a godly life . . . to the outward actions that testify of a life surrendered to the lordship of Jesus Christ—a picture of the life devoted to growing and maturing in Christ.

It is the author's prayer that the reader might be greatly encouraged and exhorted through reading this devotional book, "so that the body of Christ may be built up until we all reach unity in the faith and in the knowledge of the Son of God and become mature, attaining to the whole measure of the fullness of Christ" (Ephesians 4:12-13).

WORDS OF LIFE
Read Genesis 48–50

These commandments that I give you today are to be upon your hearts. Impress them on your children. Talk about them when you sit at home and . . . when you lie down and when you get up.

DEUTERONOMY 6:6-7

Do you like flattery, or would you rather have someone shoot straight with you? Maybe your answer is, "Well, I'd like them to shoot straight, but not too straight." The truth is sometimes hard to take.

Genesis 48–50 shows us Jacob, the ancient patriarch, gathering his sons to his side and shooting straight by giving each of them a word from God. Jacob did not hesitate to tell his sons the truth, even though, in some cases, it was not pleasant and, I'm sure, not easy to do. He is an Old Testament example of the New Testament words of Paul urging us to speak the truth in love.

Today there is such a mad scramble to protect a person's self-image that often the truth of the matter gets compromised. But in the Scriptures we see ourselves as we really are in the context of God's love and holiness.

May we lead our families into the Word and daily expose them to the truths found in Scripture. Who can know the impact it will have on their lives?

> *Lord, so often I make time for everything else but reading Your Word and listening to Your voice. Help me to put You first in my life and to lead my family by the light of Your Word. Amen.*

To Ponder: What better thing can I do than encourage my family to hunger for the eternal Word of God?

FULL OF COMPASSION
Read Exodus 21–24

We love because he first loved us.

1 JOHN 4:19

Has anyone ever told you there are two Gods in the Bible—a cruel God of the Old Testament and a loving God of the New Testament? Nothing could be further from the truth! Scripture portrays God's compassion for His creation, and especially for those who might be taken advantage of because of their weakness or position in society.

For instance, He gave protective laws concerning servants who had suffered abuse under the heavy hand of taskmasters. Look at God's concern toward the stranger, the widow, and the fatherless. He says, "Do not mistreat an alien or oppress him, for you were aliens in Egypt. Do not take advantage of a widow or an orphan. If you do and they cry out to me, I will certainly hear their cry" (Exodus 22:21-24).

Not only were the destitute, the timid, and the helpless not to be abused, but God's people were to be ready to lend them a hand—to comfort and assist them, and to show them kindness.

God's great compassionate heart is toward all His creation. For instance, the land was not to be abused or overworked. Every seventh year the land was to be given rest. So also the vineyard and the olive grove.

Scripture sets forth the God of the Old Testament as filled with compassion, care, and creative ways to watch out for those who might not be able to watch out for themselves, and puts to rest the accusations of those who portray Him otherwise.

Lord, Your love, mercy, and fairness are the same throughout the Bible. Great is your faithfulness to me!

To Ponder: God *is* love!

THE LIVING GOD
Read Exodus 32–34

This day I call heaven and earth as witnesses against you that I have set before you life and death, blessings and curses. Now choose life, so that you and your children may live.

DEUTERONOMY 30:19

Many Christians are crippled by their limited idea of God. We see the same problem in Exodus 32–34, describing a sad and bitter time in the life of God's people.

Moses was up on the mount with God, receiving the two tables of testimony—tables of stone written with the finger of God. Down below, it was another story. The Israelites decided to trade their allegiance from the true and living God to a golden calf made with hands.

"Come make us gods that will go before us," the people said to Aaron, who was in charge while Moses was away. But wait a minute. Didn't they already have a God who went before them in a pillar of cloud by day and a pillar of fire by night? Of course they did. But they wanted a god they could control. They wanted a god who would stop when they wanted to stop and go when they wanted to go.

Meanwhile, back on the mountain, the Lord spoke to Moses and said, "Go down, because your people, whom you brought up out of Egypt, have become corrupt. They have been quick to turn away from what I commanded them" (Exodus 32:7-8).

Moses immediately began to pray, and he prayed from the depth of his soul. "Oh what a great sin these people have committed!" he said. "But now, please forgive their sin" (Exodus 32:31,32).

Moses was a man who knew the Living God face-to-face in all His glory, and it made him a humble, compassionate man of prayer. He never forgot that it was God's hand that blessed his leadership. It was God's voice that led him.

Lord, You alone are the giver of life. I choose to listen to Your voice and follow You. Amen.

To Ponder: Am I following the Living God or a golden calf of my own making?

9

STAYING ON COURSE
Read 1 Samuel 20–23

For this God is our God for ever and ever;
he will be our guide even to the end.

PSALM 48:14

In today's passage we find David going to Jonathan to find out why Saul was trying to kill him. Listen to Jonathan's answer: "You are not going to die! My father doesn't do anything, great or small, without confiding in me. Why would he hide this from me? It's not so!" Was Jonathan trying to lure David into a trap? No, of course not. If David could depend on the loyalty of anyone, it was that of Jonathan. Counsel can be wrong, even when given by someone who truly loves you and has your best interests at heart.

After my wife and I became Christians, we decided that I should quit my job and we should go to Northwestern College for some Bible training. Most of our friends and relatives tried to talk us out of it. They were well meaning, but misdirected. When we need to make decisions, we need to look to the God who guides us. The Bible says "in multitude of counselors there is safety" (Proverbs 24:6 KJV).

In addition to many counselors, we also must look for direction in the Bible and from the witness of the Holy Spirit.

A Christian seeking to know the will of God is like a ship captain who must line up three lights in order to make a safe approach into the harbor. For Christians, those three lights are the Bible, the witness of the Holy Spirit, and the counsel of godly friends. When the three lights look like one, then he is on the right course.

Lord, "Your Word is a lamp to my feet and a light for my path.
. . . My heart is set on keeping Your decrees to the very end"
(Psalm 119:105,112). Amen.

To Ponder: We should carefully line up the "three lights" when seeking the right course.

OUR GREAT GOD
Read 2 Samuel 21–24

The LORD is my shepherd, I shall not be in want.

PSALM 23:1

David's life was something like a roller coaster. At one point we find him on the mountaintop, rejoicing in a great victory. Turn the page and we find him in the pit, despairing of life and harassed by his enemies. Through it all there is one constant. David knew God in a personal way, and he praised God and worshiped Him for who He is.

David's words give us a marvelous portrait of God. There is none like Him; no one can be compared to the Lord. The promises of men may go unfulfilled, but the Word of the Lord is true and trustworthy. David goes on to say: God is my rock, my strength and power, my hiding place, my fortress in whom I am safe, my high tower, my stronghold. Am I in distress? God is my deliverer. Are the fiery darts of the enemy pelting me? God is my shield. Am I pursued by the enemy of my soul? The Lord is my refuge.

What does all this mean to me? If the problems of life threaten to sink me under the load, He is my support; I can cast all my cares upon Him. If I've lost my direction in the dark, His Word is my lamp, showing me the way. If I am oppressed, He saves me from him who seeks the ruin of my soul.

If the Lord is our God, we will submit our will to Him and depend on His power, wisdom, and goodness to see us safely home.

Lord, I want to be like David. When my soul is downcast, put a song of praise in my mouth, and show me how to worship You for the great God that You are. Amen.

To Ponder: The very God that David described is *my* God. He is the same yesterday, today, and forever.

GOD IN YOU
Read 1 Kings 9–11

*What agreement is there between the temple of God
and idols? For we are the temple of the living God.*

2 CORINTHIANS 6:16

The Vietnam War memorial in Washington, D.C., has become one of
the most visited and emotional sites in the nation's capital. What sets
it apart from other memorials? Carved into that black granite wall are
more than 58,000 names of Americans who gave their lives building
a foundation for freedom.

In 1 Kings 9, we find Solomon, having built the temple, now dedi-
cating it to God. Here is God's response, verse 3: "I have heard the
prayer and plea you have made before me; I have consecrated this
temple, which you have built, by putting my name there forever. My
eyes and my heart will always be there."

Solomon built a physical temple, but only God could hallow it and
consecrate it to Himself. In the New Testament, God tells us of living
temples—the people of God. And only God can sanctify us to Himself.
He promises that those whom He sets apart for Himself have His eye,
His heart, His love, and His care upon them.

Sanctification begins with God's call to us in Christ. It is put in
motion when we respond by faith and give our lives to Him. And it
continues with God's work of molding us to be more like the person
of Jesus Christ. We must dedicate ourselves to Him and cooperate by
obeying His commands, but the sanctifying belongs to Him.

The apostle Paul wrote, "Being confident of this, that he who
began a good work in you will carry it on to completion until the day
of Christ Jesus" (Philippians 1:6).

*LORD, when I get discouraged by my inability to be holy,
remind me that I can do nothing unless You do it in me.
Amen.*

To Ponder: Holiness does not come from observing a list of do's and
don'ts; it comes from God's supernatural work in me as I obey
Him.

POWER WITHOUT END
Read Exodus 9:13-16

For the word of God is living and active. Sharper than any double-edged sword, it penetrates even to dividing soul and spirit, joints and marrow; it judges the thoughts and attitudes of the heart.

HEBREWS 4:12

A family I know was just about to leave the house to go to church when all the lights went out—the city was experiencing a power failure. *No problem,* they thought. *When we come back from church it will be restored.* Then it occurred to them they couldn't leave—they had an automatic garage door that opened on electricity. So there they stood, thwarted by a power failure.

An electrical power failure causes problems every which way you turn. The same is true of a power failure within our lives. But unlike a failing electricity source, the Bible is very clear that there's always an abundance of power available to see us through even the most trying and difficult circumstances.

For the Christian, the source of power is God, and God never runs out of power or fails in anything. If that's true, how can there ever be a spiritual power failure in a believer's life? The problem arises when we get cut off from the power supply. And one of the primary means by which God transmits His mighty power to His people is through His Word. The Word of God is food that sustains and empowers our soul and spirit.

The apostle Paul spoke of being nourished upon the words of faith. How goes it with you? Are you making time each day to nourish your soul on the Word of God? Don't let a power failure happen in your life.

Lord, thank You for Your life-giving Word. Amen.

To Ponder: For Thine is the kingdom and the power and the glory forever.

LIVING BY THE WORD
Read Deuteronomy 1–4

When your words came, I ate them; they were my joy and my heart's delight, for I bear your name, O LORD God Almighty.

JEREMIAH 15:16

In the first few chapters of Deuteronomy, as the people of God stand on the brink of the Promised Land, they are faced with a formidable foe. Their instructions do not concern the strategy and tactics of battle, but their duty to God. Why? Because if they would walk with God in obedience and faith, and keep themselves in the light of His favor and blessing, He would go before them—He would fight for them and settle them securely in the land He'd promised to faithful Abraham many years before.

The book of Deuteronomy gives one of the clearest pictures in Scripture of the importance God places on His Word. For instance, we are told that when the nation was given a king, he was to write out a copy of the Word of God with his own hand and read it every day of his life. When the people passed over Jordan, it was to be written on huge stones for the people to see—sort of like billboards along the highway. God's Word was to be read publicly at the Feast of Tabernacles by the priests to all the assembly of Israel.

Jesus, our role model, knew the Word. When He was tempted by Satan in the wilderness, all of His answers came from the pages of Scripture—in fact, from the book of Deuteronomy.

This fifth book of the Old Testament shows us the sort of attention God wants all His people to pay to the Scriptures. We are to learn His Word, remember His Word, and obey it.

God always keeps His Word. His people must do the same.

Lord, thank You that by the Holy Spirit's power Your Word gives me greater insights into Your heart and purposes. Amen.

To Ponder: If we are ignorant of God's Word, how can we recognize and enjoy the promises He has made to us?

LEST YOU BE DECEIVED
Read Deuteronomy 5–7

*I have considered my ways and have
turned my steps to your statutes.*

PSALM 119:59

In today's passage, we see that once again Moses gathered the people together to hear a second copy of the Ten Commandments read so that they might remember and obey, lest, as James 1:22 tells us, they deceive themselves.

When the people heard the commands of God, they responded in a wonderful way. They said, "It was not with our fathers that the LORD made this covenant, but with us, with all of us who are alive here today" (Deuteronomy 5:3). Don't you just love to see people take the Word of God seriously?

For years I have approached the Bible, book by book, chapter by chapter, verse by verse. I go into each chapter on four different roads. The more ways you enter, the more you see. Road one: What does the chapter say? Here I stop and write a summary in my own words. Road two: What does it say that I don't understand? Here I stop and write down the problems and difficulties. Road three: What does it say in other portions of Scripture? Here is where I cross-reference the verses in the chapter. The Bible is its own best commentary, so I want to throw the light of the rest of Scripture on the passage I'm studying. Road four: What does it say to me? Here is where I pray over the passage and write out a personal application God has shown me for my own life. And then I seek to do it.

I encourage you to make the Bible a personal message from the heart of God to you.

Lord, as I read Your Word today, I welcome Your personal word to me, and I will obey it. Amen.

To Ponder: It is not enough simply to know what the Word says; we must obey it.

A COMPASS FOR LIFE
Read Joshua 1–5

But his delight is in the law of the LORD, and on his law he meditates day and night. He is like a tree planted by streams of water, which yields its fruit in season and whose leaf does not wither. Whatever he does prospers.

PSALM 1:2-3

About all most people know of General Joshua is that he "fit the battle of Jericho, and the walls came tumblin' down" (usually as sung by a male quartet). But the first thing we're told about this man in the Old Testament was that he was on speaking terms with God.

Joshua 1:1 says, "After the death of Moses . . . the LORD said to Joshua son of Nun, Moses' aide . . ." Here is what God commanded of his newly appointed leader: "Do not let this Book of the Law depart from your mouth; meditate on it day and night, so that you may be careful to do everything written in it. Then you will be prosperous and successful" (1:8).

Joshua could have said: "What? Think about the words of the Bible, day and night? What about the invasion of Canaan? What about getting all these people across this swollen, rushing river?" But key to Joshua hearing the voice of God and getting his marching orders was his meditation on God's Word.

Years ago, when I was asked to begin a campus ministry, I spent the better part of three weeks reading the Bible, praying, and seeking how God wanted to penetrate this campus with the gospel of Jesus Christ. Out of that time, I received a solid conviction and a strategy for effective evangelism and discipleship.

In our daily walk with Christ and in protracted times alone with Him, meditation on God's Word is a key to opening the door of God's guidance. Take another look at Joshua 1:8; memorize it, meditate on it, and claim it for your own life.

Lord, I have no excuse for getting "lost" when Your Word gives such clear directions for daily walking with You. Amen.

To Ponder: Do you know how to get your direction from God?

MEDITATING ON THE WORD
Read Joshua 1:8

Be diligent in these matters; give yourself wholly to them,
so that everyone may see your progress.

1 TIMOTHY 4:15

———

I have a friend named Sam who for years has practiced meditation. He used to be part of a cult—an Eastern religion that promised inner tranquility. It was supposed to make one serene, confident, joyful. But Sam admitted his meditations resulted in none of those things. As he sat for hours in jeans and bare feet—chanting and meditating—a disturbing question tugged at his heart. *What about my sin?*

One day he met a man who spoke of his own release from the burden of sin through faith in Jesus Christ. Much to Sam's surprise, the man said he, too, practiced meditation, but of a different kind. He meditated on the Bible to find deeper, clearer insight into its teachings. Through the continued witness of this friend, Sam came to Christ, abandoned his former practice of meditation, and adopted the practice of meditation on the Word of God.

Friend, God says that if you meditate on His Word, then you will be prosperous and have success! (Joshua 1:7). The promise is plain: God's hand of blessing will be on that person's life in an extraordinary way.

The psalmist said, "Oh, how I love your law! I meditate on it all day long" (Psalm 119:97). Meditation flows from a love for the Word of God. Ask God to give you a love for His Word and you will think on it.

Lord, teach me to love Your Word. Amen.

To Ponder: "For where your treasure is, there your heart will be also" (Matthew 6:21).

WHICH WAY?
Read 1 Samuel 24–26

*I guide you in the way of wisdom
and lead you along straight paths.*

PROVERBS 4:11

———

When Saul entered the cave where David and his men were hiding, David's men reminded him this was what they had all longed for—a wide-open door to the throne of Israel. With Saul at their mercy, how easy it would have been to misinterpret the promises and the providence of God. David took guidance by two things: First, his belief that Saul was the Lord's anointed. God had made Saul king, and God would have to remove him. Second, David was restrained by a proverb of the ancients, "From evildoers come evil deeds." He depended on God to avenge the wrongs done to him by Saul.

It's easy to mistake circumstances for the will of God. Just because events fall into place that enable us to do something doesn't necessarily mean God wants us to do it.

Some years ago I was planning a preaching tour through Asia, and we were praying for the Lord to show us if my wife Virginia should go. During this process, a friend heard of the situation and sent Virginia a signed blank check with a note that said: "Why not?" We had the invitation, the money, and the desire. After several weeks of praying, Virginia still didn't have peace in the matter. She tore up the check, thanked our friend for his kindness, and wrote the people overseas that she would not be coming.

I believe the key to knowing God's guidance is for us to saturate our lives with the wisdom of the Word of God. Then, when we are faced with a decision, the blessed Holy Spirit of God can guide us with the Word we have laid up in our hearts.

Lord, You have called me to have eyes of faith. Help me not to always equate the circumstances of my life with Your perfect will. Amen.

To Ponder: In discerning the will of God, circumstances are much less important than the Word of our Father in heaven.

LIFE IS HARD, AND THEN . . .
Read Genesis 21–24

If God is for us, who can be against us?

ROMANS 8:31

When should we expect life to get easier? When we graduate—when we marry—when we retire?

Today's passage contains a story that seems to nullify God's great promise that in Abraham all the families of the earth would be blessed. He is to take his son, Isaac, into the land of Moriah and kill him— offer him as a sacrifice upon one of the mountains. Verse 1 tells us this command came to him "after these things." After what things? After all the hardships and difficulties Abraham already had gone through.

All the tests and trials we have endured will not prevent other tests from coming our way. But these things need not destroy us nor wreck our faith. On the contrary, if you and I respond as Abraham did, in obedience and faith, these tough battles and trials can be the crowning moments of our lives.

Once I drove a small car from Colorado to Arizona for my son-in-law. In New Mexico I encountered violent crosswinds. It was all I could do to keep the car on the road. Suddenly I noticed a hawk flying right in front of me with his wings spread majestically, and he wasn't moving a feather! The winds that almost blew me off the road were just carrying that hawk higher and higher. And I thought, *For Christians, tough times are supposed to do that—just bring us higher and higher, closer to the Lord.*

Christian, what winds are knocking you around today? Family matters? Finances? Ill health? When Abraham faced his toughest test, he looked to the Lord. By God's grace and strength, you and I can do that, too.

Lord, I will trust and obey You, no matter what. Amen.

To Ponder: God has determined that we should become conformed to the image of His Son.

WHEN GOD MAKES A PROMISE
Read Genesis 25–26

For no matter how many promises God has made,
they are "Yes" in Christ. And so through him the
"Amen" is spoken by us to the glory of God.

2 CORINTHIANS 1:20

When God's Word promises something, and we claim it in prayer, but nothing happens, what are we supposed to believe?

I talked to a pastor who was struggling with this issue. He was preparing a sermon on Proverbs 22:6, which says, "Train a child in the way he should go, and when he is old he will not depart from it." The pastor's struggle was that he'd seen too many children turn away from the Lord, even though they had godly parents and a solid Christian upbringing.

I assured him that I believed the promise in Proverbs 22:6 was true, but that many issues were involved. One is the God-given free will of our children. Another is that we need to keep praying for our children and grandchildren, because all the evidence isn't in yet.

In today's passage, we find Isaac, the heir to all of God's promises, facing a similar issue. The land of Canaan was being plagued by a severe famine that forced Isaac to live in the land of the Philistines. What good is a Promised Land if you can't live in it?

But God is faithful. And while Isaac was in the land of Gerar, God came to him to buck up his flagging spirits. God said in Genesis 26:3, "I will be with you and will bless you."

A great fact emerges here that stays with us throughout the rest of the Bible: Just because a person is walking by faith and claiming the promises of God doesn't mean his life will be easy and free of difficulty. But through it all is the guiding, protecting hand of God. And, in it all, we can find the unfailing promises of God.

Lord, give me a grateful heart for Your promises that I have not yet seen fulfilled. Amen.

To Ponder: When it comes to God's promises, His delays are not His denials.

GOD, HAVE YOU FORGOTTEN ME?
Read Genesis 45–47

*We have not received the spirit of the world but the Spirit who is
from God, that we may understand what God has freely given us.*

1 CORINTHIANS 2:12

Thirteen years passed from the time Joseph was sold into slavery until
he entered Pharaoh's service—years of injustice, disappointment,
and obscurity. It must have been a great day for Joseph when the mystery finally was solved, and he understood the leading of God in his
life and in the lives of his family.

Through a series of almost unbelievable circumstances, God had
worked out a plan to save the lives of Joseph's father and brothers and
their household. They now were settled safely in Egypt, with plenty of
food to eat and plenty of work to do. But the thing to remember is
Joseph's statement to his brothers: "God sent me ahead of you to pre-
serve for you a remnant on earth and to save your lives by a great
deliverance. So then, it was not you who sent me here, but God"
(Genesis 45:7-8).

Throughout the years of loneliness and all the months in an
Egyptian prison, throughout all the difficulties that could have caused
his faith to fail and his spirit to become bitter, Joseph saw the hand of
God. In his mind there was nothing for which man could take either
the credit or the blame.

Remember the account of the apostle Paul and Silas being beaten
and cast into prison at Philippi? Acts 16:25 says, "About midnight Paul
and Silas were praying and singing hymns to God." Why weren't they
complaining, griping, demanding their legal rights? Somehow, like
Joseph many centuries before, they were able to detect the merciful
hand of God in it all.

Lord, I praise You for Your hand on my life. Amen.

To Ponder: Failure to look up to God, whether your circumstances
are good or bad, can mean the difference between victory and
defeat.

21

GOOD NEWS FOR BAD PEOPLE
Read Hosea 1–3

For you know the grace of our Lord Jesus Christ, that though he was rich, yet for your sakes he became poor, so that you through his poverty might become rich.

2 CORINTHIANS 8:9

One night I was playing a game of Scrabble when the phone rang. The man on the other end of the line had called to talk to me about life after death. He was afraid he wasn't going to heaven. When I told him the only way to heaven was through faith in Jesus Christ, he said, "Yes, I've heard that, but I'm afraid I've done so much bad in my life that God won't forgive me."

Many people feel this way. But the amazing thing about the Bible's good news of salvation is how much God loves sinners. Romans 5:6 says, "Christ died for the ungodly." Jesus said that He did not come to call the righteous, but sinners, to repentance. That's the message we find in Hosea 2:23: "I will say to those called 'Not my people,' 'You are my people'; and they will say, 'You are my God.'"

The grace of God extends to everyone who turns to the Lord in repentance and faith. Listen to Jesus' words in John 5:24: "I tell you the truth, whoever hears my word and believes Him who sent me has eternal life and will not be condemned; he has crossed over from death to life."

Throughout the Bible, God tells us that no one is too bad to come to Him. No one is beyond the reach of God's grace, mercy, and love.

Lord, I praise You that Your Word says "where sin increased, grace increased all the more," and now You look at me with eyes of love because of Jesus Christ's atoning death on the cross. Amen.

To Ponder: Nothing in your past is a barrier to the grace and mercy of God.

WHO, ME?
Read Exodus 3–6

Jesus looked at them and said, "With man this is impossible, but with God all things are possible."

MATTHEW 19:26

Moses was raised as the son of Pharaoh's daughter, but through a series of circumstances he found himself on the backside of the desert, tending somebody else's sheep. It was there an event occurred that led him to become one of the greatest men the world has ever known. Here's how it happened: God called to Moses out of the midst of a bush that burned but was not consumed. When Moses saw this strange sight, he turned aside for a closer look. And God revealed Himself with these words: "I am the God of your father, the God of Abraham, the God of Isaac and the God of Jacob." Then He told Moses, "I have indeed seen the misery of my people in Egypt. I have heard them crying out because of their slave drivers, and I am concerned about their suffering. So I have come down to rescue them" (Exodus 3:6-8).

Can you imagine the joy that must have flooded Moses' heart? God Himself was going to take action to deliver the children of Israel from the hand of their oppressors. Then God said, "So now, go. I am sending you to Pharaoh to bring my people the Israelites out of Egypt."

Moses was dumbfounded. "Who am I, that I should go to Pharaoh and bring the Israelites out of Egypt?" he said. The question was so irrelevant that God didn't even bother to answer it. Instead He said, "I will be with you."

Christian, are you tempted to back out of something, to tell God to get somebody else to do it? Remember in whose power you go, and then launch out and watch the hand of God at work.

Lord, I feel inadequate for the task ahead, but I press on, knowing that You will go with me. Amen.

To Ponder: God delights in using ordinary people to do extraordinary things.

ARE WE THERE YET?
Read Exodus 13–15

*These have come so that your faith—of greater worth
than gold, which perishes even though refined by fire—
may be proved genuine and may result in praise, glory
and honor when Jesus Christ is revealed.*

1 PETER 1:7

A few years ago, a bus company coined the slogan, "Getting there is
half the fun." Their ad campaign was a failure. Why? Because hardly
anyone believes that getting there is half the fun—especially on a bus.
We're destination-oriented people.

And so were the children of Israel—there were two ways to get
out of the land of Egypt into the land of Canaan. One way took only
a few days. The other took much longer and led them into the howl-
ing wilderness. So they took the shortcut—right? Wrong. God led
them through the way of the wilderness by way of the Red Sea. Why
did He do this?

Deuteronomy 8:2 says, "Remember how the LORD your God led
you all the way in the desert these forty years, to humble you and to
test you in order to know what was in your heart, whether or not you
would keep His commands."

God was taking a group of former slaves and transforming them
into His free people, ready to possess the Promised Land. Had God led
them through the shortcut, they would have come into contact
almost immediately with the Philistines, a warlike people—fierce and
tough. They weren't ready for that. Their hands were accustomed to
the brick mason's trowel, not the warrior's sword.

In Deuteronomy it says God led His people "about." Back and
forth, here and there. But what appeared to be a "wandering" experience was really not that at all. God knew exactly what He was doing.
It wasn't the nearest way, but it was the right way.

*Lord, I feel unsettled and out of control right now, but I know
You are with me, and You will make a way through this desert.
Amen.*

To Ponder: God doesn't allow us to take shortcuts; He exposes us to
experiences that will strengthen our walk with Him.

GOD'S CARE FOR HIS CHILDREN
Read Exodus 16–18

*And my God will meet all your needs according
to his glorious riches in Christ Jesus.*

PHILIPPIANS 4:19

———————

When the Israelites' supplies ran out, they accused Moses and Aaron of leading them out in the wilderness to kill them. Their complaint was really against God, for He was the one who had brought them forth out of the land of Egypt.

Now, you'd think they would quickly learn the lesson of the bountiful provision of God! But here they are, putting on a repeat performance and forgetting the long chain of miracles whereby God had delivered them, served them, and fed them. God didn't forget His people, and once again He met their needs.

In addition to God's provision of food and water, He sent them a management consultant in the person of Jethro, Moses' father-in-law. Jethro watched Moses in action and saw that he was overworked and needed to delegate some responsibilities. He gave Moses some sound advice: "You must be the people's representative before God and bring their disputes to him" (Exodus 18:19). Then he said, "Teach them the decrees and laws, and show them the way to live and the duties they are to perform." He had to teach them the Word of God and then lead by example.

So in these three chapters, we see the God who provided food to eat, water to drink, and leadership to help meet their spiritual needs.

What is the greatest need in your life today? Maybe you need more money to meet the obligations of life. Or maybe you need a companion, friend, or advisor to help you through a time of aching loneliness or critical decision making. Whatever your need, let me encourage you to depend on God to meet it.

Lord, I trust You to meet all my needs. Amen.

To Ponder: God doesn't deal with us as we deserve. God *is* love.

Every Day with God
Read Exodus 25–27

*My heart is steadfast, O God; I will sing and
make music with all my soul.*

Psalm 108:1

———

Today's passage in Exodus, describing the tabernacle and the Holy of
Holies, is a reminder of all that God has done to make it possible for
us to have fellowship with Him. In the tabernacle, the veil separated
the holy place from the most holy place. And into that Holy of Holies
went the high priest once a year. This veil was the very one that was
torn from top to bottom when Jesus Christ died on the cross, indicating that the way now was open for the likes of you and me to enter
into that close, intimate communion with God that for centuries was
reserved for the high priest alone. It took the death of the Son of God
to make that intimate fellowship possible.

Another special feature in the temple was a courtyard enclosed
with hangings of the finest linens. The court was fifty yards long and
twenty-five yards wide. This was the court David longed for and into
which the people of God entered with praise and thanksgiving. The
court could only hold a few worshipers. But thanks be to God, in the
New Testament times the enclosure was taken down, and today there
is room for everyone who calls on the name of the Lord Jesus.

Tomorrow, when your alarm goes off, remember that Jesus Christ
died to make it possible for you to come directly into the presence of
the Lord, a privilege that once was reserved for a special few. Thank
God that today there is room for every heart that longs to enter the
place of prayer.

*Lord, thank You for that most precious of privileges—the
priesthood of the believer, that gives me perpetual access to
Your holy presence. Amen.*

To Ponder: Many Christians are missing out on one of their greatest
privileges as children of God—a daily quiet time with their heavenly Father.

BRINGING UP THE FUTURE
Read the book of Numbers

*And the things you have heard me say in the presence
of many witnesses entrust to reliable men who will
also be qualified to teach others.*

2 TIMOTHY 2:2

Do you know many people who are living with the next generation in mind? Probably not. Most of us have more than we can handle today without worrying about those who come after us.

It would seem that Moses could have been caught in the same trap with all he had to do, but he wasn't. For years, he had been investing his life in a young man named Joshua. After Moses knew that he would not enter the Promised Land, and new leadership would be needed, we find him on his knees before God, asking God to make it clear who should take his place.

When Moses prayed, God pointed to Joshua as the new leader of the people. Joshua had already proven himself a man of courage in his battle with Amalek; he was a man of humility, having spent many years as Moses' servant; and he was a man of faith, one of two men who had brought back a good report from spying out the Promised Land. Joshua was described as a man "in whom is the spirit."

It has been said that "success without a successor is failure." In the midst of your present Christian endeavors, are you training someone to continue that ministry? That's what parenting is all about. And by the way, our children are one of our greatest opportunities for developing disciples of Christ for future years.

You and I have a great responsibility to pray for the succeeding generations of leaders for the work of Christ, that His work might flourish and advance long after we are in our graves. It all depends on which generation you're living for.

Lord, I pray for the young people in our Sunday school classes and youth programs. May we teach, nurture, and love them into leadership positions for Your kingdom. Amen.

To Ponder: Who is the next-generation person you could invest your life in?

27

JUST LIKE YOU
Read 1 Kings 17–19

Elijah was a man just like us. He prayed earnestly. . . .

JAMES 5:17

If a person is going to accomplish anything in life, he's going to have to take action. And that's what I see in the life of Elijah the prophet, as we meet him in 1 Kings 17–19. At that time, Israel's sin was right out in the open, parading itself in the streets in defiance of the Word of God. And into this mess the Lord sent Elijah.

The book of James tells us Elijah was a man just like us, a man subject to like passions as we are. So often we think the people God uses are somehow different. They must have some special ability to resist temptation and stand up for what's right. But Elijah was a person with all the same emotions and struggles we have. He was also a man of action; he had a fiery spirit. He wasn't content to sit in his chamber and write memos to King Ahab. Elijah was right out there on the firing line, confronting the worst aspects of his world with the Word and the power of God.

Perhaps most important, Elijah was a man of prayer. His communion with God kept rain from the land for three-and-a-half years, then brought it back. His prayer called the fire of God down from heaven in a confrontation with the prophets of Baal on Mount Carmel. He wasn't just a loud, angry voice condemning the sins of the nation. He was a humble servant of God, on his knees, pleading with the Lord to work miracles so that his people might come to repentance.

That's exactly the kind of person God is looking for today—an ordinary person facing the same problems as everyone else, but a person of action and prayer.

Lord, make my life count for You in the things I say and do. Amen.

To Ponder: God's power is perfected in our weakness.

LIFE CHOICES
Read 2 Chronicles 21–25

Do two walk together unless they have agreed to do so?

AMOS 3:3

In today's Scripture passage, we watch an entire nation take a dramatic turn for the worse. This downward spiral is directly related to the marriage of the new king, Jehoram. While his father and grandfather had been godly men, 2 Chronicles 21:6 tells us that Jehoram "walked in the ways of the kings of Israel, as the house of Ahab had done, for he married a daughter of Ahab. He did evil in the eyes of the LORD."

The Scriptures tie Jehoram's marriage and his conduct together. The lesson is clear: The choice of a marriage partner has far-reaching effects. If you're a young person feeling the tug of the Holy Spirit upon your life to serve the Lord, your marriage partner will either double your effectiveness for Christ or kill it. There is no in-between.

I heard of a young man whose wife is an encouragement and challenge to him. One of his unmarried friends asked him, "Where did you find a girl like that?" His answer was amazing. He said, "I asked God for a wife like that. Every day since junior high school I've prayed for God's perfect choice for me. And God has answered my prayers."

According to one recent book on marriage, the statistical improbability of a person finding the right mate is astonishing. The author based his mathematical calculations on six desirable qualities, including physical attractiveness, intelligence, and concern for others. He concluded that a person would have to meet more than fifteen thousand people before encountering one with all of the above requirements. If you consider other criteria like religion and age, the chances become even less optimistic. But we're dealing with the faithfulness of God, not the chances of finding the right person.

Lord, I desire Your will for my life. Keep me in the palm of Your hand. Amen.

To Ponder: Are you asking God for His direction for your life?

COME AS YOU ARE
Read Esther 3–4

"Come to me, all you who are weary and burdened, and I will give you rest. Take my yoke upon you and learn from me, for I am gentle and humble in heart, and you will find rest for your souls."

MATTHEW 11:28-29

Today's passage in Esther is a study in contrasts. And it all centers around a contrast in kingdoms. The Scriptures go to great lengths to describe the riches of the king's palace at Shushan. There were hangings of white, green, and blue fastened to silver rings with cords of fine linen and purple. The beds were of gold and silver on a pavement of red, blue, white, and black marble. It must have been something! But one day, every child of God will see something that will make the palace at Shushan look like a doghouse. We have no concept of what the glories of heaven will be like except that they will be beyond our wildest imaginings.

The second contrast emerges when Mordecai challenged Queen Esther to approach the king. Everyone knew the dangers involved. If she came to the inner court without being called by the king, she could be put to death if the king did not hold out his golden scepter.

What a contrast to the King of kings, whose word is, "Call unto me and I will answer thee." What a contrast to the urging of Scripture to come boldly to the throne of God, where we can find mercy and grace.

We can see it in the life of Jesus as well. He was the most inclusive person who ever lived. He welcomed people others turned away—little children, lepers, tax collectors, sinners, anyone who came to Him in simple faith and need. And today, without special invitation, the Lord of glory is waiting to reveal more and more of Himself to you and me in His Word.

Lord, I am awed that Jesus died for me so that I could be Your child and have access before Your throne. Amen.

To Ponder: God wants us to come into His throne room unbidden, to "interrupt" Him with our prayers.

30

HELP FOR THE HURTING
Read Job 15–17

*Therefore confess your sins to each other and
pray for each other so that you may be healed.*

JAMES 5:16

When we hear about someone who has been brought low, either
through his own sin or through no fault of his own, do we weep over
it? Or are we quick to condemn—quick to pass on gossip? It's easy
to snicker and to take on a holier-than-thou attitude. But it's more
profitable to pray.

In today's passage, we find Job's friends doing everything but comforting him. They try to expose some hidden transgression. They cast
doubt on the integrity of his family. They bring his honesty into question and imply that he obtained his wealth by dishonest means.

Finally, Job cries out, "My friends scorn me, but mine eye poureth
out tears unto God. Oh, that one might plead for a man with God, as
a man pleadeth for his neighbor!" (16:20-21, KJV). That's the need.
Rather than punishing people with words that are as sharp as knives,
we need to pray for them with words that are directed by the spirit of
truth. It is through prayer that we can help hurting people focus their
eyes on Christ.

The Bible challenges us to run with perseverance the race marked
out for us, fixing our eyes on Jesus, the author and finisher of our
faith. And during the painful process, the Bible tells us to "consider
him who endured such opposition from sinful men, so that you will
not grow weary and lose heart" (Hebrews 12:3). Is there a person you
know who is suffering right now? Will you take a few minutes and
pray for that individual?

*Lord, just as You have showed mercy to me, give me a heart
of compassion for the frailty of others and a passion to pray
for them. Amen.*

To Ponder: It is through prayer that we can help hurting people focus
their eyes on Christ.

31

THANKS BE TO GOD
Read 2 Corinthians 12:9-10

But thanks be to God! He gives us the
victory through our Lord Jesus Christ.

1 CORINTHIANS 15:57

We all have an Achilles' heel—a weakness that's difficult to overcome. I remember when I first started an exercise program years ago. For an ex-Marine, you'd think exercise would come naturally, but there were numerous times I had trouble getting down to the gym. And even after I got there it was tough. After all, it was a workout.

In the Bible there are certain teachings that aren't easy to obey. And different teachings are difficult for different people. For some, witnessing is a scary thing. Getting up early for a devotional time with the Lord can be difficult. My difficulty can be summed up in one short statement by the apostle Paul: "Give thanks in all circumstances, for this is God's will for you in Christ Jesus" (1 Thessalonians 5:18). Friend, it's hard for me to give thanks in every circumstance.

I remember flying home one Saturday night. I was preparing a Sunday school lesson on the subject of thanksgiving. I had the tray down and was using it as a desk. I was deep in thought when the guy in front of me suddenly reclined his seat. The tray was now hugging my chest, and I sat looking at the top of the guy's head. I began to mutter and then dropped my pen. Now I really began to fume, under my breath, of course. Then it dawned on me. I was preparing to teach others about giving thanks in every situation, and I sat fretting over a pen. I began to laugh, confessed my bad attitude to God, and finished the lesson.

Sound familiar? I thought so. It's one of those tough teachings of Scripture, but it can be a reality if we walk daily as disciples.

Lord, You are so good to me, giving me the power to do those things befitting Your children. Amen.

 To Ponder: God delights in giving me His strength to overcome my weaknesses.

THE CREATION OF MAN
Read Genesis 1:26-31

*For by him all things were created: things in heaven and on earth,
visible and invisible, whether thrones or powers or rulers or
authorities; all things were created by him and for him.*

COLOSSIANS 1:16

Why does the theory of evolution get such a grip on people? I believe
it's because all people realize that if there is a God, and He made us
and gave us life, we are accountable to Him for our actions.

If He has revealed His will to us; if He has given us the Ten
Commandments; if He has given us the prophets and apostles, and
even His only begotten Son, the Lord Jesus Christ, to teach us what
is right and wrong; and if we don't want to live the way He teaches
and believe what He teaches, the simplest thing to do is deny that any
of it is true. There is no God, the Bible is a bunch of fairy tales, and
we owe our existence to a theory that tells us somehow, somewhere,
at some time there came into existence a living cell, and from this cell
man evolved by a process of natural selection.

In contrast to this theory, we have the record of the Bible, which
tells us that man is a created being. Genesis 1:27 simply and elo-
quently says, "So God created man in his own image, in the image of
God he created him; male and female he created them." You would
think man would be honored by such a statement. A college founded
by Thomas Jefferson would be a mark of prestige. A house designed
by Frank Lloyd Wright is a mark of honor. But somehow man would
rather have crawled out of the slime onto the muddy bank and eventually up into the trees with the monkeys.

Scripture is clear. We owe our life to God. And may our lives be
lived in such a way as to please Him.

*Lord, Master Potter, Your mark is indelibly fixed in the clay
that is me, and I rejoice in being created by You. Amen.*

To Ponder: It is an awesome thing to contemplate being part of the
family of God and to say by the Spirit, "Abba Father."

CALLED-OUT ONES
Read Exodus 19:1-6

They devoted themselves to the apostles' teaching and to the fellowship, to the breaking of bread and to prayer.

ACTS 2:42

———

Shortly after I became a Christian, I heard a famous preacher speak on "churchianity." He said, "Don't confuse churchianity with Christianity. They are not the same. Churchianity will not save you, because the church can't save. Only Christ can save. And Christianity is Christ."

Of course, I knew what he was saying. All the same, I grew a bit suspicious of the value of the church and the place of the church in daily life. After that night the church intrigued me, and I wanted to find its proper place in my Christian life.

If the church can't save, what can it do? Is it just a place to go once a week and see our friends and enjoy fellowship with them? Oh sure, we learn more of the Bible each week through the Sunday school class and from the pulpit, but we could do that at home in personal Bible study.

In the Old Testament the people of God were called out from among the nations to be a holy people. In the New Testament you have the same idea. Christians are said to be "called-out ones." God calls us out of darkness into His marvelous light. We no longer belong to ourselves; Christ has bought us to be His own special people, to live under His authority and enjoy His unmerited love. And we are more effective for Him when we are united.

The Bible teaches that the church is made up of every believer in Jesus Christ—anywhere in the world and throughout time. That means the congregations you and I meet with each week are members of God's unique family. Although we may not look like it, Christ calls us His beloved bride. Friend, that's identity!

Lord, thank You for the privilege of being a member of Your family. Amen.

To Ponder: God said, "Not forsaking the assembling of ourselves together . . ." (Hebrews 10:25, KJV).

GOD'S ARMY
Read 2 Kings 6:8-23

*Don't be afraid. . . . Those who are with us are
more than those who are with them.*

2 KINGS 6:16

Most nations of the world have some sort of standing army—men and women whose sworn duty it is to defend the land against enemies. They stand ready to carry out the orders of the commander in chief.

The kingdom of God also has a commander in chief, and a huge standing army as well. God is the commander. He is called the Lord of hosts, and He has at His command a host of angels standing ready in battle array to carry out His orders. Angels are more than messengers of God, they are also the army of God, committed to win the battles of God.

Frankly, I find great comfort in that picture of heaven with the host of angels surrounding the throne and sworn to instant obedience to the will of God. Why comfort? Because this army is charged with the mission of protecting you and me.

In addition to the feeling of comfort, there's also a sense of challenge. This heavenly host of the army of God should find its reflection in the church of Jesus Christ here on earth. The heavenly picture is surely given as a model for us to stand ready to fulfill the slightest wish of our great commander in chief, as He leads us to victory over the forces of Satan.

Friend, you and I are not left on this earth to fritter away our days, drifting from church to church and meeting to meeting. Like the angels of God, we are called upon to join ranks with the faithful and carry out the commission of the captain of our souls—to reveal the light of the gospel to those who dwell in darkness and the shadow of death. We're all in the Lord's army!

*Lord, help me to stand battle-ready against Satan and his
forces, having put on the full armor of God. Amen.*

To Ponder: According to the list of the armor of God described in Ephesians 6:10-18, are you missing any of your battle gear?

STREAMS OF LIVING WATER
Read Hosea 12–14

*I have been crucified with Christ and
I no longer live, but Christ lives in me.*

GALATIANS 2:20

Hosea 13:15 presents a prophecy of judgment against the nation of Israel: "An east wind from the LORD will come, blowing in from the desert; his spring will fail and his well dry up. His storehouse will be plundered of all its treasures."

Here is a picture of someone whose inner source of life and power has dried up. His life was once a blessing to those around him but has now become a curse. As I studied this passage, I was reminded of a man I knew well.

His testimony for Christ shone brightly against the dark background of the people among whom he worked—people whose lives had been ruined by drugs, alcohol, and sin of every description. This man was instrumental in leading many of these people to Christ and seeing them begin new lives. But his inner spring dried up. He left his wife and children, and dismissed his actions by saying that the love was gone and his marriage was no longer working. What happened was not a reaction to outward pressure or tragedy. It was an inward spiritual drought, brought on by his lack of daily personal fellowship with Christ.

In John 7:37-38, Jesus said: "If anyone is thirsty, let him come to me and drink. Whoever believes in me, as the Scripture has said, streams of living water will flow from within him." And then John unlocks the mystery of Jesus' words. By this, John said, Jesus meant the Spirit. The secret to a life that fulfills us and refreshes others is to live under the daily control of the Holy Spirit. Then our spring will never fail, and our well will not dry up.

Lord, may Your sweet, refreshing Spirit fill me and cause a stream of living water to flow from my life. Amen.

To Ponder: Is the flow of the Holy Spirit in your life a trickle or a stream?

OUR EVER-PRESENT HELP
Read Nehemiah 5–7

Be strong and courageous. Do not be terrified;
do not be discouraged, for the LORD your God
will be with you wherever you go.

JOSHUA 1:9

As Nehemiah struggled to rebuild the wall of Jerusalem, one of his greatest enemies was fear. First, he had to fight it among the people. In Nehemiah 4:10, we find the warlike tribe of Judah about ready to throw in the towel, saying, "The strength of the laborers is giving out, and there is so much rubble that we cannot rebuild the wall."

They also feared an enemy attack while they worked. So Nehemiah prayed, posted a guard, and encouraged the people to remember God's faithfulness. But after helping the people with their fear, the next attack came against Nehemiah himself.

Sanballat and Geshem tried to lure him into meeting with them in one of the villages. When he resisted their scheme, they created a false report about him and threatened to report him to the king. Then they tried to frighten Nehemiah into taking refuge in the temple to escape their threats of death. And was he afraid? Yes. But he didn't show it. He was not controlled by the fear. And he asked God to strengthen him (verse 9).

Christian, we do not have to be under the control of our emotions if we walk under the control of the Holy Spirit. The Bible says that one fruit of the Spirit is self-control, or self-discipline.

Paul wrote to his young friend Timothy, "For God did not give us a spirit of [fear], but a spirit of power, of love and of self-discipline" (2 Timothy 1:7). The answer to fear is not denial. Like Nehemiah, admit your fear. That's the first step. Then place your trust in the never-changing One who, right up to this day, has never lost a battle.

Lord, when I am afraid, I will trust in You. Amen.

To Ponder: Walking in the Spirit is a daily decision to hand over control of our lives to God. When we do this, there is no room for fear.

GOD'S DELIVERERS
Read Psalm 34

*Suddenly an angel of the Lord appeared
and a light shone in the cell.*

ACTS 12:7

Do you remember the television series "Hogan's Heroes"—the wild episodes of American soldiers supposedly locked in a Nazi prison? They were always breaking out of jail, but they usually did it quietly. No noise allowed.

The apostle Peter's jailbreak was quite different. Acts 12 says that King Herod threw Peter into prison with four squads of soldiers guarding him. Imagine that! Four squads of soldiers to guard one man!

A few nights later, Peter was sleeping between two soldiers and bound with two chains. The cell was guarded as well. And then the Bible tells us: "Suddenly an angel of the Lord appeared and a light shone in the cell. . . . Then the angel said to him, 'Put on your clothes and sandals.' And Peter did so. 'Wrap your cloak around you and follow me.'"

This angel broke all the rules of conventional jailbreak wisdom! First, you wouldn't shine a bright light into the cell for fear of waking the guards! Second, you wouldn't put on your sandals and clomp out of the place. You would carry your sandals and tippy-toe by the sleeping guards in your bare feet. Third, you wouldn't release the chains and let them clatter to the ground.

God can rescue you just as easily as He rescued Peter. But there are times when God's deliverance doesn't fit the mold of human wisdom. God's ways are not our ways. We must accept the fact that God knows what He's doing and fall in step with Him by faith, like Peter did.

Maybe you're facing a situation right now that needs God's touch. Ask the Lord to send deliverance, but don't be surprised if it comes in an unexpected way.

*Lord, help me to recognize Your hand of deliverance in my life
and I will give You all the praise and glory. Amen.*

To Ponder: Is there a time when God supernaturally delivered you from a dangerous situation?

CONSIDER THE CONSEQUENCES
Read Genesis 3

*Don't you know that when you offer yourselves to someone
to obey him as slaves, you are slaves to the one whom you obey—
whether you are slaves to sin, which leads to death,
or to obedience, which leads to righteousness?*

ROMANS 6:16

When someone tells us not to do something, it makes us want to do
it all the more, sort of like the forbidden fruit in the Garden of Eden.
Here was a lush, beautiful garden filled to overflowing with wonderful things to eat, and all available for the taking. But there was one tree
in the midst of the garden the Lord declared out of bounds. Adam and
Eve were not to eat its fruit.

But, of course, they did. Notice this tree and its forbidden fruit
were not evil things. But when Adam and Eve disobeyed, they knew
they were in big trouble—so big, in fact, that the effects of their sin
are still felt today by the entire human race.

Now why do you think these two indulged their appetites on something that was forbidden when they had so many other choices?

We must take very seriously the biblical admonition to be content
with our personal lot. Ask the Lord to give you the attitude of the
apostle Paul: "I have learned to be content whatever the circumstances" (Philippians 4:11).

Secondly, ask God to give you a healthy fear of the consequences
of giving in to the sins of the flesh. I've found that temptation makes
a sin seem very attractive, but it's a lie. After I've done wrong, the sin
that seemed so attractive is disgusting and short-lived.

*Lord, through your Holy Spirit, I want to be a thoughtful, obe-
dient person who considers the consequences of sin and says
"no" instead of letting desire take control. Amen.*

To Ponder: Are you content with the life God has given you?

SATAN'S LIES
Read Genesis 3–5

*Blessed is the man who does not walk in the counsel of
the wicked. . . . He is like a tree planted by streams of
water, which yields its fruit in season and whose leaf
does not wither. Whatever he does prospers.*

PSALM 1:1,3

The greatest lie ever told comes at the beginning of the saddest story ever written. "You will not surely die," the serpent said to the woman. "For God knows that when you eat [this fruit] your eyes will be opened, and you will be like God, knowing good and evil" (Genesis 3:4-5). Adam and Eve believed the lie and ate the only fruit God had kept from them.

As Genesis 3 opens, we see our first parents enjoying a life of fellowship with God in a garden home filled with His abundant provision. They were holy. They were experiencing the grace and blessing of God. Everything that surrounded them was good. But in one devastating stroke, the scene changes.

The apostle Paul gives the summary: "Therefore, just as sin entered the world through one man, and death through sin, and in this way death came to all men, because all sinned" (Romans 5:12).

There is one primary lesson in these chapters. Holiness, not sin, brings happiness. Let me repeat that. As long as Adam and Eve were walking with God in the unbroken fellowship of a holy life, they were happy. Now, how could they turn their backs on God? It seemed so senseless and absurd for them to think they could improve on what God had done.

Before it's experienced, the life of sin appears attractive, exciting, colorful, and everything you could desire. And the life of holiness appears drab, dull, and unattractive. But once the life of sin is experienced, what you desired and embraced turns to ashes.

*Lord, help me to remember that sin never delivers what it
promises, and that my greatest joy will be in the pursuit of
holiness. Amen.*

To Ponder: Satan's basic lie in his war against mankind is that we can improve our lives by disobeying God.

THE WORD CONVICTS OF SIN
Read Genesis 6–9

*What if some did not have faith? Will their lack
of faith nullify God's faithfulness?*

ROMANS 3:3

Today's passage concerning the Flood is directly related to a modern difficulty you may be facing. Maybe you've talked with someone about Christ, only to have them respond, "I don't believe the Bible." What does that have to do with the Flood, you ask?

Let me illustrate. I took a course on evolution in college. One of the professor's stated objectives was to destroy the faith of any Christian in the class. So I began to witness to him. One day when I left the room, his lab assistant followed me and expressed interest in what I had been saying. I invited him to see the Moody Science film "Dust or Destiny," which showed the remarkable wisdom in the creative acts of God.

He was impressed, and when I asked him if the film had changed his thinking, he told me it had. He could plainly see there was far more evidence for the truth of the creation story than for evolution. "But I have no intention of becoming a Christian," he said. "It would mean turning from my sin, and I'm not ready to do that." It was a moral issue, not an intellectual issue. And this is why some people are so reluctant to believe the biblical account of the Flood. It is clearly tied to the judgment of God and the sinfulness of man.

As you witness to people, you may encounter those who say, "I don't believe the Bible." When that happens, just remember that we're not out to win arguments but to win men and women to personal faith in Jesus Christ. That takes prayer and the power of the Holy Spirit. So keep sharing the truth of the Bible, even with those who say they can't believe it.

*Lord, help me to keep on telling others about Your Word—
even those people who dismiss it. Amen.*

To Ponder: Since the Holy Spirit uses the Word to convict us of sin, we should be faithful to proclaim it to others.

THE POWER OF WORDS
Read Genesis 37–40

Reckless words pierce like a sword,
but the tongue of the wise brings healing.

PROVERBS 12:18

The late Paul Little of InterVarsity Christian Fellowship used to tell us that when we speak unwisely or boastfully or pass along some gossip, it is hard to retrieve those words. It's like trying to get toothpaste back in the tube.

In the story of Joseph, we find a young man who spoke unwisely and suffered the consequences for many years afterwards.

One day Joseph and his brothers were in the field, and Joseph told them his dream: "We were binding sheaves of grain out in the field when suddenly my sheaf rose and stood upright, while your sheaves gathered around mine and bowed down to it." And his brothers, who were jealous of his favored position with their father, hated him even more. They said, "Will you actually rule us?"

Now, folks, I think Joseph was a great man, and very wise. In fact, I don't remember any other major mistake this man made. But I think what he did here was a mistake. We all know there are some things that we should simply keep to ourselves. Had he thought about it for a moment or two, he could have seen how relating his dream would promote anger and hatred and jealousy among his brothers.

As Joseph's story unfolds, the power of God turns tragedy into triumph. But the truth still comes through loud and clear that you and I need to watch what we say.

The New Testament makes it clear that the daily walk of the disciple should be characterized by lowliness and meekness, long-suffering, forbearing one another in love, and endeavoring to keep the unity of the spirit in the bond of peace (see Ephesians 4:2-3).

Lord, today may what I say honor You and encourage others. Amen.

To Ponder: Today, look for opportunities to speak healing words.

THE WELL-SPOKEN WORD
Read 2 Samuel 19–20

Do not let any unwholesome talk come out of your mouths, but only what is helpful for building others up according to their needs, that it may benefit those who listen.

EPHESIANS 4:29

In 2 Samuel 19, we see David snatching defeat from the jaws of victory. After his army triumphed over the rebellion of Absalom, David was in tears. His men had won the battle, but he was making them feel as if they'd lost. It's normal for a father to grieve the death of his son, but there was a problem here. The men in the army who had fought in this battle saw David's tears and assumed he was angry with them. The Bible says, "The men stole into the city that day as men steal in who are ashamed when they flee from battle" (2 Samuel 19:3).

I wonder how often we do the same thing with our kids. Billy comes home from school with a good grade on a math paper and we greet him with criticism for not making his bed. Susie does a great job in a school play and we're angry because she hasn't done anything on her science project. We're taking a victory and turning it into a defeat for those we love. There's a time to discuss the dirty room and the science project, but it isn't on the heels of a victory.

As parents, we often forget how much a kind word or a compliment means to our kids. It costs so little to express appreciation or to give a word of encouragement. But how often these expressions of kindness are lost because our minds are taken up with so-called "larger issues."

David finally presented himself at the head of the troops and gave them his approval. And how about the troops at your house? Today would be a great time to congratulate them on their successes.

Lord, I want to encourage people with what I say. Give me the words to speak today as I interact with my family and others. Amen.

To Ponder: There is very little happening in the world on any given day that is more important than encouraging our children.

MONEY HUNGRY
Read Judges 17–21

For the love of money is a root of all kinds of evil.

1 TIMOTHY 6:10

In Judges 18, a son steals money from his mother, but returns it for fear of a curse she pronounced on the thief. The silver in question is soon forged into the image of a pagan god, but in fact, this money had become a god in the lives of these two long before it took the form of an idol.

In chapter 19, we find the same theme, a Levite who cannot resist an offer of wages, clothing, and food. Clearly, these material concerns have crowded out his desire to serve the Lord. When a more attractive financial offer is made, he accepts it without seeking spiritual counsel or the will of God. If it would give him more money, that was all that mattered.

As the book of Judges ends, we see idolatry spread from this one household to an entire tribe. We are told that each man did what was right in his own eyes. The result? One of the blackest periods in the history of the Old Testament people of God.

When people leave the Bible and begin to make up their own rules, anything can happen. There is no sin too vile, no activity too foul. We can see it in today's headlines. And if we look closely enough, we can see the same tendencies in our own hearts. We need to fall on our knees, plead with God for mercy, and rededicate ourselves to Him.

Lord, reveal to me if there's anything that has become an idol in my life. Amen.

To Ponder: What is your attitude toward the things of this world?

LORD OF ALL
Read Genesis 1–2

*But seek first his kingdom and his righteousness, and all these
things will be given to you as well.*

MATTHEW 6:33

The Bible begins with a mystery: "In the beginning God created the
heavens and the earth." What's so mysterious about that, you say?
Did you know the Hebrew word for God in this passage is plural? All
three persons of the Trinity were involved in the creation of the
world.

The Bible says the Spirit of God moved upon the face of the waters
and God the Father created all things by Jesus Christ. "For by him" —
that is, by Jesus Christ — "all things were created" (Colossians 1:16).
That means all things spiritual and physical, including your spiritual
and physical life, came through Jesus Christ. Is it any wonder that
God's Word reminds us that in all things His Son, the Lord Jesus
Christ, must be preeminent in our lives. Just as He was Lord at creation, so He is Lord today.

Does Jesus Christ have priority in every area of your life? What
about your appointment calendar? How are you spending your time?
Is Jesus Christ squeezed out of your schedule because you're too
busy?

Christ is present in all Christians. In some, He is prominent. In
only a few is He preeminent. Why not make sure the Lord Jesus Christ
dwells supreme in the throne room of your heart.

*Lord, speak to me about the priorities of my day. Give me the
power and wisdom to glorify You in my life today. Amen.*

To Ponder: Our seemingly small troubles have eternal value with
God, and He is lovingly fitting all things together for our good.

45

WHO'S STEERING?
Read Genesis 10–11

"Whoever follows me will never walk in darkness,
but will have the light of life."

JOHN 8:12

In early biblical records, we find man doing exactly what he's doing today—making plans based on his egotistical pride and rebellious heart. In Genesis 11 we find man determined to construct a world without God, and so he began a massive effort to build a tower—the tower of Babel—to make himself a name, to take his future into his own hands, to grab the steering wheel of history so that the kingdom of human reason replaces the kingdom of God.

I know a young man who had a careful Christian upbringing. He was involved in Bible classes during the week, Sunday school, and all the right things. But during his junior high days, he decided to go his own way. And he's been doing that for years. Some time ago, I went to visit him in jail and sat by his mother. Tears were running down her cheeks, and her heart was broken for this son who had committed robbery and was now serving time.

If a man is ever to get on the right track, headed in the right direction, he must first hand the steering wheel of his life over to the Lord, with a deep commitment to go God's way. Have you ever surrendered to do the will of God, no matter what? God is waiting to fill your life with blessing and joy when you let Him do the driving.

Lord, please take control of my life, and by Your grace I will go Your way. Amen.

To Ponder: God is waiting to fill our lives with blessing and joy, but He will do that only when we've surrendered completely to Him.

OUT OF THE ORDINARY
Read Genesis 12–14

Now if you obey me fully and keep my covenant, then out of all nations you will be my treasured possession.

EXODUS 19:5

Abraham was a most remarkable man. From Genesis 12 to the end of the Bible, he and his descendants are almost the only subject of the divinely inspired Word of God.

Here is a man whom both Christian and Jew claim as the father of their faith. He is even mentioned in the Koran, the holy book of the Muslim religion, in 188 verses. What was it that made Abraham so remarkable? *He simply did what God said to do.*

As Hebrews 11:8 says, "By faith Abraham, when called to go to a place he would later receive as his inheritance, obeyed and went, even though he did not know where he was going." Abraham's willingness to pack up his family and all his belongings to move to an unknown land is one of the first indications of his commitment to the Lord.

Maybe the Lord has spoken to you recently through His Word about mending a relationship with a friend or family member, or about meeting Him faithfully every morning in a quiet time of prayer. Perhaps He has spoken to you about sharing Christ with a neighbor or coworker.

Most of us don't have spectacular calls from God. But we can obediently answer all those ordinary calls. And that kind of obedience makes an impact on life. God called; Abraham obeyed. Simple faith, simple obedience. An extraordinary result.

Lord, increase my faith to follow You wherever You lead. Amen.

To Ponder: Sometimes what God asks us to do goes against all human logic; that is when God is most honored by our obedience.

LORD OF YOUR HEART
Read Exodus 7–10

*The Lord came and stood there, calling as at
the other times, "Samuel! Samuel!" Then Samuel said,
"Speak, for your servant is listening."*

1 SAMUEL 3:10

Have you ever tried to reason with someone and had them mock you and turn you down flat? When Moses and Aaron went to Pharaoh with the message from God: "Let my people go," the demand was met with scorn and ridicule. Pharaoh said he didn't know the Lord, wouldn't obey His voice, and wouldn't let Israel go.

Pride. Defiance. Self-confidence. Arrogant spirit. I'm sure it was beneath Pharaoh's dignity to enter into a contest with this Lord who claimed to be the God of a rag-tag gang of slaves who were under Pharaoh's absolute control. Pharaoh was certain that if push came to shove, he would be the victor. He had wealth in abundance. He had a standing army of thousands of well-trained warriors and hundreds of chariots. And what did this Lord, about whom Moses spoke, have going for Him? Nothing. No money. No army. Nothing. Or so it appeared.

This God of whom Pharaoh spoke so disparagingly was the Lord of hosts, the creator of heaven and earth, the Lord God Almighty. There was no way Pharaoh was going to win. Even when God displayed His power through the plagues, Pharaoh was unmoved. Now before we get too amazed at the hardness of Pharaoh's heart, we need to look inside ourselves. Perhaps the Lord has been speaking plainly to us through His Word and His servants, but we haven't yet obeyed.

I can't think of anything more dangerous, more foolhardy, than to hear the voice of God and do nothing in response. In our daily walk of discipleship, may God deliver us from the Pharaoh syndrome and help us obey when He speaks.

*Lord, sharpen my hearing to hear Your command, and soften
my heart to obey it. Amen.*

To Ponder: "Do not put the Lord your God to the test" (Matthew 4:7).

TODAY'S WALK
Read Deuteronomy 8–11

"Remain in me, and I will remain in you. No branch can bear fruit by itself; it must remain in the vine. Neither can you bear fruit unless you remain in me."

JOHN 15:4

The key to making it over the long haul in the Christian life is to make it over the short haul. Today is all we have. Yesterday is gone. Tomorrow never comes. When you go to bed tonight and then wake up, what day will it be? Not tomorrow, but today.

In 1 Corinthians 10:12, Paul says, "If you think you are standing firm, be careful that you don't fall!" That's a warning about not walking with God today.

Some time ago, I was speaking at a Christian college and a student asked me if working too hard was the cause of burnout. My response was that hard work is not the cause of burnout. Burnout occurs when we become so occupied with our work that we don't have time for God.

In today's passage, we see God's warnings to His people not to forget Him when they enter the Promised Land and settle down. Deuteronomy 8 opens with these words: "Be careful to follow every command I am giving you today, so that you may live and increase and may enter and possess the land." He tells them to remember the way He led them in the desert for the past forty years and to let that be a motivation for their continuing love and obedience to Him each day.

As Christians, our walk of daily discipleship is one of dependence on God. What I did last week, or what I hope to do tomorrow, is not important. What's important is whether or not I walk with the Lord in faith and obedience today.

Lord, keep my heart and mind focused on today and what You would have me accomplish. Amen.

To Ponder: If a person will walk with Jesus today, he will walk with Jesus for eternity.

LEAVING THE PATH
Read 2 Samuel 11–14

*Against you, you only, have I sinned
and done what is evil in your sight.*

PSALM 51:4

Every time I read the story of David and Bathsheba, I watch in horror as David, the man of God, falls into immorality and murder. What prompted this godly man to fall into such sin? I believe the Bible gives us a number of reasons.

First of all, he was not where he was supposed to be. This was the time of year when kings went forth to battle. David, as commander in chief, should have been with his soldiers, leading the army on the field. When we wander away from our duty, we can easily fall into sin.

Second, it appears that David was indulging a slothful spirit. Why do I suspect that? Because the record tells us that David arose from his bed at eventide. He had dozed away the whole afternoon! David's bed of sloth soon turned into a bed of lust.

Third, he gave in to a wandering eye. A missionary friend of mine pointed out that it's the second look that can get you. When the women of the night passed by, he couldn't help but see them, but he could keep from the second look. And so, David was tempted by what he saw.

His next step downward was the murder of Uriah, Bathsheba's husband and one of David's loyal men. It's almost impossible to commit only one sin. They seem to multiply as we try to hide the results of the first one.

I wish all this had never happened in David's life, but it did, and this account is written for our admonition that we might take heed lest we fall. The next time Satan comes to you with an offer to leave the narrow path, seek God's power to resist. Then look down the road and don't take that first step.

*Lord, as I meditate on Your Word, give me a heart of wisdom
to recognize when my foot leaves Your path. Amen.*

To Ponder: God has made a way of escape from your temptations (see 1 Corinthians 10:13).

HIS YOKE IS EASY
Read James 1–5

Then you will know the truth, and the truth will set you free.

JOHN 8:32

Whenever I'm driving an automobile and I see a law enforcement officer, I slow down. It's an automatic reaction. I may be going twenty miles per hour under the speed limit, but the sight of a cop always causes me to touch the brakes and make a quick mental inventory of any driving laws I might be breaking.

This is a strange reaction because I'm a very cautious driver. I haven't had a traffic ticket in years. In fact, my kids call me the world's greatest yielder. Nevertheless, the sight of a police car makes me nervous.

Now, with that in mind, take a close look at James 1:23-25:

Anyone who listens to the word but does not do what it says is like a man who looks at his face in a mirror and, after looking at himself, goes away and immediately forgets what he looks like. But the man who looks intently into the perfect law that gives freedom, and continues to do this, not forgetting what he has heard, but doing it—he will be blessed in what he does.

Most people do not associate law with liberty; they associate law with restrictions—just as I still do when I see a police car.

God promises a life of freedom and blessing to the person who looks into the Bible in a special way. The person who glances at the Bible quickly, occasionally, and flippantly is not the one who profits. It is the person who reads the Word carefully and who obeys it wholeheartedly.

Lord, thank You for the truth of Your Word that sets me free from the law of sin and death. Amen.

To Ponder: How would you explain Jesus' words, "My yoke is easy and my burden is light" (Matthew 11:30) to the person who wants to run his own life?

SPIRITUAL HEALTH
Read Leviticus 11–15

But just as he who called you is holy, so be holy in all you do;
for it is written; "Be holy, because I am holy."

1 PETER 1:15-16

Today, through the research of medical scientists, we are well aware of the fact that some foods are good for us and some are not. For the health and welfare of the Israelites out there in the burning desert, with no refrigeration or other means of keeping food from spoiling, God gave certain laws that were designed to help them remain healthy and free of disease.

I suppose that among those ancient people were some who questioned God's wisdom. Why can't I eat a vulture or a mouse or a lizard? Well, it seems to me the best answer is simply that God said not to. But it was much more than just what was on the menu. God told them, "I am the LORD your God; consecrate yourselves and be holy, because I am holy" (Leviticus 11:44).

God set these people apart so their lives would reflect two things: His holiness and love. This process of being set apart begins in us when we come to grips with the fact that we are not our own because we've been bought with the blood of Christ. The process continues with daily choices to glorify God in every area of our lives because we belong to Him.

God wants you and me to live lives unspotted by the flesh— untainted by the world in which we live. God has called us to shine as lights so that those who live in darkness might find their way home.

Lord, thank You for the instructions in Your Word that are designed to protect my spiritual health and well-being. Amen.

To Ponder: God's plan for making us holy is not an event but a process that involves daily choices in every area of life.

STANDING WITH THE LORD
Read 1 Kings 20–22

He who unites himself with the Lord is one with him in spirit.

1 CORINTHIANS 6:17

In the record of 1 Kings 22, when King Ahab assembled his four hundred prophets and asked if he should go to war, the prophets all said yes and predicted victory. But Ahab's ally, King Jehoshaphat, wanted a second opinion, and he called for Micaiah, prophet of the Lord.

The messenger who summoned Micaiah urged him to agree with the other prophets, but Micaiah said, "As surely as the LORD lives, I can tell him only what the LORD tells me" (1 Kings 22:14). When Micaiah prophesied defeat and ruin for Israel, he was beaten and ridiculed by the other prophets, then sent to prison with nothing but bread and water. But his prophecy came true, and King Ahab was killed in battle.

This passage presents a powerful challenge in our day of R-rated ethics. How will we respond when everyone else around us is saying something's right when we know good and well it's not. Will we take a stand for what we believe, even when it risks ridicule or personal loss?

Christian, there are times when we've got to step out from the mooing herd and take a solitary stand for the truth of God. Everybody else may be doing it; everybody else may be saying it; everybody else (even other Christians) may be calling it right, but if the Word of God says otherwise, you and I must not be swayed by the foolishness of this world.

Lord, Give me the strength to say and do what I know is right, even if I have to stand alone. Amen.

To Ponder: God calls us to live on the basis of conviction, not convenience.

PURE EYES
Read Job 29–31

*Do not love the world or anything in the world. If anyone
loves the world, the love of the Father is not in him. For
everything in the world—the cravings of sinful man, the
lust of his eyes and the boasting of what he has and does—
comes not from the Father but from the world.*

1 JOHN 2:15-16

I had a Christian friend who contracted polio during the late 1950s
and was confined to an iron lung. I remember visiting him when he
had wasted away to nothing but skin and bones. I asked him what was
the most difficult thing he faced in his ordeal, and he said, "The lust
of the flesh."

I was stunned. Here was this guy on his deathbed, still fighting the
same thing you and I struggle with. You see, the lust of the flesh is a
battle fought in our minds. And one of the ways the enemy launches
his attacks is through what we see.

Listen to Job's words in 31:1: "I made a covenant with my eyes
not to look lustfully at a girl." Job began at the right place, his eyes.
He did not allow his eyes to stimulate his mind to lustful thoughts and
impure desires.

Now obviously we can't go through life blindfolded. We will catch
glimpses of many people each day. But it is not the first glimpse that
causes the problem. It is the second look that we are to avoid. Where
did the first sin have its beginning? Genesis says that the woman saw
that the forbidden tree was good and pleasant to the eyes. So what we
would not lust after, we must not gaze upon.

Let's take stock of our visual consumption. Where does our
glance stop and our gaze begin? How about the magazines we read,
the television programs we watch, and the videos we rent? Remember
Job's words: "I have made a covenant with my eyes."

*Lord, knowing the cost You paid on the cross, please keep me
from the second glance that leads to lust. Amen.*

To Ponder: If we want to keep our hearts set on God, we must guard
our eyes.

WORDS OF WELFARE
Read Job 35–37

Out of the same mouth come praise and cursing.
My brothers, this should not be.

JAMES 3:10

Years ago, my cousins Eva and Dean raised large hunting dogs. Most nights these dogs would bark at the moon, protesting its appearance. I suppose dogs were doing the same around the world. Quite possibly, the moon was being barked at twenty-four hours a day. But I noticed something about the moon. It was totally unaffected by it all.

That is what Elihu is saying about God in Job 35:5: "Look up at the heavens and see; gaze at the clouds so high above you. If you sin, how does that affect him? If your sins are many, what does that do to him?" Our good deeds and our bad deeds have no effect on our unchanging God. He is not added to or diminished by our successes or failures.

But Elihu also pointed out that our actions, good and bad, can vitally affect the welfare of the men and women around us. A wicked person can rob someone of his wealth, his peace of mind, or his good name and reputation. On the other hand, a good person, through kind words and acts of love and concern, can help others find peace of mind and soul.

It's a simple yet profound reminder that while the nature of God is completely out of reach of our sins and our service, the lives of people are greatly affected by what we say and do. So let us praise the God who cannot be changed and love the people who can.

Lord, keep me from speaking words that wound; instead, help me to speak words that promote the welfare of others. Amen.

To Ponder: "A word aptly spoken is like apples of gold in settings of silver" (Proverbs 25:11).

GRACE FOR TODAY
Read Psalms 78–83

"For I know the plans I have for you," declares the LORD,
"plans to prosper you and not to harm you,
plans to give you hope and a future."

JEREMIAH 29:11

One of the greatest hindrances to the people of God is longing for "the good old days." Why? Because in the midst of a faith journey, whenever we look back and long for the comfort and security of things gone by, we limit God. We see this in Psalm 78 where we read that in the desert the children of Israel "turned back and tempted [tested] God, and limited the Holy One of Israel" (78:41, KJV).

How on earth could someone limit an all-powerful God? Could a person stand on a railroad track and limit the progress of an oncoming freight train by holding out his hand to stop it? Yet the psalmist tells us these people whom God was leading through the wilderness were actually able to limit Him.

For one thing, they despised the food God gave them and longed for the leeks and garlic of Egypt. By that act, they claimed they knew better than God what was good for them. God was fulfilling His promise to feed them, but they wanted a more interesting menu. Pride and rebellion became a way of life as they doubted God's power and ridiculed His wisdom. They were constant grumblers because God did not always grant their desires. That was Israel's sin.

One lesson from this passage comes forth loud and clear. We had better stop arguing with God, even if our argument seems more logical than what He has revealed. When God calls us to move ahead in faith, let us not hang back in fear, clinging to a comfortable memory of the past.

Lord, I'm often guilty of the same sin as that of the children of Israel when I grumble about my life. Increase my faith that You are working out what is best for me, and help me to see this day through Your eyes. Amen.

To Ponder: God is out to help us, provide for us, comfort us. He desires what is best for us, according to His wisdom.

WISE LIVING
Read Proverbs 1–4

The fear of the LORD is the beginning of knowledge, but fools despise wisdom and discipline.

PROVERBS 1:7

There is a tremendous contrast between the book of Psalms and the book of Proverbs. Part of this contrast comes from the differences in the two principal writers, David and Solomon. Both were kings who loved the Lord. But David was a man of war, a soldier who fought the battles of Israel. Solomon spent time contemplating the great questions of life and applying his God-given wisdom to the difficult issues of everyday existence.

I believe there's a lesson for us here as Christian parents. It has to do with allowing our children to be themselves and not trying to force them into the same kinds of educational and career choices we made for ourselves.

Apparently, David was quite happy to see Solomon develop into a much different kind of person than he had been. But David did try to pass on important spiritual principles to his son. David prayed that Solomon would be a righteous man who loved God and kept His commandments. And in the first nine chapters of Proverbs, we see Solomon seeking to pass along those same spiritual principles to his own son. The first nine chapters of Proverbs could well be called a manual for young men and women, to guide them in their growing-up years.

If you are a parent with young people in the home, you might want to have a family meeting and suggest reading a paragraph or two of the first nine chapters of Proverbs out loud, then talking about what you read. The time might prove so valuable that you'll continue the practice and finish the whole book! Let's help our children to be themselves and encourage them to follow the Lord with all their hearts.

Lord, show me how to encourage my children to be comfortable with who they are and to follow You wholeheartedly. Amen.

To Ponder: God has a special job for you that no one else can do.

THE MARKS OF A NEW LIFE
Read Genesis 32–36

Dear friends, do not be surprised at the painful trial you are
suffering, as though something strange were happening to you.
But rejoice that you participate in the sufferings of Christ, so that
you may be overjoyed when his glory is revealed.

1 PETER 4:12-13

You know, a lot of strange and sometimes exciting things can happen
to you when you're traveling. In Genesis 32, we find Jacob traveling
back home, and he has an experience that is more than just exciting.
Jacob is met by a host of angels. Then he receives word that his
brother, Esau, is heading his way with four hundred men, and he
assumes he's in for a battle, which causes him great fear and distress.
But the most amazing thing of all happened while he was alone at
night. He had a wrestling match with an angel, in which he prevailed,
his life was preserved, and God blessed him.

In that encounter with God, his life was changed for all time. No
longer would he be Jacob—the con man, liar, thief. He was now Israel,
a prince who had power with God. But note something significant. He
doesn't begin to beat his chest and flex his muscles and announce to
one and all that he had wrestled with God and prevailed.

In deep humility and wonder he says, "It is because I saw God face
to face, and yet my life was spared" (32:30). Immediately, he begins
to show the marks of a new life. He is a different person.

Today you may be facing a similar encounter with God. It may
have come through a sickness, a heartache, the loss of a job, or some
other difficult circumstance. And it hurts. But the very encounters we
resist because of their pain are the ones that can lead us to a changed
life and a deeper fellowship with the Lord.

Lord, I submit to your correction as to a dear and loving
Father. Amen.

To Ponder: We are never closer to God than when we are resisting in
a spiritual battle through the power of the Holy Spirit.

MEETING WITH GOD
Read Leviticus 1–3

Very early in the morning, while it was still dark, Jesus got up, left the house and went off to a solitary place, where he prayed.

MARK 1:35

———

In today's passage we find a lesson that could do more than anything I know to end spiritual burnout among Christians. We see the tabernacle set up to be a place of fellowship and communion between God and His people. It was there they rendered their various religious duties to God. It was also there that God revealed His will to them.

Leviticus 1 begins with the words, "The LORD called to Moses and spoke to him from the Tent of Meeting." The word translated "called" means God spoke in a still, small voice. No lightning and thunder as on Mount Sinai. This was the gentle voice of God.

I have found it a great advantage to have a place set aside in my home where I start the day with a time of Bible reading and prayer. For a few minutes each day that place becomes my holy ground.

Several years ago, we had a home in Omaha where fifteen people were living, including my family. To find a little nook or cranny without a body was a real challenge. But one young man was determined to have a daily time alone with God. So he cleaned up a little storage closet next to the furnace room, put a map of the world on the wall, and placed a little rug on the floor so he could kneel and pray. Other people complained about the house being too crowded, but he'd found his place to privately meet with God. If you want to have a daily quiet time, there's really nothing that can stop you.

Lord, let me hear your still, small voice today as I meditate on Your Word. Amen.

To Ponder: Where can you stake out a place as holy ground to meet the Lord on a daily basis?

DAMAGE CONTROL
Read Numbers 5–8

Get rid of all bitterness, rage and anger, brawling and slander, along with every form of malice. Be kind and compassionate to one another, forgiving each other, just as in Christ God forgave you.

EPHESIANS 4:31-32

In Numbers 5–8 the Lord establishes certain laws for the removal of anything that is unclean from the place where the people are camped. This has a powerful application for you and me in our daily walk of discipleship. One of the most urgent matters we face every day is the removal of anything in our lives that might hinder our fellowship with Christ and ruin our testimony before others.

Some years ago, a violent windstorm caused great damage to the city of Colorado Springs. It broke windows, loosened shingles, and tore down electrical lines. A friend of mine and his wife were driving home from church the next morning when they saw a tree that everyone in the city had admired for its greatness and beauty. It had stood in splendor for years. Now it was flat on the ground. Then my friends noticed that the trunk was hollow.

Something had attacked the tree from the inside and destroyed the inner core. Looking at the tree from the outside revealed no evidence whatsoever that anything was wrong. But after many years of silent destruction, the tree had toppled in the wind.

A type of hollowness can happen in the life of a believer if there is an absence of deep abiding in Christ. When the believer suddenly faces something that reveals the depth of the problem, the sin is exposed, and that which may have looked great from the outside is shown for what it really is.

Lord, show me if there is anything in my life that Satan could use to damage my fellowship with You and destroy my testimony. Amen.

To Ponder: Is your inner life rooted and grounded in a vital, personal fellowship with Christ?

DEVOTED TO THE WORD
Read Numbers 9–12

Yet I hold this against you: You have forsaken your first love.

REVELATION 2:4

———

Numbers chapter 9 begins with the concerns of certain men that they would not be able to partake in the celebration of the Passover. What a blessing it is in the life of the church when people are *eager* to be involved in the activities of the people of God! What a blessing to see people hungering and thirsting after God's Word and concerned about those things that might hinder them from enjoying all that is available from the gracious hand of God.

During the years I was involved in a ministry with cadets at the Air Force Academy in Colorado Springs, we had a team of about forty guys. They were all sharp, but a couple of those guys were especially eager learners. I remember waking up from a nap one Sunday afternoon to find the two of them sitting at the foot of my bed, notebooks and pens in hand, waiting to talk about some aspect of their Christian faith.

Now these guys were near the top of their class academically and could easily have had a know-it-all attitude, but they didn't. As I've watched them over the years, that same quality of being an eager learner has propelled them into great responsibility and leadership in their jobs and churches.

How's your heart for learning today? Are you still excited about the Bible and the things of the Lord or has it all grown a little moldy and stale? You know, one of the root meanings of the word *disciple* is pupil, or learner. In our life of daily discipleship, we need a continuing hunger to learn from the Master.

Lord, I'm eager and ready to learn from Your Word today. Teach me what I need to know. Amen.

To Ponder: What have you learned from God's Word lately?

A THANKFUL SPIRIT
Read Numbers 21–25

Through Jesus, therefore, let us continually offer to God a sacrifice of praise—the fruit of lips that confess his name.

HEBREWS 13:15

In Numbers 21, we find the children of Israel murmuring and complaining for lack of bread, although manna was in constant supply. When they despised God's provision and called it "light bread," fiery serpents came among them and killed many of those who shook their fists in the face of God.

When Moses prayed, the Lord gave Him instructions to set up a serpent of brass on a pole so that if a serpent bit anyone, that person could look up at the serpent of brass and live. (The acts of Moses are a clear picture of Christ, and so is the brass serpent itself.) Immediately, those who had looked upon Moses as their enemy now sought him out as their intercessor and their advocate with God.

One of the most difficult, continuing battles we face as Christians is the battle against a thankless spirit. In Romans 1:21-31, we're given a long list of people's heinous crimes and sins against God. On that list are the words, "For although they knew God, they neither glorified him as God nor gave thanks to him." Now that puts a thankless spirit in some pretty bad company.

How do we turn our grumbling and discontent around and receive life with a grateful heart? How do we develop a thankful spirit? We simply have to see all that we have as the gracious provision of God and thank Him for it each day.

Lord, I thank You for my life and for all that I have. There's nothing that comes my way that doesn't go through Your hands. Amen.

To Ponder: Thankfulness in any situation depends a lot on your perspective.

THE WORD, PRAYER, AND OBEDIENCE
Read Deuteronomy 27–30

*If we claim to have fellowship with him yet walk in the
darkness, we lie and do not live by the truth.*

1 JOHN 1:6

Have you ever considered that God wants to turn every location of
your daily life into a personal fellowship hall with Him? He wants
every area, from the kitchen sink to the freeway, to be filled with His
presence and joy. How do you do that? There are three avenues—the
Word, prayer, and obedience.

In Deuteronomy 27:2, God gave these instructions: "When you have
crossed the Jordan into the land the LORD your God is giving you, set up
some large stones and coat them with plaster. Write on them all the
words of this law. . . ." (27:2-3). This was a sort of rough-hewn monu-
ment indicating that the Word of God needed no embellishment.

In addition, they were to establish an altar and offer sacrifices. In
this way, they responded to His Word—they prayed—and communion was established between God and His people.

The third element was to do all the commandments God had
given them. Obedience is a vital link in a life of fellowship with God.
Why? Because there is no fellowship with a superior apart from it. If
you want to test that out, when you go to work tomorrow and the
boss tells you to do something, tell him to hang it on his beak. There
probably won't be the same quality of fellowship the two of you have
enjoyed on other occasions.

Obedience, along with the Word and prayer, is vital to our daily
walk of discipleship. Wherever you are today—at home, in your car,
in a hospital, at a military barracks—it can become your "fellowship
hall" with the Lord.

*Lord, I know that when I don't feel Your presence beside me,
I'm the one who moved away. Help me to be faithful to meet
with You in every area of my life. Amen.*

To Ponder: Jesus said, "If you love me, you will obey what I command" (John 14:15).

WALKING WITH GOD
Read 1 Samuel 9–12

Therefore, my dear brothers, stand firm. Let nothing move you.
Always give yourselves fully to the work of the Lord, because you
know that your labor in the Lord is not in vain.

1 CORINTHIANS 15:58

King Saul had a fantastic start in life. He wasn't seeking to be king of Israel, but when he was chosen, he accepted it as a call from God and got under way with the job. When Saul was anointed king, 1 Samuel 10:9 says, "God changed Saul's heart," and he began to demonstrate many wonderful qualities early in his reign.

When public announcement was made of his appointment, some people despised him and publicly humiliated him. But instead of flying into a rage and defending his wounded ego, he held his peace. And when the people of Jabesh-Gilead were threatened, he called Israel together, led them in battle, and delivered his brothers out of the hand of their oppressors. After he had led the army to victory, he gave the glory to God and forgave those who had mocked his leadership.

Saul started out as a man of humility, mercy, and courage. But a day came when his heart turned away from the Lord. Of course it didn't happen all at once, and that's just the point. The most important day in your Christian life is today. You may have gotten off to a great start when you gave your life to Christ a few years back, but what are you going to do today? Will you make time for personal fellowship with the Lord today? Will you share your faith with a friend today? Will you trust God to carry you through the difficult circumstances today?

Lord, please give me Your strength to walk today in fellowship with You. Amen.

To Ponder: "Encourage one another daily as long as it is called Today, so that none of you may be hardened by sin's deceitfulness" (Hebrews 3:13).

GOD'S ESSENTIAL LINK
Read Genesis 15–17

"Come, follow me," Jesus said,
"and I will make you fishers of men."

MATTHEW 4:19

How important do you think you are to God's eternal plan for reaching the world? A lot of Christians I know would say, "I don't think that I'm important at all." But that feeling usually comes when people forget a key element in the plan—the fact that God uses people.

In Genesis 15–17, we have an incredible event. The Most High God—the possessor of heaven and earth—is speaking to one of His creatures, Abram, and giving him a promise that will have a tremendous impact on all generations to come. One part of the promise had to do with the Promised Land that Abram's descendants would one day possess. But the other part had far-reaching implications too. In Abram "shall all families of the earth be blessed." God was about to use this one life to start a fire that would warm the hearts of people in all the nations of the earth, throughout history.

And friend, you are a vital part of this four-thousand-year-old promise. How? "If you belong to Christ, then you are Abraham's seed, and heirs according to the promise" (Galatians 3:29). Christian, you are a vital link in God's purpose.

If God wants to reach your neighbor, He may want to use you. You're the one who took over a casserole when his wife was sick. You've baby-sat their kids. You've fried hamburgers together in the backyard. You've built a relationship that can become a natural bridge for sharing the good news of Christ. And you may be the only Christian with that kind of relationship.

Do you see yourself as a vital link in that ancient chain God began with Abram and continues with the Great Commission of Jesus Christ?

Lord, open my eyes to the opportunities around me to proclaim Your salvation. Amen.

To Ponder: God has enabled you to reach some people more effectively with the gospel than anyone else could.

THE PRIESTHOOD OF BELIEVERS
Read Exodus 19–20

*To him who loves us and has freed us from our sins
by his blood, and has made us to be a kingdom
and priests to serve his God and Father.*

REVELATION 1:5-6

Before the Ten Commandments were given, God communicated a powerful truth to His people. He said in Exodus 19:5, "Now if you obey me fully and keep my covenant, then out of all nations you will be my treasured possession. Although the whole earth is mine, you will be for me a kingdom of priests and a holy nation."

God told them plainly what He expected and required of them—obedience. Next, He claimed His sovereignty over all of creation and every man, woman, and child in it. His people were to be a peculiar treasure—a kingdom of priests to whom the oracles of God were given and through whom the Redeemer would come to bless all nations; a kingdom of priests who would be God's personal emissaries to the rest of the heathen world.

Christian, this is still the Lord's desire. His people—all of us—are to be witnesses and take the light of the gospel of the glory of Christ to those who sit in darkness and the shadow of death.

Just before His ascension into heaven, our Lord said, "But you will receive power when the Holy Spirit comes on you; and you will be my witnesses in Jerusalem, and in all Judea and Samaria, and to the ends of the earth." Not just the missionary, not just the pastor, but all of us—a kingdom of priests who are to spread the knowledge of God far and wide.

*Lord, before You may I own my failures as well as my successes.
Empower me to do Your will. Amen.*

To Ponder: We are priests unto God, and His personal emissaries to the world.

WIDENING THE FELLOWSHIP
Read Joshua 18–21

*"I tell you . . . there will be more rejoicing in heaven
over one sinner who repents than over ninety-nine
righteous persons who do not need to repent."*

LUKE 15:7

I attended a Christian conference where two men gave a testimony on
the subject of evangelism. The first man told of a meeting at which
the speaker asked everyone to jot down the names of five friends who
were nonChristians, and then begin praying for them on a regular
basis. He and his wife just stared at each other. They didn't have five
nonChristian friends.

They began to look for ways to meet nonChristians. The husband
went to the local gym and met a worldly young lawyer, who was quite
skillful in asking argumentative questions. The Christian was quite
skillful in answering them from the Scriptures. The lawyer eventually
came to Christ, and these two men now were telling *their* story.

Testamonies like theirs are rare nowadays. I'm afraid we're like the
children of Israel in today's passage, wherein Joshua said to them, "How
long will you wait before you begin to take possession of the land that
the LORD, the God of your fathers, has given you?" (Joshua 18:3).

Seven tribes had not yet claimed their inheritance. Apparently,
they had no desire to be scattered abroad and break up the old gang.
They had lots of spoil from the cities they had taken and could live the
good life in ease and comfort. They had plenty to eat, were safe, and
enjoyed each other's company.

Joshua's question is pertinent to us today. How long will we sit
around in our cozy little fellowships? There are thousands of lost men
and women who need us to reach out in friendship with the gospel of
Christ.

*Lord, please help me to break out of my "Christian cocoon"
and give me a vision for the lost. Amen.*

To Ponder: Our churches aren't meant to be a safe haven against the
world but a place to refuel before going out again to share the
gospel.

LIFE INVESTMENT
Read 2 Kings 1–3

*I will open my mouth in parables, I will utter hidden things,
things from of old—what we have heard and known,
what our fathers have told us. We will not hide them from
their children; we will tell the next generation the praiseworthy
deeds of the LORD, his power, and the wonders he has done.*

PSALM 78:2-4

What do you want to leave behind when your life on earth is over?
Let's look at what Elijah the prophet left behind. In today's passage,
we find him on his last day on earth, visiting the schools of the
prophets where young men trained. We see Elijah's final investment
in the life of Elisha. Never underestimate the power of one life invested
in another. When I was a twenty-four-year-old student at Northwestern
College in Minneapolis, one man taught me most of what I know about
the Christian life.

Don Rosenberger had been sent by The Navigators to teach
courses on personal Bible study and follow-up. Over a period of two
years he did much more than deliver classroom lectures on the subject.
He spent personal time with me and invited me to minister with
him to others.

I had never before heard of the principle of multiplying myself
through the lives of others. But Don took this vision and applied it to
daily life.

Paul wrote to Timothy, "And the things you have heard me say in
the presence of many witnesses entrust to reliable men who will also
be qualified to teach others" (2 Timothy 2:2). Are you investing yourself
in someone? For Elijah, it was Elisha. He left behind one young
man who would have a double portion of his spirit and carry on the
work of God. Who will you leave behind?

*Lord, keep me faithful to teach others who will in turn teach
others the truths of Your Word. Amen.*

To Ponder: Are you taking the time to invest your life in teaching
someone God's truths?

68

LIFE EXAMPLES
Read 2 Kings 9–12

For this reason I am sending to you Timothy, my
son whom I love, who is faithful in the Lord. He will
remind you of my way of life in Christ Jesus, which
agrees with what I teach everywhere in every church.

1 CORINTHIANS 4:17

When we talk about spiritual leaders who train their successors, you might be saying, "I can barely get my own work done every week. How can I train someone else?"

Let me offer a couple of suggestions. First, involve someone in your ministry, whatever it is. If you teach Sunday school, ask someone to assist in what you're doing. That gives him or her a chance to observe you in action—and to help.

Second, get involved together in things other than spiritual activities. Throughout the books of First and Second Kings, we see Elijah and Elisha involved in training the young men in the schools of the prophets. But we also see Elijah investing himself in one man, Elisha, who would carry on the ministry when he was gone.

Moses and Joshua, Elijah and Elisha, and Paul and Timothy must have enjoyed a tremendous friendship that developed over years of shared experiences. A lot of principles of Christian living are caught rather than taught.

If you feel that your life isn't good enough to be observed and imitated by others, join the club. No one does. By the grace of God, we can be challenged to a deeper walk with the Lord as we seek to help others. Our lives are honed as we share our victories and defeats and grow together.

Whatever your ministry, let me challenge you to include someone young in it, and you will prepare someone who will keep on serving the Lord in the generation to come.

Lord, with Your help, I want to invest the life You're working
in me with others. Amen.

To Ponder: As Jesus spent time with the disciples, they internalized a message that would turn the world upside-down.

WHEN YOUR MINISTRY CHANGES
Read 2 Kings 13–17

Always learning but never able to acknowledge the truth.

2 TIMOTHY 3:7

———

George Sheffer died of a heart attack at age seventy. He had been with Young Life since its beginning in the early forties and had invested himself in people all over the world. There were more than a thousand people at his memorial service.

During the last four years of George's life, he spent a lot of time in Africa, sharing his vision of youth ministry with men and women in Kenya, Uganda, Tanzania, and Malawi. He had just returned from Africa the night he went home to be with the Lord. During his final years, George drew experiences from the treasure house of a lifetime of sharing Christ with others. He adapted his ministry and remained useful to the Lord right up to the end.

In 2 Kings 13, we see Elisha at a turning point. He has fallen ill, and the last part of his prophetic service is hidden from us. After sixty years as a prophet, he is no longer a prominent figure on the stage of Israel. Was he less useful to God? Of course not. But his ministry had changed. In his younger days, Elisha was out front, making a tremendous impact on the society around him. In his latter days, it seems he gave himself to the young men in the schools of the prophets, to prepare them for their service for God.

If you are a young person just getting started in your work for Christ, focus on learning what God has to teach you. As time goes on, give yourself to putting into practice what God has taught you. In your declining years, spend time teaching the next generation what you have learned.

Lord, as my circumstances change, help me to adapt and change my focus so that I can stay useful to You. Amen.

To Ponder: What are some ways a person can serve the Lord in any season of life?

LEADING WITH HEART
Read 2 Chronicles 29–32

Never be lacking in zeal, but keep your
spiritual fervor, serving the Lord.

ROMANS 12:11

Isn't it good to see people give it all they've got, whatever they're doing? That's what we see in today's section of Scripture concerning King Hezekiah. Second Chronicles 31:21 tells us, "And in every work that he began in the service of the house of God, and in the law, and in the commandments, to seek his God, he did it with all his heart, and prospered" (KJV).

This is God's evaluation of Hezekiah's life: he sought the Lord and served Him with all his heart.

When Hezekiah came to the throne, he found the nation in shambles. But his first priority was not the government or the economy, but the spiritual health of the people. He challenged the priests and the Levites to sanctify themselves and get their hearts right with God, pointing out two current examples of their spiritual apathy: the lamps had not been lit and the incense was not being burned. The lamps speak to us symbolically of the Word of God, while incense evokes the prayers of the people of God rising before the throne of grace.

Hezekiah experienced his leadership by calling the priests and the people back to personal worship and spiritual discipline. And when the priests responded to Hezekiah's challenge and the people began to worship God again, the Bible tells us there was great joy in Jerusalem, unlike anything since the days of Solomon.

How's it going in your life today? Do you live like Hezekiah, "with all your heart?" In particular, is your spirit aflame with zeal for God? If not, why not ask Him to rekindle that fire through the study of the Word and the exercise of prayer.

Lord, create in me a desire to live for You with my whole heart.
Amen.

To Ponder: If we ask for cleansing, God will bring us back to the high road of fellowship with Him.

THE GOOD SEED
Read Matthew 12–15

For we are to God the aroma of Christ among those who are being saved and those who are perishing.

2 CORINTHIANS 2:15

I am convinced that lay men and women need to recapture a biblical view of their role in the kingdom of God. In Matthew 13, Jesus uses a parable about sowing seed to introduce a tremendous concept concerning the kingdom of God. "The field is the world, and the good seed stands for the sons of the kingdom" (13:38).

Here Jesus points out the magnitude of the job: "The field is the world"—a world of people who need the message of the gospel. And what is the Lord's plan for accomplishing this? Planting good seed that will be fruitful and multiply throughout that needy world.

All too often we see the good seed as those among us with unique gifts and abilities that enable them to fulfill the roles of Bible teachers, seminary professors, missionaries, or pastors. Now, it's a great privilege to pray for full-time Christian workers, support them financially, and encourage them in their work. But that's not all God has called us to do.

Jesus said, "The good seed stands for the sons of the kingdom." Christian, that's not just the people who can sing, preach, and translate the Bible into another language; it's all of us who know Him. We are the good seed of the kingdom He wants to scatter throughout the world to bring the message of salvation to the lost. Christian, you are important to God, and He has a job for you to do.

Lord, as I live and work among people, help me to reproduce the good seed in the world until we crowd out the tares. Amen.

To Ponder: Jesus desires to fulfill His Great Commission through all of us, not just a select few.

THE ROAD TO GREATNESS
Read Matthew 20–23

"Whoever serves me must follow me; and where I am, my servant also will be. My Father will honor the one who serves me."

JOHN 12:26

Here are the words of Jesus to His disciples about greatness in His kingdom: "You know that the rulers of the Gentiles lord it over them, and their high officials exercise authority over them. Not so with you. Instead, whoever wants to become great among you must be your servant, and whoever wants to be first must be your slave—just as the Son of Man did not come to be served, but to serve, and to give his life as a ransom for many" (Matthew 20:25-28).

I remember a week of meetings in Arizona with the Wycliffe Bible Translators. One day we were going through the food line for dinner when I noticed that Kenneth Pike was serving the beans. Now, Dr. Kenneth Pike, Ph.D., is recognized as one of the world leaders in the field of linguistics. This man is a genius, one of a kind. He could have easily been at the head table because of his position and prestige. Instead, he had chosen to serve others.

The Upper Room Discourse in John 13 opens with Jesus washing His disciples' feet in an act of love and service. He was teaching His disciples by example to prepare them to be leaders in His kingdom. But it took time for the disciples to understand what true leadership was. James and John had just asked the Lord if they could sit on either side of Him in His glory. Jesus countered with the command to serve.

In the kingdom of God, Jesus turned the organizational chart upside-down and put Himself on the bottom. If you're not getting credit for your good work as a Christian, keep on serving. Jesus says you're on the road to greatness.

Lord, help me to understand the paradoxical laws of Your kingdom and to want to live no other way. Amen.

To Ponder: Service is the law of greatness in the kingdom of Christ.

THE PLUM ASSIGNMENT
Read Mark 8–10

*However, I consider my life worth nothing to me, if only I may
finish the race and complete the task the Lord Jesus has given
me—the task of testifying to the gospel of God's grace.*

ACTS 20:24

For many people, being a servant of Jesus Christ sounds romantic
and idealistic. But serving Christ is a demanding proposition, as we
see in Mark 10:32-34 (KJV).

> And he took again the twelve, and began to tell them what
> things should happen unto him, saying, "Behold, we go up to
> Jerusalem; and the Son of Man shall be delivered unto the chief
> priests, and unto the scribes; and they shall condemn him to
> death, and shall deliver him to the Gentiles, and they shall mock
> him, and shall scourge him, and shall spit upon him, and shall
> kill him; and the third day he shall rise again."

Before these remarks, Jesus and His disciples had been in Galilee.
The people had been friendly and had turned out in large numbers.
The ministry had gone well, and the disciples may have begun to
think that serving Jesus was a great idea. Friendly people, big crowds.
And then one day Jesus dropped the bombshell: "We're leaving Galilee
and going up to Jerusalem!"

I can almost hear the disciples saying, "The ministry is going great
here in Galilee. Here they like us; up there they hate us and are liable
to kill us."

The principle emerging from this story is that a servant of Christ
cannot choose his place of service, nor the type of service he will ren-
der to the Lord. God chooses both of these things. But along with
God's choice, He gives us the wisdom and strength we need.

Lord, give me willingness to do what You call me to do. Amen.

To Ponder: There may be times when we go to a seemingly unattractive place with no idea of what lies ahead. But there is no
greater joy than following the orders of the Master.

TO LOVE IS TO GIVE
Read John 17:25-26

Husbands, love your wives, just as Christ loved
the church and gave himself up for her.

EPHESIANS 5:25

I greeted our youngest boy with, "Son, what did you do in school today?" To my utter surprise, he said the teacher had them write a definition of love.

That sounded more like an assignment for a college-level sociology or philosophy class than a bunch of eight-year-olds. But I controlled my surprise and said, "What did you write?"

"Well, it sure could have been better."

"But what did you say?"

"Well," he replied, "it sure could have been longer."

"Yes, I suppose it could have, son, but what was it you put down?"

"I put down 'To love is to give!' "

I was dumbfounded! "Wow!" I said, "that was great! How did you come up with such a wonderful answer as that?"

Now it was his turn to look startled. "Dad," he said, "don't you know John 3:16? 'For God so loved the world that He gave His only begotten son that whosoever believeth in Him should not perish but have everlasting life'?"

For God so loved the world that He *gave*. Now Christian, that is one of the most significant truths contained in the whole Bible.

Wouldn't it be wonderful if all the people of the world understood love in that way? Most people see love in the light of getting rather than giving. And L-O-V-E is usually spelled L-U-S-T. Is there anything we can do to help our kids see things in the right perspective? Mom and Dad, show affection for each other. Let your kids see a tender pat on the shoulder, an affectionate hug, and tender kiss.

Let them see love that focuses on the needs of others.

Lord, may I grow in selfless love, the kind of love with which
You love me. Amen.

To Ponder: Love is not self-seeking (from 1 Corinthians 13:5).

SERVANTHOOD
Read 2 Corinthians 1

Let no one seek his own, but each one the other's well-being.

1 CORINTHIANS 10:24 (KJV)

———

Most people would agree that the truly great people of this world are remembered not for what they took out of life but for what they gave. How do you acquire a servant's heart or help others develop a servant's heart? I believe the first step is to become sensitive to the needs of other people and then take the initiative to set the whole thing in motion.

The China Inland Mission used the dinner table to train people in servanthood. They had a rule that when the members of the mission gathered for the evening meal, no one was allowed to ask to have any food passed to them. Everyone learned to be alert to the needs of others and to watch for the empty plate.

Think for a moment of the words of Jesus, "I lay down my life for the sheep. . . . No one takes it from me, but I lay it down of my own accord" (John 10:15,18). Jesus came into the world to meet the needs of others and exercised the initiative to meet those needs.

Friend, do you think your dinner table could become a training ground to develop the Christlike attitude of a servant's heart in your own life, and in the lives of your family? Remember what Christ told His disciples, "For he who is least among you all—he is the greatest" (Luke 9:48). The same is true for His disciples today.

Lord, help me to put others' needs above my own. Amen.

To Ponder: How is your family's dinner table different from or similar to the one practiced at the China Inland Mission?

HUMILITY
Read Philippians 2:1-11

But when his heart became arrogant and hardened with pride, he was deposed from his royal throne and stripped of his glory.

DANIEL 5:20

We were on our way to Steamboat Springs for a few days of skiing. The road was icy, and the wind was blowing so hard we went gliding right off the road into the snow. Some of us got out and tried to push the car back onto the road. The combination of slickness and a large snow bank was too much resistance for us. The car wouldn't budge.

Eventually, a good Samaritan in a four-wheel-drive truck came along and pulled us out.

As I look back on that experience, I am reminded of the words of the apostle Peter recorded in 1 Peter 5:5. "Young men, in the same way be submissive to those who are older. All of you, clothe yourselves with humility toward one another, because, 'God opposes the proud but gives grace to the humble.'"

It's frightening to think of going through life pushing against something you can't budge. God resists the proud. And I'm sure we'd agree that when a person has God resisting Him, he's in for a hard struggle. So we each have a choice. Do we want to struggle through life, fighting God in our pride and arrogance, or do we want to go through life in the enabling power of His grace, experiencing His love, mercy, power, and blessing?

How wise it is to walk humbly with our God—and our neighbors—relying on Him to enable rather than resist us in our journey through life.

Lord, keep me from a haughty spirit; I desire to walk humbly with You. Amen.

To Ponder: The same God who resists the proud pours out His grace to the humble.

THE JUDGE OF THE EARTH
Read Genesis 18–20

He is the Rock, his works are perfect, and all his ways are just.
A faithful God who does no wrong, upright and just is he.

DEUTERONOMY 32:4

One evening Virginia and I had dinner with friends who were hosting members of a professional basketball team and their coach. After the meal, my friend asked me to share with the group my personal experience with God. When I was finished, I asked them if they had any questions. Immediately, the coach's hand went up. "What about the heathen in Africa?" he said. "Do you mean to tell me that God will send all those people to hell, even though they have never had a chance to hear the message?"

"Let me answer by asking you a question," I said. "Do you believe God is a God of love?" He did. "Do you believe God will treat people fairly?" He did.

"Then you believe exactly what the Bible teaches, because the Bible says, 'Will not the Judge of all the earth do right?' So leave the heathen in the hands of God. He will do what is right, not by your standards but by His. Your concern should be for your own soul, because now you've heard the message, and God calls upon you to repent and believe the gospel."

"Will not the Judge of all the earth do right?" (Genesis 18:25). Abraham felt initially that it wouldn't be right for God to judge Sodom and Gomorrah and destroy the righteous along with the wicked. But as Abraham talked with God, he found the answer to his question.

Christian, are you harboring the thought that God has treated you unfairly? Perhaps in your health, the job promotion that never came, finances, problems with your kids. Identify and surrender that issue to the Lord. The Judge of all the earth has done right in your life, too.

Lord, your compassions never fail. They are new every morning. Great is Your faithfulness (from Lamentations 3:22-23). Amen.

To Ponder: Let me examine my ways and test my thought patterns beside God's great love and faithfulness.

THE LAMB OF GOD
Read Exodus 11–12

*John saw Jesus coming toward him and said, "Look,
the Lamb of God, who takes away the sin of the world!"*

JOHN 1:29

Hundreds of years before the crucifixion, God told Moses to gather the
people of Israel together in preparation for their departure from Egypt.
They were to sacrifice a lamb without blemish and without spot, eat
the flesh of the lamb, and sprinkle the blood on the doorposts of their
home. This lamb was, of course, a symbol of the Lord Jesus. "For
Christ, our Passover lamb, has been sacrificed" (1 Corinthians 5:7).

The lamb without blemish and without spot represented Christ's
sinless life, the just one paying the penalty for the unjust. The lamb
was to be set apart four days prior to the feast. Christ was sacrificed
at the Passover, and He entered Jerusalem four days before the day the
paschal lamb was set apart. The lamb was to be roasted with fire,
denoting the sufferings of Christ. Not a bone of the lamb was to be
broken, a prophetic picture of Christ on the cross.

Then the people of God were to sprinkle the lamb's blood on the
doorposts of the houses as an open witness to everyone. I'm sure the
Jews might have thought, *Wouldn't that give the Egyptians one
more thing to ridicule—"What are these crazy Jews doing now?"*
Some may have been tempted to sprinkle the blood out of sight—the
closet door perhaps. Wouldn't that be just as good? No, it must be outside for all to see, denoting our open profession of faith in God and
obedience to His Word.

Christ was crucified publicly, openly, for our sin. And the Bible tells
us that our witness for Him should be public and open for all to see.

*Lord, thank You that Your blood cleanses me from all unright-
eousness. Amen.*

To Ponder: Do I live in such a way that my life is a clear testimony of
salvation through Jesus' shed blood?

GOD PAID OUR DEBT IN FULL
Read Leviticus 6–17

By one sacrifice he has made perfect forever
those who are being made holy.

HEBREWS 10:14

I often tell the story of the young man brought before a judge for an offense. He is given the verdict—thirty dollars or thirty days. The young man, who is now sorry for what he did, has no money to pay his fine. So the judge steps down, removes his robe, takes out his own wallet, and pays the fine. With the verdict he has satisfied the law; out of love, he has paid the young man's penalty and set him free. That's exactly what God did for you and me in Jesus Christ.

The Old Testament record of the Day of Atonement—God's way of reconciling people to Himself—and the New Testament account of Christ's death are like reading two books at once: the Old Testament message is clarified by the New. The New Testament tells us that Christ entered once into the holy place and obtained eternal redemption for us (see Hebrews 9:11-28).

There is another New Testament picture that emerges from the Old. On the Day of Atonement, two goats were provided for the people—one for a sin offering, its blood sprinkled before the mercy seat and on the altar. The other was a scapegoat. The sins of the nation were confessed over it, and then it was sent into the wilderness, signifying that because of their sin, they deserved to be banished from the presence of God. Both symbolized Christ: "The Lord has laid on him the iniquity of us all" (Isaiah 53:6); "We have been made holy through the sacrifice of the body of Jesus Christ once for all" (Hebrews 10:10).

Through Christ's atonement, our sins are covered, forgiven, and removed. We can find rest for our souls and enjoy the incredible privilege of walking daily with God.

Lord, thank You for securing eternal redemption and delivering me from the curse of the law. Amen.

To Ponder: "Jesus paid it all" gives us great comfort. "All to Him I owe" gives us great motivation.

DISPELLING THE DARKNESS
Read Leviticus 24–27

*"Neither do people light a lamp and put it under
a bowl. Instead they put it on its stand,
and it gives light to everyone in the house."*

MATTHEW 5:15

In today's passage about the tabernacle, we read that the lamps were
to burn continually. They were to be tended and supplied with oil so
their light would never go out. Throughout the Bible, lamps are used
to picture our lives as believers.

Jesus said, "Let your light shine before men, that they may see
your good deeds and praise your Father in heaven" (Matthew 5:16).
Where does a lamp do the most good? Outside at high noon or in a
dark place where there is no other source of illumination? Yet how
many times we complain when God puts us in a situation where we
are about the only source of light.

I have to smile when I think of a young Marine named Tony, who
is having a profoundly positive effect on the men around him. His life
is a light in a dark place. When Tony first made his faith in Christ
known, a lot of his fellow Marines laughed at him. But Tony didn't
react. He continued to live for Christ, doing his job with everything
he had. He was promoted to the rank of sergeant at the age of twenty,
an almost unheard of thing in the Marines.

We may work in an office with people who have no regard for God.
Life in a college dorm or a military barracks can seem like a black hole.
But that's where a lamp is needed most. A lamp doesn't have to make
noise, have a fancy exterior, or call attention to itself. It just has to provide illumination in the deep shadows of life.

*Lord, let the contrast of my light against the darkness around
me cause people to ask about its source. Amen.*

To Ponder: The darker the area around me, the brighter my light will
shine.

BARREN NO MORE
Read 1 Samuel 1–3

*Pray in the Spirit on all occasions with
all kinds of prayers and requests.*

EPHESIANS 6:18

When we meet Hannah in 1 Samuel 1, we find her in the temple of the Lord, pouring out her heart to God. The Bible says she was in bitterness of soul and prayed to the Lord and wept much. Hannah was unable to have children, and her physical barrenness had become intolerable to her.

As she poured out her heart to God, she was completely oblivious of how she appeared to others. Eli the priest thought she was drunk. But God answered Hannah's prayer for a child and she became the mother of Samuel.

I wonder how long it has been since you and I prayed like that because of our spiritual barrenness. I believe that one of the secrets to a fruitful Christian life is to become so fed up with our fruitless life that we will approach the Lord on our knees and pour out our hearts to Him in prayer.

We often pray for other reasons—when we face financial difficulty, when a cherished relationship is in trouble, when our physical health fails. Out of our personal anguish we will fall on our faces and pour out our souls to God. But will we do it because of our lack of spiritual fruit? Only if God so convicts us that it produces a genuine grief of soul.

Christian, when we begin praying for God to use us and make us fruitful for His glory, something wonderful is going to happen.

Lord, create in me a grief for my lack of spiritual fruit. Amen.

To Ponder: Do I have a personal longing for the salvation of souls?

A PICTURE OF GRACE
Read Ezekiel 12–15

*There came a man who was sent from God; his name was John.
He came as a witness to testify concerning that light, so that
through him all men might believe.*

JOHN 1:6-7

Years ago I was asked to lead a daily vacation Bible school program, so I began to look around for some means of making the gospel clear to the kids. One elderly lady suggested I use a flannelgraph, and she showed me how to explain the gospel in pictures. It was a smashing success, as thirteen children and three teachers came to Christ.

Now, the use of visual aids is not a new idea. In fact, God was using the concept in Ezekiel's time to get people's attention and communicate His message. In Ezekiel 12:3, the Lord said to Ezekiel, "Therefore, son of man, pack your belongings for exile and in the daytime, as they watch, set out and go from where you are to another place. Perhaps they will understand, though they are a rebellious house." The Lord had him pack his belongings, leave his home, dig through a wall, tremble as he ate his food, and shudder in fear as he drank his water—all to foretell the confusion and fear that was about to come on the people.

When it comes to visual aids, the Lord can use anything. But the most effective visual aid is the godly life of the believer. Friends of ours lost their nine-year-old son to leukemia. After the funeral, they went away to a mountain lodge. One morning at breakfast, a woman pressed them about what they'd been through. She was astounded by their peace and confidence in God. "I want to know why you don't hate God," she said.

You see, when you and I show peace, joy, purpose, and contentment—all those things the world craves—we are demonstrating the truth of the gospel and the power of God.

Lord, let my life be a picture of Your love and grace. Amen.

To Ponder: Our lives are the best visual aid some people will ever see.

DID YOU GET THAT?
Read 2 Chronicles 6–9

*Yet he saved them for his name's sake,
to make his mighty power known.*

PSALM 106:8

One of the dangers we face as Christians is becoming so familiar with certain words and phrases that we fail to consider their meaning. For example, we know that God is an infinite being who is so powerful and so immense that the heavens cannot contain Him. He is infinitely above and beyond the boundaries of creation. Great! But what does that mean?

Some time ago, a Canadian astronomer working on a mountaintop in Chile sighted a supernova. It was the first such sighting since 1604. A supernova is an exploding star that in one second releases a burst of atomic particles with a force equal to all the energy the sun will give out in its lifetime of ten billion years—multiplied by 100. Did you get that? If this is what the creation can do, then what can God the Creator do?

How could the infinite God of the universe live in the temple built for Him by Solomon? It is part of the mystery of His promise. The New Testament tells us that God was pleased to have all His fullness dwell in Jesus Christ. And that by faith, Christ lives in the heart of every child of God. You see, once again we are faced with a familiar phrase, the meaning of which we may fail to grasp.

Although God is infinitely above and beyond our finite understanding of Him, He hears our childlike prayers and accepts our childlike praise. All our plans, all our plots and schemes, all our thoughts and aims and affections are uncovered and laid bare before Him who loves us, and to whom we must give account.

Lord, infinite God . . . mighty in power . . . Creator of heaven and earth, the sea, and all that is in them; thank You for living within my heart through faith in Jesus Christ. Amen.

To Ponder: What does it mean to me that the infinite mighty Creator loves me?

LOVING THE ONE YOU SERVE
Read Song of Songs

God is love. Whoever lives in love lives in God, and God in him.

1 JOHN 4:16

There were some great love songs in the forties: vocalists with the Glenn Miller band sang about that gal from Kalamazoo; the Tommy Dorsey Orchestra extolled the virtues of Marie; the Andrews Sisters exhorted the soldier to not sit under the apple tree with anyone else but the girl he left behind. During the war years, one song promised that one day there would again be bluebirds over the white cliffs of Dover. When the war finally ended, Perry Como sang that we would be together till the end of time.

When my wife and I became Christians and headed off to Northwestern College to study the Bible, I saw an amazing thing. Hundreds of young men and women assembled every morning during chapel hour and sang love songs to God! This opened up a whole new musical world to me. I learned songs like "My Jesus, I Love Thee" and "Jesus, Lover of My Soul."

We find another love song in the Song of Songs. As the bride extols the virtues of the bridegroom and pledges her undying love for him, we see an application to the church as a whole and to each Christian.

Remember the question Jesus asked Peter: "Do you love me?" Together Jesus and the Twelve had fed the five thousand, healed the sick, raised the dead, even walked on water together. Yet Jesus asked, "Do you love me?" And the Lord is still asking the same question of you and me today. We may have served the Lord, but Solomon's Song reminds us of the heart of the matter. Do we love Him? Christian, if you do, tell Him today. You might even want to sing a love song to your Lord.

Lord, I love You and I give you first place in my heart. Amen.

To Ponder: How do I express my love to God?

CAN GOD BE TRUSTED?
Read Isaiah 36–39

You are my hiding place; you will protect me from trouble and surround me with songs of deliverance.

PSALM 32:7

As I've talked with people and listened to their prayers, many of them are concerned with seemingly impossible situations: long-term unemployment, terminal illnesses, rebellious and estranged children.

These are real issues in today's world. The international scene is filled with chaos, hate, and mistrust. There seems to be no power on earth that can turn things around to bring peace and tranquillity. It all seems overwhelming. And it is, except for God.

In Isaiah 36, we find that King Sennacherib of Assyria had captured all the fortified cities of Judah and then laid siege to Jerusalem. He sent his field commander to call for King Hezekiah's surrender because, humanly speaking, there was no way Hezekiah and his people could survive.

Notice Hezekiah's reaction in 37:1,20: "He tore his clothes and put on sackcloth and went into the temple of the LORD . . . and Hezekiah prayed, 'Now, O LORD our God, deliver us from his hand, so that all kingdoms on earth may know that you alone, O LORD, are God.'" God answered Hezekiah's prayer in a miraculous way.

Can God be trusted? Listen to Hebrews 13:5 from the *Amplified Bible*: "For He (God) Himself has said, I will not in any way fail you nor give you up nor leave you without support. [I will] not, [I will] not, [I will] not in any degree leave you helpless, nor forsake nor let [you] down.'"

Lord, nothing is too hard for Thee. Amen.

To Ponder: When life gets overwhelming, I always have the choice to go before God in prayer and cast myself on His mercy and strength.

THE GOD OF THE SECOND CHANCE
Read 1 Samuel 4–8

Our God is in heaven; he does whatever pleases him.

PSALM 115:3

Have you ever tried to manipulate God? For example, some people think that by tithing they can force God to bless them financially. Others believe that by doing evangelism or serving sacrificially, they can guarantee that God will give them what they want. It's true that God blesses those who tithe, and He honors the humble service rendered for Him. But we do not manipulate God through religious ritual of any kind.

Today's passage begins with the people of God going out to battle apart from the Lord's command and suffering defeat. But rather than repent of their sin, they blamed the whole thing on God. When they decided to try again, they thought they would guarantee success by performing a religious ritual—taking the ark of the covenant into battle with them. They thought they had God in a box. Thirty thousand of Israel's soldiers were killed, and the ark was captured by the Philistines.

Many years after this devastating defeat, Samuel sensed that the people were ready to return to the Lord, and he said to them, "If you are returning to the LORD with all your hearts, then rid yourselves of the foreign gods . . . and commit yourselves to the LORD and serve him only, and he will deliver you out of the hand of the Philistines" (7:3).

You may have left the Lord behind a long time ago. But it's not too late for the deep, genuine repentance that God responds to with mercy and love. We cannot manipulate God, but we can love and serve Him with all our hearts. And we can praise Him that He is the God of the second chance.

Lord, I repent of my attempts to force You to bless my actions; thank You for giving me a second chance. Amen.

To Ponder: It is my heartfelt repentance, not a religious ritual, that moves the hand of God.

A HEART AFTER GOD
Read 1 Samuel 16–19

Therefore we do not lose heart. Though outwardly we are wasting away, yet inwardly we are being renewed day by day.

2 CORINTHIANS 4:16

Most of us put a lot of stock in outward appearance. While there's nothing wrong with combing our hair and smelling good, it says a lot about our basic orientation to life. We are most concerned with how other people see us.

Not so with God. When the Lord sent Samuel to the house of Jesse in Bethlehem to anoint one of his sons as king, Samuel was impressed with Eliab, but God said to Samuel, "Do not consider his appearance or his height, for I have rejected him. The LORD does not look at the things man looks at. Man looks at the outward appearance, but the LORD looks at the heart" (1 Samuel 16:7).

Does that mean that a big, good-looking guy cannot be a spiritual leader? No, of course not. It just means that God looks for something deeper than that: a heart that is given to Him.

David, who wasn't even invited to the event, was finally brought in from the pasture where he was tending the sheep, and the Lord said, "Rise and anoint him; he is the one." There was something within David that only the Lord could see.

What does God see when He looks at us? Hearts that are filled with the Word and given to prayer? And what about our opinion of others? Are we so turned off by someone's outward appearance that we write them off before we discover their inner beauty?

It is one of the great ironies of our day that we spend buckets of money on our bodies, which are, in effect, wasting away. At the same time, we often neglect the inward person, which the apostle Paul says should be renewed day by day.

Lord, help me today to see as You see, and to live my life in light of Your perspective. Amen.

To Ponder: What does God see when He looks at me today?

THE BARREN PLACES
Read Esther 1–2

*Blessed is the man who trusts in the LORD, whose
confidence is in him. He will be like a tree planted
by the water that sends out its roots by the stream. It
does not fear when heat comes; its leaves are always green.*

JEREMIAH 17:7-8

As far as I know, the book of Esther is the only book in the Bible in
which the central figure rose to prominence by winning a beauty contest. But Esther never considered her promotion selfishly. In fact, she
put everything on the line, including her life, to do the will of God in
a very difficult situation.

For Esther and her people, the Jews, circumstances were bad.
They had been taken captive from their homeland many years before
and were second-class citizens in this place. Now a plot was being
hatched to exterminate them from the face of the earth. But the hand
of God was leading Esther and her Uncle Mordecai in what seemed to
be a God-forsaken place.

I remember the first time I drove across the desert from Arizona
into California. My first reaction was, "This is a God-forsaken place."
Every plant seemed to have sharp needles or stickers on it and just
didn't appear very attractive to me. But that was before I learned to see
the beauty God has created in the desert.

In a similar way, there are times when we look at the landscape of
our lives and think, *God is nowhere to be found.* That just isn't true.
Just as you can see in the book of Esther many evidences of God's
mercy, grace, and love, you can see the hand of God in your own life
if you look for it. Start today with a prayer that God will make you
aware of those times when He intervenes in your life.

*Lord, thank You that even in the barren places of my life, Your
hand upholds me and will lead me to a green place once
again. Amen.*

To Ponder: God is with me in my desert experiences, ultimately turning them into places of beauty and joy.

GOD'S UNFAILING LOVE
Read 1 Thessalonians 4:1-11

How great is the love the Father has lavished on us,
that we should be called children of God!

1 JOHN 3:1

Bible scholars and theologians usually list the attributes of God under two headings: His natural attributes and His moral attributes.

His natural attributes tell us of a God who is all-knowing, all-powerful, ever-present, eternal. His moral attributes tell us of a God who is holy, righteous, faithful, full of mercy and kindness, and who is love. To contemplate any one of these attributes by itself staggers us. But it is His undying love for us that thrills our hearts.

Some years ago my wife and I were visiting the home of friends who live in Oklahoma City. We arrived midafternoon, and my wife went into the living room to join a ladies' Bible study. I went into the back bedroom to prepare a message I was to give that night at a church banquet.

Some of the ladies had brought their children, who were playing just outside my window. A little boy named Jimmy shouted at a little girl, calling her names. "You're a dummy," he said. "You're nothing but a silly dummy. And you're ugly. And I don't like you, you dummy."

Suddenly I heard the little girl say with a sweet little voice, "Jimmy, I love you."

I thought, *You what!? You love him? After all those cruel names he called you?*

And then it occurred to me, God says the same thing to us, all the time. People all over the world carve out images of God in the form of a snake or an ox or a dog, and say, in effect, "God, you are nothing but a dog. You're a snake. You're a dumb ox." And God looks down from His throne in heaven and reaches out to them in mercy and kindness and says, "I love you."

Lord, You are absolute power and absolute holiness, yet You love me—though I am totally unlovable—with absolute love. Amen.

To Ponder: "For God so loved the world that he gave his one and only Son, that whoever believes in him shall not perish but have eternal life" (John 3:16).

THE LIFE-CHANGING WORD
Read 2 Kings 22–25

The law from your mouth is more precious to me
than thousands of pieces of silver and gold.

PSALM 119:72

Several years ago, a fifteenth-century Gutenberg Bible was sold at Christie's Auction house in New York for $5.4 million, more than double the previous record for a printed book. Now that's a dramatic response to the Bible, but not nearly as dramatic as what we see in today's passage.

King Josiah had arranged to have the temple repaired, and as the workmen went about their tasks, they found a book. But it wasn't just any old book; they found The Book! For some reason, it had been lost or mislaid or tossed in a corner by those who didn't know the value of it. Or perhaps it had been hidden by some idolatrous priest who hoped it would never again see the light of day.

Shaphan the scribe brought the Scriptures to King Josiah and read to him. We are told in 2 Kings 22:11 that "when the king heard the words of the Book of the Law, he tore his robes." He realized that he and his people were not living in obedience to God's commands, and that they needed to repent and turn to the Lord.

Scripture says, "Pray without ceasing." When you read that, is your prayer life affected? Scripture says, "Desire the sincere milk of the Word." Will those words affect the way you arrange your schedule to have more time for personal Bible study? When it comes to God's Word, let's be changed by what we read.

Lord, I look forward to my transformation as I daily read Your
life-changing words. Amen.

To Ponder: If the world will pay five million dollars for a closed Bible, how much more should we value the Word of God that is free and open to us!

STRIKING IT RICH
Read 1 Chronicles 1–9

*Ezra had devoted himself to the study and observance of the Law
of the LORD, and to teaching its decrees and laws in Israel.*

EZRA 7:10

A friend of mine was sorting through a box of old financial records
several months after his father died and came across copies of his parents' income tax returns for the past thirty years. One year his father
had earned less than $200. His mother's salary from teaching school
had been their only income. If my friend had read that income tax
return as a child, it would have meant nothing to him. But as an
adult, those records were a revelation, filled with deep meaning.

A lot of people would put the genealogies of 1 Chronicles 1–9
in the same category as old income tax returns. Some would question the value of lists of names and a discussion of who were the
parents of whom. But a lot of what we see in the Bible depends on
our maturity and perspective. After reading the Scriptures several
times, we should begin to recognize names and recall incidents
from their lives. But if we confine our Bible reading to favorite portions of Scripture, we will miss much of the blessing of the entire
Word of God.

Here in 1 Chronicles, we have little spiritual nuggets tucked away,
awaiting our discovery and application. As you read the Bible, don't
skip the portions that seem obscure. Read them carefully, prayerfully,
and expectantly. And God will be faithful to teach you the lessons He
has tucked away for those who wait on Him.

*Lord, I long to dig deeper in Your Word and find the rich
spiritual nuggets I've overlooked in the past. Help me to
learn to mine all the lessons in Your Word. Amen.*

To Ponder: We cannot neglect any portion of God's Word without loss
to our spiritual growth and hindrance to our usefulness.

A HEART TO KNOW GOD
Read 2 Chronicles 13–16

Direct me in the path of your commands, for there I find delight.

PSALM 119:35

King Asa was a man whose primary aim in life was to please God and do the things of which the LORD approved. In 2 Chronicles 15:1, the prophet Azariah told Asa, "The LORD is with you when you are with him. If you seek him, he will be found by you, but if you forsake him, he will forsake you."

Asa set His heart to know God and His ways. He spent the first years of his reign purifying the worship of God throughout the land. When he was attacked by a neighboring king with a vast army, Asa turned to God in prayer. And the Lord delivered him. Now, is it possible for you and me to have that kind of relationship with God and that kind of guidance from Him? Of course it is.

One of the great keys to finding guidance from God is to dig into the Word in a consistent and systematic way. God does not reveal His inner thoughts to the casual reader. We must set our hearts to know God and His ways. It takes time, but the promise is "seek and ye shall find." If we're studying the Word and walking with Christ in daily discipleship, then guidance will come as the natural outgrowth.

Lord, I want to faithfully study Your Word so I can know Your ways and obey them. Amen.

To Ponder: When you face difficult decisions, do you use the Bible like the Yellow Pages?

ONLY TRUST HIM
Read Ezra 1–6

I gain understanding from your precepts;
therefore I hate every wrong path.

PSALM 119:104

Who do you think will be president two hundred years from now? Impossible to answer, you say. The person hasn't even been born yet. It would be like the signers of the Declaration of Independence predicting the election of our president two centuries in advance.

But this is exactly what we have in Ezra, chapter one. Some two hundred years before it happened, the prophet Isaiah wrote that Cyrus, king of Persia, would issue a proclamation throughout his kingdom—and put it in writing—that the captive Jews were to be released to go back to Jerusalem and rebuild the house of the Lord. When Isaiah wrote that, there was no Cyrus, king of Persia. He hadn't been born yet.

What a record we have here of the love and faithfulness of God! His people were in captivity because they had rebelled against Him and abandoned His Word. But God had not abandoned them. You see, many years before, He had sent His prophets, and they were not heeded. So God sent the king of Babylon, who took the people of Israel into captivity. One way or another, God will be listened to and make people realize that He is the Lord.

Through all the years of captivity, God was at work to bring His children's hearts back to Him and to bring them back to the Land of Promise. What an amazing record of the reliability of the Word of God. And what a challenge for us to put our complete confidence in it.

Lord, by the Holy Spirit's help, I will obey Your Word. Amen.

To Ponder: The messengers of the justice of God will be sent to those who despise the messengers of the mercy of God.

FROM THE MOUTH OF GOD
Read Psalm 119:137-152

I delight in your decrees; I will not neglect your word.

PSALM 119:16

There is a worldwide hotel chain that promises "No Surprises." Every room in every hotel in every city of every country is identical.

It reminds me of my days growing up on a farm in Iowa. When the mailman drove into our farm and parked his Model T Ford by the gate and handed us the package from Sears and Roebuck, we knew exactly what would be inside. Whatever Ma ordered, that's what came. It was absolutely reliable.

So it is with the Bible. There are two forms of evidence put forth to back up the conclusion that the Bible is the Word of the living God.

The first is what Bible teachers call internal evidence—statements found in the Bible that claim it is the Word of God; the second is external evidence, such as the unity of its message—fulfilled prophecy and the like. Let's look for a moment at the internal evidence.

Hundreds of passages in the Bible declare the Bible is God's Word. Jeremiah quoted the Lord as saying, "I have put my words in your mouth." When the apostle Paul proclaimed the Scriptures to the Thessalonians, he was thankful they received it not as the word of men but as it is in truth, the Word of God (1 Thessalonians 2:13). Jesus referred to the writings of Moses as the Word of God (Mark 7:6-13).

We see some of the external evidence when we test the Word of God in the everyday affairs of life. It proves reliable and trustworthy, doing just what it says it will do, every time, no surprises.

Lord, "Your promises have been thoroughly tested, and your servant loves them" (Psalm 119:140).

To Ponder: The Word of God lights our path and directs our feet.

SCRIPTURE MEMORY
Read Proverbs 22:17-18

*Let the word of Christ dwell in you richly as you teach and
admonish one another with all wisdom, and as you sing psalms,
hymns and spiritual songs with gratitude in your hearts to God.*

COLOSSIANS 3:16

Dawson Trotman, founder of The Navigators, loved to tell us about a
letter he received from an eighty-year-old woman who had begun to
memorize Scripture and was finding it an enjoyable way to know
God's Word. For years she had told herself she couldn't memorize—
that Scripture memory was for children. She had convinced herself
she couldn't remember the reference, so even if she did memorize a
verse, she wouldn't know where it was located. But she did learn to
memorize Scripture, and so can you.

Dawson's own testimony tells what the memorized Word can do,
whether a person believes it or not. Through a series of circumstances—on his way to jail as a teenager—he promised God that if He
got him out of the scrape he was in, he would go to church. Well, God
did keep him out of jail, and Dawson kept his promise to God by going
to a young people's meeting in a nearby church. The kids in the group
were having a contest. One of the ways you got points for your team
was to memorize ten verses from the Bible. So that week, on his way
to his job at the lumberyard, Daws memorized them. When he went
to the meeting the next Sunday night, he was the only one who had
memorized the ten verses. And he wasn't a Christian!

After he became a Christian, Daws gave himself to helping Christians
write the Word on their hearts through Scripture memory. Friend, have
you discovered the joy of hiding God's Word in your heart?

*Lord, help me to learn Scripture. When You look into my
heart, may You be pleased to see the Scripture I have hoarded
up against the day of need. Amen.*

To Ponder: When the Devil tempts us, how can we effectively rebuke
him if we don't know Scripture?

TIME FOR A GROWTH SPURT?
Read Hebrews 5–7

*I want to know Christ and the power of his resurrection
and the fellowship of sharing in his sufferings.*

PHILIPPIANS 3:10

One Sunday evening years ago, I went with Dawson Trotman, the founder of The Navigators, to a church where he was speaking. In his usual no-holds-barred manner, Daws began to talk about spiritual maturity. Right at the end he made a startling statement.

"Folks," Dawson said, "If some of you were as immature physically as you are spiritually, you would fall off the pew you're sitting on." Many of the congregation had known the Lord for twenty, thirty, even forty years!

Dawson often said things like that because he loved people and wanted them to wake up and become all that God wanted them to be. He closed his message by quoting Hebrews 5:12-14: "Though by this time you ought to be teachers, you need someone to teach you the elementary truths of God's word all over again. You need milk, not solid food! Anyone who lives on milk, being still an infant, is not acquainted with the teaching about righteousness. But solid food is for the mature, who by constant use have trained themselves to distinguish good from evil."

Christian, let me encourage you to look at yourself in the mirror of God's Word. What do you see? A person who is skillful or unskillful in the use of the Word? Can you hear God's voice and follow His guidance from the Word? Are you able to open the Bible and share the message of Christ with those who need it? Babyhood is wonderful, but don't drag it out over the years. Get going; get growing toward spiritual maturity in Christ.

Lord, I don't want to be an everlasting "baby" when it comes to understanding Your Word. Teach me, by Your Holy Spirit, to skillfully apply Your precepts in my life. Amen.

To Ponder: The contrast between spiritual infancy and spiritual maturity is not expressed by years in the faith but in familiarity with and obedience to the Word of righteousness.

KILLING GIANTS
Read Numbers 13–16

"I tell you the truth, if you have faith and do not doubt,
not only can you do what was done to the fig tree,
but also you can say to this mountain, 'Go, throw yourself
into the sea,' and it will be done."

MATTHEW 21:21

In Numbers 13, we arrive at a memorable and melancholy moment in the life of the people of God. Just when they were about to set foot in the Promised Land, they turn back from the borders of Canaan and are sentenced to wander and perish in the wilderness for their sin of unbelief and their complaining spirits.

You remember the story. Twelve leaders were dispatched to spy out the land. They had been charged with the responsibility of finding out whether the inhabitants of the land were strong or weak; whether the land was good or bad; whether the cities were fortified or simply a cluster of tents; whether it was a bountiful land. After forty days, they returned.

Their report? "The land . . . does flow with milk and honey . . . but the people who live there are powerful, and the cities are fortified and very large. We even saw descendants of Anak there . . . people of great size. . . . We seemed like grasshoppers in our own eyes, and we looked the same to them."

When the Israelites heard this, they broke out in shouts of fear and dismay. The Bible says they forgot God and despised the pleasant land. They murmured in their tents and didn't listen to the voice of the Lord. They saw the task and they saw themselves, but they didn't see God. And from that perspective it all seemed too much.

Some things in life are too big to handle without the Lord. But with Him, you are able to see that difficulty in light of His power, to claim what He has promised, and to possess it.

Lord, I want to walk by faith and not by sight. Amen.

To Ponder: God delights in overcoming great obstacles for us when we step out by faith and rely on Him.

A PICTURE OF FAITH
Read Numbers 34–36

"If you believe, you will receive whatever you ask for in prayer."

MATTHEW 21:22

If you were the commander of an army on the brink of war, wouldn't you appoint some commanders and generals and get organized for the fight? That's what's happening in Numbers 34–36, but instead of organizing for war, Moses takes the list of names the Lord gives him and appoints those who will be involved in dividing the land that is still in the hands and under the control of the Canaanites.

This whole scene is a picture of faith. The Israelites knew they were going to possess the land—not by the skill of sword and bow, but by the power and favor of God. Their faith was not arrogance or presumption. This business of possessing the Promised Land was not their idea, but God's. They were acting on God's orders to accomplish His mission in the world.

That's exactly the way we should respond to God's commands in the Bible. God commands us to share the good news about Christ with other people; to be kind and compassionate to one another; to forgive each other; to live godly lives in a dark world. We have been called into a spiritual warfare whose battlefields are the ordinary, nitty-gritty situations of everyday life. If we wait until we think we're well trained or skilled enough to accomplish all that, we'll never do anything.

In the light of faith and history, that little get-together to divide up an unconquered land doesn't seem so strange after all.

Lord, I delight in doing Your will, even when it might not seem like the rational thing to do. Amen.

To Ponder: Is my faith centered on God, who enables me to do what He has commanded me to do?

FAITH THAT DEFIES REASON
Read Joshua 6–8

Trust in the LORD with all your heart and lean not on your own understanding; in all your ways acknowledge him, and he will make your paths straight.

PROVERBS 3:5-6

It may often appear to us that God is leading in a direction that doesn't make any sense at all. But God is not a combination of theology and logic. He is God.

A case in point is the crossing of the Jordan River, recorded in today's passage. To the mortal mind, God's timing was all wrong. Actually, it was the perfect time. If they had crossed when the river was normal, the landing probably would have been opposed. Crossing at harvest time, there was plenty of food for the millions of Israelites. And the miracle of crossing a flooded river would cause the enemy to tremble at God's power.

To capture the great walled city of Jericho, God again chose a strange approach that defied human reasoning. Instead of preparing battering rams to knock down the wall or using ladders to scale the wall, or digging trenches under the wall, the ark of God was carried by the priests around the city once a day for six days. On the seventh day the ark was carried around the city seven times while the soldiers marched in silence and the priests blew the trumpets of ram's horns. When the command was given to shout, the walls fell down flat. What a glorious picture of obedience and faith!

Maybe the Lord is leading you down a road that seems to make no sense at all. It may be the road of forgiving someone who has deeply hurt you. Or it could be the path of persevering in your Christian witness in spite of opposition and ridicule. Whatever it is, you can be sure that as you walk in faith and obedience, God will enable you to do it.

Lord, I look forward to the day when I will see the whole of life through Your eyes. Amen.

To Ponder: There is no such thing as good or bad timing to a God with no beginning and no end.

100

REDEEMING LOVE
Read Ruth 1–4

Love never fails.

1 CORINTHIANS 13:8

Every cloud is supposed to have a silver lining. That's what the book of Ruth is, in a time characterized by religious and moral corruption, national disunity, foreign oppression, and sin of every kind.

In the book of Judges, we see that everyone did what was right in his own eyes. Living in that time could be compared to flying an airplane in the severest storm. The dark clouds spit lightning, and wind batters the plane as the turbulence intensifies. But the book of Ruth takes the plane above the clouds into sunshine and smooth air.

Judges ends with selfishness and spiritual anarchy; Ruth begins with the unselfish devotion of a young widow to her mother-in-law. At the end of Judges, it seemed all beauty and virtue had disappeared from the earth. But in Ruth we see the people seeking God and His way.

Redemption is a key concept in the book of Ruth, appearing over twenty times. Boaz is the kinsman redeemer, a person responsible to protect the interests of needy members of the extended family: to provide an heir for a brother who had died, to buy back the land a poor relative had sold outside the family, and to redeem a relative who had been sold into slavery. We see Naomi transformed from grief and despair to joy and hope. In Ruth herself, we see the reward of unselfish service, simple faith, and obedience. It all combines as a portrait of God's redemption of us.

The book of Ruth is a reminder that God is at work, even in the bleakest of circumstances.

Lord, You are my silver lining. I rejoice in Your selfless love that brought me to Yourself through my Redeemer, the Lord Jesus Christ.

To Ponder: When we are in the midst of the storm—without hope—it is Christ who lifts us above the dark clouds and saves our souls from certain death.

PRESENT FEAR OR PRESENT FAITH?
1 Samuel 27–31

*Those who trust in the LORD are like mount Zion, which
cannot be shaken but endures forever. As the mountains
surround Jerusalem, so the LORD surrounds his people
both now and forevermore.*

PSALM 125:1-2

———

There's something interesting about fear. While you'd think it would diminish with age and maturity, it seems to grow bigger. Maybe it's because we're more aware of all the things that could happen.

Take the young guy careening around the streets in his automobile. He doesn't have a fear in the world. Before I get in the car, I make sure I've got the insurance paid up, I fasten my seat belt, and I take a lot of time and trouble to make sure everything is okay.

Today's Scripture passage begins with David under the control of unwarranted fear. I can hear you saying, *Unwarranted?* Wasn't King Saul out to slay him? Yes. Wasn't Saul's army much greater in number than the men around David? Yes. Did not Saul's jealousy and anger burn night and day against David? Yes.

Here's why I say his fear was unwarranted: Didn't God choose David to be king, and didn't Samuel, under the direction of God, anoint him to be king? Of course he did. And that fact gives clear assurance that David would be preserved until the time came for him to ascend the throne. He had no reason to trust Saul, but he certainly could trust the Lord. His fear stemmed from his weakened faith.

David didn't consult the Lord, he consulted his own heart, which in this instance led him astray. Young David faced Goliath with a slingshot, while Saul and the rest of the army cringed in fear. Now David had fallen victim to the same kind of dread.

Past faith is no answer to present fear. If we are to finish the race and end well, we can't trust our feelings, we must trust the word of the Lord.

Lord, renew my faith in Your presence in my life today. Amen.

To Ponder: When fear overtakes us, we can rest in the assurance that God has promised to be with us always—and He never breaks a promise.

NOTHING BUT GOD
Read 2 Samuel 15–18

*[I show] love to a thousand generations of those who
love me and keep my commandments.*

EXODUS 20:6

Have you ever been disappointed by the actions of people you love
and depend on, and for whom you have the highest hopes and expectations? It hurts when a friend whispers about you or a child lies to
you or a spouse breaks a promise.

But consider the life of David. Today's passage is filled with his disappointments from family, associates, and friends. God told David He
would punish him for his sin in the matter of Uriah by raising up evil
against him out of his own household.

Immorality and murder were David's sins and, although forgiven,
those sins occurred among his children years later when Amnon
defiled his sister Tamar and Absalom murdered Amnon in revenge.

These were the beginnings of David's punishment at the hand of
God. And I'm sure he suffered deeply from the thought that his own
bad example had brought his children to this wickedness. But in the
midst of it all, David learned there was one who would never fail
him—his God.

Listen to David's words: "My soul finds rest in God alone; my salvation comes from him. He alone is my rock and my salvation; he is
my fortress, I will never be shaken. . . . My salvation and my honor
depend on God; he is my mighty rock, my refuge. Trust in him at all
times, O people; pour out your hearts to him, for God is our refuge"
(Psalm 62:1-2,7-8).

Christian, have you learned that lesson? What are your disappointments today? They hurt, I know, but now is the time to follow
David's example. Respond to God with thanksgiving and joy!

*Lord, I often rely on people, things, and systems that are unre-
liable. Today I renew my total dependence on You. Amen.*

To Ponder: Your worst circumstances may be God's best opportunity
to bring new meaning to your life.

PRAYER
Read Job 23

*"My Father, if it is possible, may this cup be taken
from me. Yet not as I will, but as you will."*

MATTHEW 26:39

The woman was scared out of her wits. Here she was, on a lonely
road, in the middle of nowhere, with a car that wouldn't run, and
night coming on. She began to pray that God would send an angel to
help her. She scanned the road in both directions, but there was no
sign of anyone.

She closed her eyes and prayed some more. "Lord, please send an
angel who can help me." Again she scanned both ways and saw a
speck way down the road, coming toward her. She took heart and
began to pray even more fervently. As the speck grew larger, she saw
the biggest, burliest, long-haired, bearded man she had ever seen—
a rough, tough, mean-looking guy on a motorcycle, wearing the
leather jacket of the Hell's Angels.

He stopped and came toward her. "You got trouble?" he asked.
"Yes, m-my car quit," she replied. "Well, let me have a look," he said.
He lifted the hood, made a few adjustments, turned the key, and the
car started.

"There," he said. "You shouldn't have any more problems with it,
but just in case, I'll follow you to the next town." When she pulled into
an all-night service station with a mechanic on duty, her benefactor
went on his way. God had sent an angel, but not exactly the kind she
had in mind.

Christian friend, it is so easy to want to tell God how to answer our
prayers. "God, please do this for me, and do it in this way." Wait a
minute! Since when does the creature give orders to the Creator? Can
the piece of pottery critique the potter?

*Lord, please forgive the many times I devise the answers to my
prayers and expect You to cooperate. Teach me to pray in Your
will and accept Your answers with thanksgiving. Amen.*

To Ponder: Perhaps God has already answered your prayer, but you
can't see it because you're dictating the answer.

THE POWER OF INTERCESSORY PRAYER
Read Job 40–42

*And he saw that there was no man, and
wondered that there was no intercessor.*

ISAIAH 59:16 (KJV)

———

All of us like to see people get along, and a public quarrel is especially embarrassing. I must confess that I was a bit uneasy at times as Job's story unfolded. It bothered me to hear him utter words he would regret later on. It also bothered me to hear Job and his friends quarreling. And I must admit it bothered me to see that good man in such agony of body, mind, and spirit. But in the end, all things worked together for good.

Two major lessons stand out in these final chapters. One is found in Job 42:5-6, where Job says, "My ears had heard of you but now my eyes have seen you. Therefore I despise myself and repent in dust and ashes." This is the response of those to whom God makes a deeper revelation of Himself.

If pride is a troublesome problem for you, spend some time in the presence of Jesus Christ, God's perfect revelation of Himself. Read the Gospels of Matthew, Mark, Luke, and John. Ask God to help you see the greatness of the majesty of Christ and the ugliness of sin. When we see God as He is, and we see ourselves as we are, we will fall before Him in repentance.

The second lesson is found in 42:10: "After Job had prayed for his friends, the LORD made him prosperous again and gave him twice as much as he had before." Job's troubles began in the malice of Satan; his release had its roots in God's mercy. And when did the Lord turn everything around? When Job prayed for his friends.

Ask God to help you see the power of intercessory prayer and how He delights to see us on our knees praying for one another.

*Lord, let me see You as You are so that I can worship You in
truth. Amen.*

To Ponder: To see God as He is enables us to pray for our friends as
they are.

105

HINDRANCES TO PRAYER
Read Psalm 19:12-14

*The end of all things is near. Therefore be clear
minded and self-controlled so that you can pray.*

1 PETER 4:7

I watched a football game in which the quarterback threw a pass to one of his teammates, who headed for what appeared to be an easy six points. As he raced toward the end zone, two huge linebackers caught him from behind.

I thought, *It's the same in our life of daily discipleship!* We're frequently tackled as we endeavor to live the Christian life. Take prayer, for instance. What are the primary obstacles to a powerful prayer life? Let's consider three possibilities.

First, from Psalm 66:18: "If I had cherished sin in my heart, the Lord would not have listened. . . ." The apostle John put it another way: "[We] receive from him anything we ask, because we obey his commands and do what pleases him" (1 John 3:22). Sin blocks our forward progress in prayer.

A second obstacle is unbelief. James tells us to go to the Lord in prayer, but he says we must "believe and not doubt, because he who doubts is like a wave of the sea, blown and tossed by the wind. That man should not think he will receive anything from the Lord" (James 1:6-7).

A third hindrance is neglect of the Word: "He that turneth away his ear from hearing the law—even his prayer shall be abomination" (Proverbs 28:9, KJV). Neglecting the Word of God and its application to your life will hinder your prayers because prayer is based on faith, and our faith is firmly built on the Word of God.

*Lord, search my heart and convict me of any sin that may be
hindering my communion with You.*

To Ponder: When our prayer life isn't what it should be, we should investigate these three areas: sin, unbelief, and a neglect of God's Word.

WHY LIVE FOR GOD?
Read Psalms 36–41

O you who hear prayer, to you all men will come.

PSALM 65:2

Why do the lives of the ungodly often seem better than ours? Well, in the short run, the wicked often seem to prosper. But we must look at life from the perspective of the long run and see that the essence of life and morality boils down to determining the God-given purpose for life, and living accordingly.

I was lifting weights with a young man who was questioning why he should live a life of faith. He had been a Christian for about two years and was growing in his faith, but lately life didn't seem so good. He had watched his parents come to the verge of divorce, and he was praying hard for them, but God had done nothing to stop their fighting. It seemed like the Lord wasn't paying any attention to the things that mattered deeply to him. He began to feel, *Why live for God if He isn't interested in me, doesn't answer my prayers, and nothing seems to be going right?* But as he considered what he would go back to if he turned away from the Lord, he had to admit there weren't any good alternatives. Like Peter, he knew that Christ alone had the words of eternal life.

Although our motives for following the Lord should not be centered on our personal well-being, it is still a part of what God cares about in our lives. The psalmist finally got perspective on the prosperity of the wicked when he considered the brevity of life and the total insecurity of living without God. Why live for God? Psalm 37:37,38 says: "There is a future for the man of peace. But all sinners will be destroyed."

Lord, instruct my mind and heart to keep me from envy when I see prosperity and ease surrounding the ungodly. Amen.

To Ponder: "For evildoers shall be cut off: but those that wait upon the LORD, they shall inherit the earth" (Psalm 37:9 KJV).

LIVING PRAYER
Read Psalms 55–59

*Now when Daniel learned that the decree had been published, he
went home to his upstairs room where the windows opened toward
Jerusalem. Three times a day he got down on his knees and
prayed, giving thanks to his God, just as he had done before.*

DANIEL 6:10

———————

Can you picture this? Every day the chief executive officer of a large
multimillion-dollar corporation goes into his office to tend to the business of the day. And every day, shortly after he arrives, one of the factory workers comes bursting into his office and tells the man his
problems.

Again, at noon, when the executive is ready to leave for lunch, the
factory worker comes in with a new set of problems. That night, after
the executive has gone home, the factory worker comes charging into
the man's home and lays out a whole new set of difficulties and personal needs. The worker does this every day.

Do you think the chief executive officer would soon tire of this and
figure out a way to keep the man away from him? Not if the chief
executive was God. Look at Psalm 55:17: "Evening, morning and
noon I cry out in distress, and he hears my voice." What David is
telling us is that he begins the day with God, lives the day with God,
and ends the day with God. He prays without ceasing.

For some years, I was associated closely with a young man from
Great Britain named David Steel. David skipped lunch and spent the
noon hour on his knees. When anyone would ask, "Where's David?"
we would simply say, "He has an appointment over the lunch hour."
I'm not suggesting this as a pattern for everyone to follow. But I am
pointing out that if a person wants to do something badly enough, it
can be done. Let me encourage you to memorize Psalm 55:17 and see
what the Holy Spirit might lead you to do in the practice of prayer.

Lord, ignite in me a passion to pray without ceasing. Amen.

To Ponder: When it comes to prayer, no time is unreasonable or
unseasonable with God.

STRENGTH FOR THE JOURNEY
Read Psalms 67–72

Hear, O LORD, and answer me, for I am poor and needy.

PSALM 86:1

I spoke at a conference of missionaries in South America, some serving in places where literally every day people were being murdered by drug dealers. There were political tensions, besides all the problems that come with trying to serve people and communicate Christ in a foreign culture. I sensed this was a gathering of wounded warriors who needed a time of refreshment and encouragement.

The first night they sang the whole time, choosing songs of comfort, encouragement, love, and faith. None of the songs had to do with marching to victory and charging the enemy. These people were trying to survive another day, and they needed the comforting hand of God.

Psalm 67:1-2 has the same ring to it as the beginning of that missionary conference. Notice that the little word *us* appears three times in the first verse. "May God be gracious to us and bless us and make his face shine upon us." Why? Is it simply that they want all the benefits of the blessing of God for themselves, with no thought to the needs and welfare of others? No, just the opposite. Verse 2 ends: "that your ways may be known on earth, your salvation among all nations." It's like the winter snows in the high country of the Colorado Rockies. All winter long the snow piles up on the peaks. Then the warm spring sun melts the snow and it flows down to the valleys, watering the farmland and greening the pastures.

The prayer of verse 1 is motivated by the desire to see the whole world benefit from the blessing God brings His chosen people. But it has to begin with His people and must be true in our lives before we can pass it on to others.

Lord, let me serve, but only with Your blessing. Amen.

To Ponder: People will be attracted to the true and living God when they see His hand at work in the lives of His people.

EMPOWERED BY THE SPIRIT
Read Zechariah 3–4

"Not by might nor by power, but by my Spirit,"
says the LORD Almighty.

ZECHARIAH 4:6

One of the best-known verses in the Bible regarding the Holy Spirit is recorded in Zechariah 4:6. The word *might* comes from a Hebrew word meaning "a powerful force, an army, a band of trained, valiant soldiers." It also encompasses other resources, such as riches. The word translated *power* means "to be able to reach our goals by human ability—our own wisdom or clever manipulation of others." Zechariah is saying that we do not do the work of God by either great human strength or great human ability; we do it by the enabling of the Holy Spirit.

Exodus 31:1 says: "Then the Lord said to Moses, 'See, I have chosen Bezalel . . . and I have filled Him with the Spirit of God, with skill, ability and knowledge in all kinds of crafts—to make artistic designs for work in gold, silver and bronze, to cut and set stones, to work in wood, and to engage in all kinds of craftsmanship. . . . Also I have given skill to all the craftsmen to make everything I have commanded you.'"

My daughter, Becky, observed that God had to empower them by the Holy Spirit for the artistic work. For the past four hundred years they had done nothing but sit in the slime pits of Egypt and make mud pies. But when God called them to engage in works of artistic craftsmanship, He gave them the power of the Holy Spirit to do it.

When we are born again by faith in Jesus Christ, from that moment on we are to rely on the Holy Spirit's power and live under His control.

Lord, take control of me and use my life to bring glory to You.
Amen.

To Ponder: Is there any area of your life where you're not relying on the Holy Spirit's power?

FROM DARKNESS TO LIGHT
Read Mark 5:1-20

"So if the Son sets you free, you will be free indeed."

JOHN 8:36

———

Every night for three nights we had listened to the slow beat of the African jungle drum and the piercing screams of the people as they shattered the night with the terrifying sound of the African death wail. A woman had died giving birth to a child, and those nearest her gathered night after night to scream for hours. In their screams, we could detect the horror that held them—the hopelessness, the agony of spirit, the fears that Satan whispered to their lost souls. And we were made very much aware in a new and powerful way of the hate, the cruelty, and the delight Satan displays in tormenting those who belong to Jesus. His foul, ugly personality came through loud and clear in the din of the death wail that kept us from sleeping.

Scripture records a visit of the Lord Jesus to the country of the Gadarenes. Mark 5:2,5 tells us, "When Jesus got out of the boat, a man with an evil spirit came from the tombs to meet him. . . . Night and day among the tombs and in the hills he would cry out and cut himself with stones." What did Jesus do? Jesus took one look at the man and knew that those who said he must be bound in chains were wrong. In fact, what he needed was to be set free. And that's what Jesus did.

Satan has our world bound in sin, and Jesus is the only one who can deliver them. While they cry out in hopeless despair, He has sent us out with the message of hope, found only in the gospel of the Lord Jesus Christ that can deliver anyone—anytime—anywhere.

Lord, thank You for setting me free from the vise-like grip of Satan, so that I can tell others where freedom lies. Amen.

To Ponder: Do you know someone crying out for release from Satan's grasp?

JESUS IS GOD
Read John 17

Thomas said to him, "My Lord and my God!"

JOHN 20:28

A friend's cat came home one day proudly carrying a chipmunk in its mouth. My friend grabbed the cat and forced it to drop the chipmunk. She then picked up the poor animal, stroked it gently, said some soothing words, and put it into a box for recovery.

After an hour or so, the chipmunk seemed alert, so my friend reached in to check, and the chipmunk bit her finger to the bone! Why? Because my friend couldn't communicate with chipmunks! While this lady had saved its life and meant it only good, the chipmunk didn't get the message.

That's why Jesus became a man—to communicate with us and be the bridge between God and man. Jesus Christ is God. He claimed to be, and those who knew Him best said He was. He did the things that only God can do. But He was also man. The Bible says He was God in the flesh, God's son, a descendant of David on the human level, but the Son of God.

God has been here, and that's the good news. Jesus said, "Anyone who has seen me has seen the Father" (John 14:9). Friend, let me tell you something: If you believe that, it will change your life!

Lord, I bow my heart to You and confess that You are my Redeemer and my God. Amen.

To Ponder: Every knee shall bow, and every tongue confess that Jesus Christ is Lord, to the glory of God the Father (see Philippians 2:9-10).

OUR HELPER
Read Romans 8:22-27

I lift up my eyes to the hills—where does my help come from? My help comes from the LORD, the Maker of heaven and earth.

PSALM 121:1-2

All during my growing-up years, I was picked on by kids at school. I was small. I was weak. I was skinny. And I was always getting pushed around.

After graduation from high school in 1943, I joined the Marines. I was hoping they could toughen me up and help me learn how to hold my own. I always had a secret desire to be a rough-and-tumble guy. In fact, I even had a nickname picked out for myself—Nails. I always wanted to be known as "Nails" Eims, as in "There's a guy tough as nails." But my nickname in the Marines was Chick.

To hold my own in the tough outfit I was in, I made friends with the biggest, strongest, roughest guy in the battalion. Nobody picked on me because they knew they would have to answer to my unofficial bodyguard, the one who was always ready to come alongside and help. And nobody wanted to tangle with him.

That is exactly what God has provided for the protection and ministry of His children. The apostle John referred to the Holy Spirit as the comforter, or helper. The word translated comforter and helper from the Greek is the word *paraclete,* which means the one who comes alongside to help.

Christian, do you see the significance of that? Since the day of Pentecost, there has never been a one-on-one witnessing situation. There can't be, because the minute you begin to share Christ with someone, a third person—the Holy Spirit—comes alongside to speak to him and convict him of his need for Christ.

Lord, thank You for the Holy Spirit, my ever-present helper and comforter. Amen.

To Ponder: The Holy Spirit never leaves us to cope alone; He even perfects our prayers to the Father.

OUR BIBLE TEACHER
Read John 14:16-17; 16:13-15

You gave your good Spirit to instruct them.

NEHEMIAH 9:20

Years ago, our son Randy and his wife, Jackie, told us about a supper time when little one-year-old Clayton laid down his spoon, looked up at his parents, and jabbered away with a great deal of emotion and earnestness. "Blah, blah, blahppety blah blah," he said.

Finally Clayton ended his oration, leaving his parents completely in the dark as to what he'd been saying. Because Christine had listened so intently, Randy thought maybe she knew what Clayton had said and could act as interpreter. So he asked her, "Christine, do you know what your little brother just said?"

She nodded. "Clayton said, 'Blah, blah, blahppety blah blah.'"

It took her parents a few minutes to regain their composure.

As I listened to this story, I was reminded of the fact that to gain an understanding of the Bible, there must be an interpreter and teacher. The apostle Paul made it plain that without the help of the Holy Spirit, the Scriptures would remain a mystery. According to 1 Corinthians 2:14, "The man without the Spirit does not accept the things that come from the Spirit of God, for they are foolishness to him, and he cannot understand them, because they are spiritually discerned."

The Bible is just so much gibberish, like a baby jabbering away, to anyone who is not a Christian and not taught by the Spirit. But when we are born again, it is a whole different story. As the Spirit of God casts light upon the Scriptures, the teaching is made clear and plain, and the Bible can then be applied to our lives.

Lord, thank You for the truths of Your Word revealed to me by the Holy Spirit. Amen.

To Ponder: Apart from the Holy Spirit's work in revealing the meaning of Scripture to us, we can have no true understanding.

THE HOLY SPIRIT'S MISSION
Read John 16:5-16

And [Christ] is the head of the body, the church; he is
the beginning and the firstborn from among the dead,
so that in everything he might have the supremacy.

COLOSSIANS 1:18

One summer my wife and I attended an opera in the magnificent opera house in Vienna, Austria. We arrived early to take a look around, then the usher showed us to our seats way up in the third balcony, practically to the roof.

To be honest, I wasn't enjoying the opera that much. It was sung in German—which I didn't understand—and the plot was hard to follow. When I heard some movement behind me, I glanced over my shoulder and saw the spotlight operator, whose job was to follow the lead character with this huge, thousand-watt light. He never let the spotlight stray from the central figure, who moved back and forth on the stage or among the rest of the characters in the story.

It reminded me of a great spiritual truth about the Holy Spirit. The Bible teaches that in all things the Lord Jesus Christ is to have pre-eminence. Just as the spotlight operator in Vienna would not have gone down on the stage to share the spotlight with the central figure of the opera, neither does the Holy Spirit share the spotlight with the Lord. It is the Holy Spirit's mission to remain in the shadows and do all within His power to point men and women to the Lord.

This doesn't mean the Holy Spirit is less important than the other two members of the Godhead; the Holy Spirit is co-equal with the Father and the Son. But the Spirit has a role to carry out—to point us to Christ.

Friend, if you yield yourself to the ministry of the Holy Spirit, you'll fall more and more in love with Jesus, and want above anything else to live for Him alone.

Lord, be glorified in my life. Amen.

To Ponder: If we have submitted to the ministry of the Holy Spirit, the Lord Jesus Christ will have front and center place in our hearts.

ALL 'FESSED UP
Read Leviticus 4–7

God made him who had no sin to be sin for us,
so that in him we might become the righteousness of God.

2 CORINTHIANS 5:21

In the Old Testament, God required sacrificial offerings so that the sin that separated the people from Him could be forgiven and fellowship with God could be restored.

Note carefully the order of offerings in Leviticus 5–7. The sin offering had to be made before the burnt offering. Why? To make peace with God before offering service to God. And by the way, if the person brought an offering of fine flour, it was not to be doctored up with oil or frankincense. Why? Apparently the flour itself did not taste very good, reminding the person of the pollution and loathsomeness of his sin. To add oil and frankincense would have made it taste and smell better. But God wanted the people to see their sin as it really was.

Do you remember reading about the Garbage Barge? This huge floating barge carried three thousand tons of trash, piled in eighteen-foot stacks. For nearly six months it wandered from city to city, trying to find a place to unload. No one would take it until finally the city of New York said, "Okay, you can unload it here. We'll take it and get rid of it." What a relief it must have been after six thousand miles with that boatload of smelly trash.

That's what our spiritual lives would be like without the grace and forgiveness of God. What a relief to see the beauty and simplicity of God's forgiveness, which He offers us in Jesus Christ. First John 1:9 says, "If we confess our sins, he is faithful and just and will forgive us our sins and purify us from all unrighteousness." That's the Christian's bar of soap, and we should use it every time any sin interrupts our fellowship with God.

Lord, how awesome that You welcome me back to Your side when I confess my sin and repent of it. Your forgiveness means everything to me. Amen.

To Ponder: Have you become a kind of spiritual garbage barge because of unconfessed sin?

PRIDE'S END
Read Leviticus 8–10

*There are six things the LORD hates, seven that are detestable to
him: haughty eyes, a lying tongue, hands that shed innocent
blood, a heart that devises wicked schemes, feet that are quick to
rush into evil, a false witness who pours out lies and a man who
stirs up dissension among brothers.*

PROVERBS 6:16-19

In Leviticus 8–10, we see that the consecration of the priests contained a strange ritual. God instructed Moses to kill a ram, take the blood, and put it on the ears, hands, and feet of Aaron and his sons. They were set apart for God through this anointing, and dedicated to His service in all they did.

Soon after this, Leviticus 10 records that Aaron's sons are killed for offering strange fire before God. God had not authorized them to burn incense on the solemn day of inauguration. That was to be performed by the high priest alone; they were to assist him. We know from the New Testament that the priests were to burn incense only when it was their lot, and this was certainly not Nadab and Abihu's.

As I've pondered these events I've wondered, *Was there an element of pride in the lives of these two sons of Aaron?* They had a tremendous honor bestowed upon them, but had it gone to their heads?

Can you think of anything good that cannot be ruined by pride? I can't. May God grant us the grace to face our areas of personal pride, confess them, forsake them, and walk each day humbly with the Lord.

Lord, help me to walk humbly with You. Amen.

To Ponder: God is especially angered and grieved when we, His children, exhibit prideful behavior.

AVOIDING SLOW LEAKS
Read Leviticus 18–20

Avoid every kind of evil.

1 THESSALONIANS 5:22

———

A quick read through Leviticus 18–20 raises some questions: How low can society go? How deep into sin? How polluted can the human spirit become? How degraded the human race? There are laws and commands in this passage that stagger the mind, and the Lord speaks plainly and bluntly to His people. "You must not do as they do in Egypt, where you used to live, and you must not do as they do in the land of Canaan, where I am bringing you. Do not follow their practices. You must obey my laws and be careful to follow my decrees. I am the LORD your God" (Leviticus 18:3-4).

So they were neither to retain the idolatry of Egypt nor take on the moral standards of the land to which they were going, and they were to abstain from the corruption of their own fleshly desires.

A scientist told me about a 32-inch steel pipe carrying 1,800 pounds of steam pressure that suddenly exploded. People were burned. The room was destroyed. The force was so powerful that the insulation was peeled off the walls. The cause? A small impurity in the weld. The impurity was so tiny no one noticed it. But it blew a thirty-foot hole in that huge steel pipe.

In the Christian life, a blowout begins with a small, slow leak. If we are to avoid visible sins such as immorality and dishonesty, we must deal with the little things—the tiny impurities in the welds of our souls. May God give us wisdom and courage to confront those things that look small but can be used by the Devil to destroy us.

Lord, search me and see if I am harboring any tiny impurity in my life that could devastate my walk with You. Amen.

To Ponder: Sin always begins as a tiny impurity, but contains the potential for destruction on a massive scale.

LINGERING SIN
Read Numbers 31–33

Return, O Israel, to the LORD your God.
Your sins have been your downfall!

HOSEA 14:1-2

Years ago, I memorized Numbers 33:55 as a warning to my own soul: "But if ye will not drive out the inhabitants of the land from before you, then it shall come to pass that those whom ye let remain of them shall be as pricks in your eyes, and thorns in your sides, and shall vex you in the land wherein ye dwell" (KJV).

I memorized that verse because I was working with a group of guys and was trying to get across to them the importance of confessing sin to God—of keeping short accounts with the Lord and living a clean life before Him.

If you and I harbor sin in our lives, this verse says our vision for the work of God will be clouded, our forward progress will be hindered, and the sin that remains in our lives will be a constant vexation to us, both in our fellowship with God and in our service to Him.

Some people hear this verse and think back to a time in their lives when they should have dealt with a certain sin, and didn't. They become tremendously discouraged when they see what has happened in their lives and the wasted years of being out of fellowship with the Lord. That may be exactly how you're feeling.

Psalm 119:97 says, "Oh how I love thy law, it is my meditation all the day" (KJV). One reason I love this verse is because it's first-person singular, present tense. Oh, how I love thy law means it is right now—currently, today—my meditation. That can be your experience, too, if you choose it. It's never too late to come back to where you once were with the Lord.

Lord, reveal to me my unconfessed sin so that I may stay in close fellowship with You and be effectively used in the lives of others. Amen.

To Ponder: God can't use us to accomplish His purposes if we have lingering sin in our lives.

RESISTING TEMPTATION
Read Deuteronomy 12–16

You shall have no other gods before me.

EXODUS 20:3

Remember the bumper sticker, "I can resist anything but temptation?" The land to which the people of God were marching was filled with places dedicated to false gods—places that tempted God's people to turn from worship of Him. These places were to be destroyed. Why? Because God told His people they should have no other gods before Him—there is only one true and living God. He commanded the people to tear down these altars and pillars and images, to keep the Holy Land from being polluted by these hideous reminders of ungodliness.

God has commanded the same of us. But if we harbor evil in our lives and do not strive after holiness, we pollute our lives just as the altars to false gods polluted the Promised Land. Unfortunately, false gods don't come with horns and a tail. False gods come all wrapped up in something pretty. From what I understand about the cherubim and seraphim, and all God's angelic creation, I guess there's nothing prettier than an angel. And the Bible says that "Satan himself masquerades as an angel of light" (2 Corinthians 11:14).

Even though we understand this, God says temptations will come. And often they will come from unexpected places. So you and I must be on our guard. We must be careful of the books we read, the forms of entertainment of which we partake, the magazines to which we subscribe. Our directions are clear. Resist the Devil. Avoid the things of the world. Flee youthful lusts. And the Word of God will be used by the Holy Spirit to feed us and make us strong, and guide us along the right path.

Lord, when I am tempted, open my eyes and turn me from the glittering baubles to treasure everlasting. Amen.

To Ponder: We will never know the power of God in casting out false gods unless we choose to turn that power on.

PUTTING THE WORD INTO PRACTICE
Read 2 Chronicles 10–12

I urge you to live a life worthy of the calling you have received.

EPHESIANS 4:1

Each day we arise from our beds with the opportunity to walk with God or to walk in disobedience. And each day our practice of the fundamentals of Christian living will determine which way we go.

I know a man who has walked closely with God for over fifty years. And every time I'm with him, I feel like I'm in the presence of the Lord Himself. Why is that? Because this man has lived a life of daily obedience to the Word of God, and the Lord has made Himself so real to the man that you can sense God's presence in his life.

I know another man who used to preach a tremendous sermon on the dangers of lust and overfamiliarity with women. But some time ago he walked out on his wife and kids, and today his life is in absolute shambles. I hate to say it, but when I'm with him, I want to poke him in the nose. His problem is not a lack of knowledge—he had one of the best sermons I've ever heard on walking with God and not falling into sin. His problem is that he stopped practicing what he knew.

The Bible urges us this way: "Do not merely listen to the word, and so deceive yourselves. Do what it says" (James 1:22). Progress comes only as we practice the fundamentals in real life.

Lord, teach me to abide in Your Word. Amen.

To Ponder: As you interact with people and deal with situations today, ask yourself the question: "What would Jesus do (say)?"

A PARENT'S LEGACY
Read 1 Kings 1–4

*I have no greater joy than to hear that my
children are walking in the truth.*

3 JOHN 4

What are you hoping to pass on to your children? In 1 Kings 2:2-3 we read the charge David gave Solomon: "I am about to go the way of all the earth," David said. "So be strong, show yourself a man, and observe what the LORD your God requires: Walk in his ways, and keep his decrees and commands, his laws and requirements . . . so that you may prosper in all you do and wherever you go."

The Scriptures tell us that Solomon loved the Lord and walked in the statutes of David, his father. Solomon was a wise man, a rich man, the leader of a powerful nation, and yet he was a humble man before God.

How can we pass those things on to our children? Let me suggest a couple of biblical principles. First, we must pass on spiritual qualities by example. Solomon had observed his father's life and knew David was far from perfect. But he'd also observed his father's repentance and obedience. When David spoke to his son about walking in the commandments of God, Solomon had a strong example to follow.

A second principle involves prayer. I know a woman in Iowa who has prayed for her son one hour a day from the time he was born. The thrust of her prayer? That he would be a godly man, walking with the Lord and being used by Him. When I see that man's life today and all that God is using him to do, I realize she gave him something through her prayers that few children ever receive.

Be an example of Christlikeness and also pray regularly for your loved ones. There is nothing greater you can leave them.

Lord, help me to live as a godly example before my children and to pray for them daily as they learn to walk with You. Amen.

To Ponder: What example are you passing on to your children?

MAKING LIFE DECISIONS
Read 1 Chronicles 17–21

"But many who are first will be last, and the last first."

MATTHEW 19:30

For several years, I was involved in a ministry with cadets at the United States Air Force Academy. Just before graduation, the cadets who were headed for pilot training filled out a "dream sheet" of where they would like to be assigned. Many guys chose a location because of climate and the facilities.

We had three Christian guys involved in our Navigator ministry who requested Del Rio, Texas. A lot of their classmates thought they were crazy. Del Rio was a small town on the Mexican border. It wasn't close to any major cities, and the climate was mostly hot. These three guys had prayed about it and thought Del Rio would be a good place to minister. We called them the Del Rio trio, and they went there with a heart to witness to their classmates and have an impact for Christ.

I know a church in Pittsburgh with a pastor who challenged the members to pray about how they could have a greater impact on the people in the neighborhoods around their church. Out of that challenge, a number of families actually moved to the lower-income neighborhood in which the church was located, so they could minister more effectively to the people there.

First Chronicles 17:1 says, "After David was settled in his palace, he said to Nathan the prophet, 'Here I am living in a palace of cedar, while the ark of the covenant of the LORD is under a tent.' " Here was a man of great wealth, popularity, and power, asking not what he could do to fill his coffers with more gold or enlarge the borders of his kingdom, but what he could do to serve and honor the Lord.

Lord, when I make decisions, help me to go beyond my own interests and consider what You want. Amen.

To Ponder: Does the Great Commission have any effect on your major life decisions?

JEHOSHAPHAT'S EXAMPLE
Read 2 Chronicles 17–20

So then, just as you received Christ Jesus as Lord, continue to live in him, rooted and built up in him, strengthened in the faith as you were taught, and overflowing with thankfulness.

COLOSSIANS 2:6

When I was growing up on a farm in Iowa, we had a neighbor who, every time something unusual or exciting happened, would shout "Jumpin' Jehoshaphat!" But a reading of 2 Chronicles 17–20 lets us know that Jehoshaphat was not known for his ability in jumping, but for his walk with God.

He wisely took precautions to fortify the land against invasion. But more than that, he walked in the ways of David, his father. And even here Jehoshaphat was selective, following the positive example of David while avoiding his weakness and sin. When King Jehoshaphat gave himself to the laws of God, the Bible says he put his heart in it. The New Testament describes this as fervent in spirit, serving the Lord.

Jehoshaphat tore down the place of false worship and then sent men throughout the cities of Judah to teach the people from the Book of the Law. In gratitude, the people sent him presents and he had riches and honor in abundance. But his heart was not lifted up in pride. He continued to walk humbly with God.

How often we read in Scripture that riches and honor prove to be a stumbling block, leading a person to pride, false security, and even immorality. But not this man. These things simply oiled the wheels of Jehoshaphat's obedience.

It is so easy to approach the Christian life in a series of fits and starts and try to make progress in leaps and bounds. What is really needed is for us to walk calmly and steadily each day in the ways of the Lord.

Lord, thank You for recording the example of King Jehoshaphat in his love for Your ways and his steady walk with You. Amen.

To Ponder: What is the first thing you would do if the Lord gave you a million dollars?

UNDER GOD'S GRACIOUS HAND
Read Ezra 7–8

*In everything that he undertook in the service of God's temple and
in obedience to the law and the commands, he sought his God and
worked wholeheartedly. And so he prospered.*

2 CHRONICLES 31:21

Have you ever looked at someone who was being used by God in a
special way and wondered why the Lord seems to have His hand on
that man or woman? Why is God using that person and not someone
else? What is the secret of their spiritual success?

Ezra 7:9 says of Ezra, "The gracious hand of his God was upon
him." And the reason is found in the next verse: "For Ezra had
devoted himself to the study and observance of the Law of the LORD,
and to teaching its decrees and laws in Israel."

First, Ezra prepared his heart. This implies that Ezra prayed.
Second, Ezra sought the law of the Lord through His written Word.
Third, when God spoke to Ezra from His Word and revealed His will,
Ezra did it. Obedience was a lifestyle with this man. And fourth, Ezra
was diligent to share God's truth with others.

These four disciplines are no mystery, and they certainly aren't
for Ezra alone. Leighton Ford has a beautiful way of summarizing
these four spiritual disciplines: study the Bible through; pray it in;
live it out; pass it on. Prayer, the Word, obedience, and witnessing.
Four simple, ordinary, everyday practices by which you and I can
experience the gracious hand of the Lord our God on our lives. May
God grant us the grace to pay the price in time and energy to see it
happen.

*Lord, please keep Your gracious hand on my life so that I
might live by Your direction and power. Amen.*

To Ponder: Describe what your life would be like if your approach to
the Word was to study it through, pray it in, live it out, and pass
it on.

BEYOND GOOD INTENTIONS
Read Nehemiah 11–13

*"You call me 'Teacher' and 'Lord,' and rightly so,
for that is what I am."*

JOHN 13:13

Back in Nehemiah 9:38, we find a group of people who made a binding agreement and put in writing their intention to keep the Law of the Lord. They had searched God's Law to find out what it taught, then searched their own hearts to discover where they were falling short. After listing a number of things that were examples of their failures, they put in writing exactly what they were going to do about it.

Written applications should be part of every Bible study. As we see where we fall short or receive a new challenge in following the Lord, we should write down what we plan to do about it. But that's not enough. In Nehemiah 13, we see that the people got off to a great start by putting their intentions in writing, but stumbled in putting them into practice.

When Nehemiah returned to Jerusalem after being gone for awhile, he discovered the people had broken every promise they had made. They were giving their sons and daughters in marriage to the pagans around them; they were conducting business on the Sabbath; they had failed to give their tithes and offerings to the house of God; and they were not maintaining regular worship.

You know, sin dies hard. It can rear its ugly head at the most unexpected times and in the most unexpected places. It begins with little sparks that seem so insignificant, and then the fire grows quickly out of control before we realize it. If we're to make progress in the Christian life, we must deal with sin quickly and forcefully. When we study the Word, we are challenged and encouraged. But we make progress by application and obedience.

*Lord, as I read Your Word and learn Your will, help me turn
my good intentions into obedience. Amen.*

To Ponder: What good intention have you been meaning to carry out?

UNBROKEN FELLOWSHIP
Read Jeremiah 50–52

We must pay more careful attention, therefore, to what we have heard, so that we do not drift away.

HEBREWS 2:1

In the last chapters of Jeremiah, God is trying to get the attention of Babylon and warn the people that if they continue to follow their current lifestyle, the curtain will fall and the show will be over.

In Jeremiah 51:33, we find an example of God's warning: "This is what the LORD Almighty, the God of Israel, says: 'The daughter of Babylon is like a threshing floor at the time it is trampled; the time to harvest her will soon come.'" The Babylonians did not heed the warning, and in the years to come, the prophecies of Babylon's shocking destruction were all fulfilled.

What are the warnings you and I must not ignore in our walk of daily discipleship? What are the signs that we may be getting sidetracked from the Lord's plan for our lives? Is it getting easier to skip a daily quiet time of prayer and Bible reading? Are we passing up opportunities to share our faith with others? What about our prayer life and our thoughts?

I know a husband and wife who were growing spiritually and were very active in their church. But when the man was promoted at work, they moved into a higher financial bracket, found a new set of friends, and became more sophisticated in their attitude toward the things of God. Soon, golf and tennis took the place of Sunday morning worship. The Bible study group they attended went by the wayside. When their pastor visited them and urged them to return to the Lord, they let him know his warnings were not welcome.

In our Christian faith, the bottom line is not a list of things to do, but a person to love.

Lord, You are the strength of my life. May I not be tempted to put other things ahead of fellowship with You. Amen.

To Ponder: God's warning signs are designed to point us toward the person of Jesus Christ and our fellowship with Him.

THE "GRAY" AREAS
Read Ezekiel 44–48

*Finally, brothers, whatever is true, whatever is noble, whatever
is right, whatever is pure, whatever is lovely, whatever is
admirable—if anything is excellent or praiseworthy—
think about such things. Whatever you have learned or
received or heard from me, or seen in me—put it
into practice. And the God of peace will be with you.*

PHILIPPIANS 4:8-9

In Ezekiel 44:23, God gave this command to the priests of the sanctuary: "They are to teach my people the difference between the holy
and the common [profane] and show them how to distinguish
between the unclean and the clean." Note carefully that the priests
were to teach the people, not simply tell them. It's the difference
between telling a person what to avoid and helping him learn why he
should refrain from things that displease the Lord.

Now let's talk about the gray areas. How can we discern right
from wrong in these things? The apostle Paul said, " 'Everything is
permissible for me'—but not everything is beneficial. 'Everything
is permissible for me'—but I will not be mastered by anything"
(1 Corinthians 6:12). Here is a simple guide to discern right from
wrong. First, we can ask ourselves, will this draw me closer to the
Lord or take me farther away from Him? Second, does this practice
have an addictive quality that is likely to get me into its grip?

In Ezekiel's day, the responsibility to teach the people to discern
good and evil was given to the priests of the sanctuary. Today, this is
not something we can hand off to the pastor or Christian worker. All
believers carry the responsibility to set an example of biblical behavior others can follow. And we are to teach them how to discern the
way for themselves.

*Lord, I confess there are gray areas of behavior and attitudes
I'd like to hold on to. By Your Holy Spirit, I will set them aside
for the sake of others and to honor You. Amen.*

To Ponder: Are there gray-area behaviors in your life that you should
reconsider in light of how they might affect others?

DEVOTION TO GOD
Read Daniel 1–3

They could find no corruption in him, because
he was trustworthy and neither corrupt nor negligent.

DANIEL 6:4

———————

Daniel was a young man who, from the world's point of view, "had it all." Before the fall of Jerusalem, he was a member of the royal family in Israel. When he was taken captive to Babylon, he was selected for special training in the court of the Babylonian king. Daniel 1:4 describes the qualifications of Daniel and the others selected for this training: "Young men without any physical defect, handsome, showing aptitude for every kind of learning, well informed, quick to understand, and qualified to serve in the king's palace."

What a list! I'm sure any major corporation in the world would have been delighted to hire one of these men and make him part of the organization. But other than Daniel and three of his friends, we don't even know their names. Why? Because they apparently lacked the one major characteristic God looks for, and that He found in Daniel and the other three—a commitment to holiness in the sight of God.

The Scriptures portray Daniel as a man of both wisdom and piety. This is an interesting combination; often those who are endowed with wisdom and natural abilities are not celebrated for their devotional lives. In Daniel, God found a young man who could serve in the corridors of power because he wasn't enamored with it all. He was surrounded by the good life, and was able to turn his back on it out of devotion to God.

If God has given you some of the same gifts and abilities he gave Daniel, thank God for His goodness to you. But remember that it wasn't Daniel's IQ and good looks, but his prayer and piety that made him useful to God.

Lord, thank You for the gifts and abilities You've given me to use for Your service. Help me to stay unimpressed by what the world offers me. Amen.

To Ponder: "Often those who are endowed with wisdom and natural abilities are not celebrated for their devotional lives." Why is this statement true?

LEAVING THE LIGHT
Read Hosea 7–8

*"This is the verdict: Light had come into the world, but men loved
darkness instead of light because their deeds were evil."*

JOHN 3:19

For those people who think that the God of the Old Testament is a
God of wrath and judgment, with no mix of compassion and love, I
recommend reading the book of Hosea. Admittedly, God does eventually unleash His wrath on those who disobey, but it is not His first
impulse.

Day after day, sometimes year after year, He pleads with His
people to repent and turn to Him. But finally the day of reckoning
comes. In the section of Scripture before us, we find these words: "I
wrote for them the many things of my law, but they regarded them as
something alien" (Hosea 8:12). God had become a stranger—an
alien—among His own people. Hosea records that the Word of God
did not fit the people's lifestyle. They were glued to their idols. Sin and
immorality were the order of the day. At long last these people had
made their final decision: sin, rather than God.

You can be assured that the final act on their part did not happen
overnight. It was a long time coming. And it started with a slight devi-
ation from the path—a small sin, an act that looked quite harmless.
But it resulted in disorder. So Hosea makes this chilling statement:
"My God will cast them away, because they did not hearken unto him;
and they shall be wanderers among the nations" (9:17 KJV).

Christian, take stock. Are you toying with something that displeases the Lord? Take steps to nip it in the bud. Put it to death before
it gets a stranglehold on your life.

*Lord, have mercy on my wayward heart and draw me back
to You. Great is Your faithfulness to me. Amen.*

To Ponder: Does my lifestyle fit with God's Word?

JESUS, OUR EXAMPLE
Read Luke 19:1-10

He who walks with the wise grows wise,
but a companion of fools suffers harm.

PROVERBS 13:20

The Bible may seem to contain some contradictions, but God has taken precautions to keep His Word free from error. As we study it, we understand the paradoxes.

Take, for instance, the matter of the biblical teaching about separation from sin. We are told in Hebrews 7:26 that Jesus is holy, blameless, pure, set apart from sinners. Yet in Hebrews 4:15, we read that Jesus "has been tempted in every way, just as we are—yet was without sin."

He was without sin, separated from sinners—sinless. Yet one of the major accusations by His enemies was that He associated with sinners. Listen to the words found in Luke 15:1-2: "Now the tax collectors and 'sinners' were all gathering around to hear him. But the Pharisees and the teachers of the law muttered, 'This man welcomes sinners and eats with them.'"

In one place in the Bible we learn that Jesus was "set apart from sinners." In another place we read that He associated with sinners. In fact, in one place we are told that He went home with Zacchaeus, who was a widely known, rich, eccentric sinner. And again His enemies used the situation to condemn Him (Luke 19:1-10).

Jesus' words clear up the problem. He said, "For the Son of Man came to seek and to save what was lost" (Luke 19:10). "It is not the healthy who need a doctor, but the sick. . . . For I have not come to call the righteous, but sinners" (Matthew 9:12,13).

Jesus was on a rescue mission. But while he was on that mission, he did not engage in the sin of those he came to save. That's our example of the separated life.

Lord, keep me separated from sin, but not from the sinner
who needs to know about You. Amen.

To Ponder: What does it mean that we are to love sinners?

FOR THE SAKE OF OTHERS
Read 1 Corinthians 7–10

*Do you not know that your body is a temple of the
Holy Spirit, who is in you, whom you have received
from God? You are not your own; you were bought
at a price. Therefore honor God with your body.*

1 CORINTHIANS 6:19-20.

Many things are not specifically forbidden by the Bible. But the
absence of a definite prohibition is not the only consideration in our
choice of behavior. Beyond what may be permissible in our own eyes,
the book of 1 Corinthians leads us to consider two other factors.

The first factor is other people. In 1 Corinthians 8:12-13, the
apostle Paul says: "When you sin against your brothers in this way and
wound their weak conscience, you sin against Christ. Therefore, if
what I eat causes my brother to fall into sin, I will never eat meat again,
so that I will not cause him to fall." Paul was referring to eating meat
that had been offered to idols, a real issue in his day. But he extended
the application to forgoing any behavior that would cause a brother in
Christ to stumble.

A second factor is the question, "Will this glorify God?" In
1 Corinthians 10:31, Paul wrote, "So whether you eat or drink or whatever you do, do it all for the glory of God." We should be concerned not
only with possible negative effects of our behavior, but with the goal
that everything we do brings honor and glory to God.

Christian, are you willing to subject your personal choices for the
good of others? When you're making a choice about a certain behavior, ask yourself, how will it affect other Christians, and will it bring
glory to God. The Lord is still looking for people who are willing to pay
the price to honor Him in all they do.

*Lord, please show me any behaviors or attitudes that I should
abandon, and then give me Your strength to do it. Amen.*

To Ponder: Is there anything you should set aside out of reverence for
God and conscience for others?

CHRIST IN YOU
Read Galatians 1–6

*Set an example for the believers in speech, in life,
in love, in faith and in purity.*

1 TIMOTHY 4:12

———

You may have heard it said, "You are the best Christian someone will ever know." As you go about your daily life, there's someone watching you who thinks that everything you do is right. It may be a coworker, a neighbor, or one of your own children. It should cause each of us to begin every day with a prayer that God would help us live so that the people watching us won't be led astray.

Would you believe the apostle Peter once became a bad example to the Christians around him? Here is how the apostle Paul relates the story in Galatians 2:12-13:

> Before certain men came from James, "[Peter] used to eat with the Gentiles. But when they arrived, he began to draw back and separate himself from the Gentiles because he was afraid of those who belonged to the circumcision group. The other Jews joined him in his hypocrisy, so that by their hypocrisy even Barnabas was led astray.

Even Barnabas—one of the earliest missionaries and the leader of the missionary team of Barnabas and Saul—was led astray by Peter's bad example. But the positive effect of Peter's life far outshines the negative example here. Apparently, Peter accepted Paul's reprimand, changed his behavior, and learned from his mistake. Yet the incident stands as a reminder that our lives are open to the eyes of all around us.

If there's something in your life that needs to change today, listen to God, admit your mistake, and turn around. It will be a powerfully good example to others.

Lord, help me to live as an example to others. Amen.

To Ponder: Would you change anything about your life if you took seriously the statement, "You might be the best Christian someone will ever know"?

GROWING DEEP ROOTS
Read Isaiah 28–30

*And in him you too are being built together to become a dwelling
in which God lives by his Spirit.*

EPHESIANS 2:22

In today's passage of Scripture, the prophet Isaiah presents the first principle of spiritual growth: We must begin with a sure foundation. Here are the words of Isaiah 28:16: "Therefore thus saith the Lord GOD, Behold, I lay in Zion for a foundation a stone, a tried stone, a precious cornerstone, a sure foundation" (KJV). In the New Testament we read that this foundation is Jesus Christ. Our precious Lord Jesus is this living stone, chosen by God. In 1 Corinthians 3:11, the apostle Paul wrote, "For no one can lay any foundation other than the one already laid, which is Jesus Christ."

I recall Dawson Trotman telling about a young man he once met. Daws had preached on the need for spiritual growth, and the young man came to him after the message and said, "Mr. Trotman, I want to grow, and I want to grow fast. I don't want to go through all those things you mentioned tonight such as Bible study, morning prayer, and Bible reading." He was looking for some way to take a great leap forward and arrive at spiritual maturity overnight.

In a microwave society, we keep looking for shortcuts and instant results. But there are no shortcuts to spiritual maturity. Spiritual growth is slow, but if we meet the conditions, it is sure. Involve yourself in those things that will get your roots down into Christ. The basics of church attendance, meditation on the Word, prayer, Bible study, and Scripture memory will provide the framework for you to build every day on the solid foundation of Jesus Christ.

*Lord, thank You for my salvation. Now, by Your Holy Spirit,
I want to go on and become fully equipped to be a useful
steward. Amen.*

To Ponder: As new Christians, we face two dangers. One is being satisfied that we are saved and never wanting to grow in Christ. The other is wanting to grow too quickly.

MAKING DISCIPLES
Read 1 Kings 5–8

"Then the master told his servant, 'Go out to the roads and country lanes and make them come in, so that my house will be full.'"

LUKE 14:23

Most Old Testament Jews failed to grasp God's vision regarding their places of worship. But King Solomon had a clear understanding of the temple and its purpose. Here is Solomon's prayer in 1 Kings 8:27: "Will God really dwell on earth? The heavens, even the highest heaven, cannot contain you. How much less this temple I have built!" Solomon also had no desire to monopolize the knowledge of God and have this knowledge confined to Israel. His prayer in 1 Kings 8:43 is that "all the peoples of the earth may know your name and fear you."

Solomon did not pray that all the nations of the earth might be subject to Israel and that he might reign over them, but that they might be subject to God and that God might reign over them. This ministry of making the Lord known to all people was to be the great destiny of the Jewish nation. Somehow, they completely missed the boat.

As time went by, they kept trying to scale God down. They tried to stuff their great and awesome God into this little temple and make Him their private possession. They tried to turn Him into a little tribal god to whom no one but them had access. How easy it is to repeat that same mistake today.

We need a vision for our lives and churches like the vision Solomon had for the temple. He understood it was not to be a little golden box in which the people could hide from the rest of the world, but a place where the nations of the earth might come and learn to pray to Him who would hear them and forgive their sin.

Lord, help me to see my church as more than a place where I go to be blessed. Help me to see it as a place where all may come to be saved and equipped to minister. Amen.

To Ponder: We are to gather together to worship and to develop resources we can use to tell the world about salvation through Jesus Christ.

135

MOURNING INTO GLADNESS
Read Nehemiah 8–10

*He has sent me to . . . provide for those who grieve in
Zion—to bestow on them a crown of beauty instead of
ashes, the oil of gladness instead of mourning, and a
garment of praise instead of a spirit of despair.*

ISAIAH 61:1,3

Did you know that the chemical composition of tears is affected by
what makes us cry? Tears of frustration have a different composition
than tears of grief or joy. And some kinds of crying are better for us
than others.

In today's passage, we have the beautiful lesson that God can
turn our tears of mourning into tears of joy. When Ezra read the book
of the Law, the record says the people wept. And at that point,
Nehemiah moved into the picture and challenged them to receive the
Word with joy.

When Nehemiah saw the people weeping, he told them to rejoice,
remembering that the joy of the Lord was their strength. Then he
told them to send portions of food to those for whom nothing was
prepared.

When I consider my giving to the Lord's work, I think of
Nehemiah and the people of God in this situation. They began with
tears as they heard the reading of God's Law and sensed their own
need. As they experienced the grace and forgiveness of God, their tears
were turned to joy. And out of that joy, they were challenged to give
generously to people in need. What a great picture of God's gracious
dealings with us. From our tears of mourning, God brings tears of joy
that overflow in generosity to others.

*Lord, thank You for a heart of mourning for my sin and a
heart of joy for Your forgiveness. Give me a heart of praise
for Your bounty, so that I can share my abundance with
others. Amen.*

To Ponder: When our sin has been confessed, repented of, and forgiven, our spirit can wear the garment of praise.

FRUIT OF THE VINE
Read Hosea 9–11

*"This is to my Father's glory, that you bear much fruit,
showing yourselves to be my disciples."*

JOHN 15:8

There is a description of God's people in Hosea 10:1 that is truly tragic. The Lord said, "Israel is an empty vine, he bringeth forth fruit unto himself" (KJV). The word *empty* in the original Hebrew means "luxuriant, spread out, full of leaves," but void of fruit to the glory of God. Instead it is filled with that which glorifies and pleases self. What a picture! Here are a people who claim a relationship with God, but the entire focus of their lives is on themselves.

The tragedy revealed in today's passage is that God expected His people to bear fruit to His glory. Instead, they lived completely for themselves. In Romans 14:7-8, Paul presents the attitude we should have: "For none of us lives to himself alone and none of us dies to himself alone. If we live, we live to the Lord; and if we die, we die to the Lord. So whether we live or die, we belong to the Lord."

You and I are not at our own disposal. Dead or alive, we are God's. Our first concern should be His will, on earth as it is in heaven. And one way you and I bring glory to Him is by bearing fruit. By bearing fruit, I mean reproducing after our own kind, producing other Christians. As a result of our lives and witness, people should be coming to Christ. That is the fruitfulness that glorifies God.

Christian, beware a life that appears luxuriant, pleasing to the eye of men, but displeasing to God.

Lord, I want to bear fruit to sustain others. Prune me with Your love and care. Amen.

To Ponder: No one plants a vineyard for ornamental reasons; the only purpose of a vine is to bear fruit.

FOLLOWING JESUS
Read Matthew 1–4

"If you remain in me and my words remain in you, ask whatever you wish, and it will be given you. This is to my Father's glory, that you bear much fruit, showing yourselves to be my disciples."

JOHN 15:7-8

Once, when I was speaking to a group of people on what it means to be a disciple, I tried to boil it down to its absolute essence—following Jesus. When the meeting was over, a woman from the audience came up to me and said, "You know, I had no idea it was so simple. We tend to complicate it."

In Matthew 4:19, we find these words of Jesus to His first disciples: "Come, follow me, . . . and I will make you fishers of men." What did that mean to the people who heard those words? It meant to remain close to Jesus every day, walking with Him, talking with Him, obeying Him, asking questions, learning from Him, being led by Him. The invitation was easily understood. The Lord wasn't talking to the priests in their long robes in Jerusalem, He was speaking to some fishermen by the Sea of Galilee. And in Matthew 4:22, we read that Peter and Andrew "left the boat and their father and followed him."

The word that summarizes all of this for you and me is the word *fellowship.* To live in fellowship with Christ means to move through the day in obedience to Him—seeking His will and not our own, loving Him and not the things of this world, spending time with Him in prayer, and reading His Word. It means to seek first the kingdom of God. And that's the heart of the whole thing.

Lord, as I spend time with You, help me to respond to Your leading in my life—every day. Amen.

To Ponder: If you are praying for God to teach you, are you willing to respond to what He directs?

LOVE ONE ANOTHER
Read Matthew 5–7

Instead, speaking the truth in love, we will in all things grow up into him who is the Head, that is, Christ. From him the whole body, joined and held together by every supporting ligament, grows and builds itself up in love, as each part does its work.

EPHESIANS 4:15-16

My wife and I were in Great Britain on a preaching tour shortly after a violent windstorm had swept the land, flattening more than a million trees. An official investigation discovered that the trees had been planted just far enough apart that their roots were not intertwined with each other. Each tree stood alone, with no help from the tree next to it, and over a million were lost.

When we as Christians become estranged from each other, the whole church is weakened and becomes more vulnerable to the attacks of Satan. The only way we can stay together is to be constantly involved in the process of being reconciled to each other.

Reconciliation involves confession, forgiveness, and restoration. We need each other; we need the binding of heart to heart, from which we gain strength; we need to experience the love of Christ through the concern and prayers of our brothers and sisters in the faith.

The process of being reconciled is a lot like digging up an old minefield. When anger, bitterness, and hatred are buried inside us, they keep exploding and injuring others. Jesus said, "Blessed are the merciful, for they will be shown mercy. . . . Blessed are the peacemakers, for they will be called sons of God" (Matthew 5:7,9).

Is there someone you need to be reconciled with today? Is there a long-buried spiritual mine you need to dig up and defuse before it injures someone? We need each other. Alone, we are as vulnerable as those trees in England. But standing together, we are strong in fellowship and love.

Lord, help me to live in unity with my brothers and sisters in Christ and to keep no account of wrongs against me. Amen.

To Ponder: To understand the importance God places on unity between believers, read His instruction in Matthew 5:23-24.

OUR TRANSFORMATION
Read Matthew 16–19

For God, who said, "Let light shine out of darkness,"
made his light shine in our hearts to give us the light of
the knowledge of the glory of God in the face of Christ.

2 CORINTHIANS 4:6

What's the most mind-boggling experience you've ever had? For me, I think it was my first trip to the Holy Land, where I actually looked at things Jesus saw and walked to places where He walked. But just think of the way Peter, James, and John must have felt as they were with Jesus on the Mount of Transfiguration (see Matthew 17:1-2). Jesus' glory, which was usually veiled, was briefly displayed for the disciples to see. I'm sure their minds were boggled when they were permitted to see Him as He really is.

Did you know that you and I, as followers of Christ, are involved in a process of transfiguration as well? The word *transfigured* is the same word used by the apostle Paul in Romans 12:2, where he exhorts us to be transformed by the renewing of our minds. We are not to be conformed to the world but transformed more and more into the likeness of Christ. In 2 Corinthians 3:18, we read that this is accomplished by the Spirit of the Lord as the new nature of Christ is manifested in us. For us as believers, this is a gradual experience. And although it happens over a period of time, the results are clearly evident as we grow toward maturity in Christ.

Christian, that's why our walk of daily discipleship is so important. Spiritual growth does not automatically happen with age. It comes only as we yield to the Lord, obey Him, and are transformed into His likeness.

Lord, may the world clearly see You in my life. Amen.

To Ponder: "But we have this treasure in jars of clay to show that this all-surpassing power is from God and not from us" (2 Corinthians 4:7).

HEARING GOD'S CALL
Read Isaiah 5–8

Therefore, since we have been justified through faith, we have
peace with God through our Lord Jesus Christ, through whom we
have gained access by faith into this grace in which we now stand.
And we rejoice in the hope of the glory of God.

ROMANS 5:1-2

"Here am I, send me." The prophet Isaiah first spoke those words in
the year King Uzziah died. King Uzziah was a man greatly used of
God, until pride captured his heart and the Lord set him aside. It was
after his death that Isaiah saw the Lord, high and lifted up, surrounded by angels who were saying, "Holy, holy, holy is the Lord of
hosts: the whole earth is full of His glory" (Isaiah 6:3, KJV).

When Isaiah found himself in the presence of the holy God, his
heart melted within him, and he cried, "Woe to me! I am ruined! For
I am a man of unclean lips, and I live among a people of unclean lips,
and my eyes have seen the King, the LORD Almighty" (6:4). Isaiah was
overwhelmed by God's sovereignty, power, and holiness.

Then the Lord spoke to him, giving assurance that Isaiah's sin was
forgiven and his iniquity purged, and asked the questions: "Whom
shall I send? And who will go for us?"

Have you seen this pattern in God's call? "In the year that King
Uzziah died . . ." God often speaks to us in times of great personal cri-
sis and transition. It seems we're often more attentive to His voice
during those hard times.

"I saw the Lord seated on a throne, high and exalted." Isaiah saw
God's holiness and majesty, and his own unworthiness.

"Your guilt is taken away." After Isaiah experienced God's forgiveness, he was free to answer God's call.

If God is calling you for some special service, you will find no
greater joy than to answer, "Here am I, send me."

Lord, here am I, send me. Amen.

To Ponder: How will you be able to tell if God is calling you?

TO THE ENDS OF THE EARTH
Read Isaiah 49–51

May the LORD, the God of your fathers, increase you a thousand times and bless you as he has promised!

DEUTERONOMY 1:11

Did you know that the Great Commission appears in the Old Testament? Notice the words of Isaiah 49:6: "It is too small a thing for you to be my servant to restore the tribes of Jacob and bring back those of Israel I have kept. I will also make you a light for the Gentiles, that you may bring my salvation to the ends of the earth."

This passage speaks of Jesus Christ. His objective is to bring God's salvation to the ends of the earth. And Christ made that possible by His death on the cross and His resurrection from the dead. It was the risen, triumphant Christ who commanded His disciples to "Go and make disciples of all nations."

Let me tell you about a lady named Mrs. Nellie Myrick. She was living in an old soldier's home in the middle of Iowa. It was a pretty gloomy place. But in her room, what a different story! The day my friend and I visited her, she was cutting pictures from Christmas cards to send to missionaries, who would use them in telling the story of Jesus to children. Every picture went out with her prayers.

We discovered that her radio was broken, and she couldn't listen to the Christian radio programs that gave prayer requests for missionaries. We took the radio and got it fixed, and she again was able to hear her programs and pray for the specific requests she heard.

Now here was a lady in very limited circumstances who was serious about the Great Commission. She was doing what she could, where she was, with all her heart. I wonder what would happen in the world today if more of us did the same.

Lord, infuse my heart with a desire to do whatever I can to turn people to Your light. Amen.

To Ponder: In the hand of God, our resources and abilities are multiplied for His kingdom.

SPIRITUAL MULTIPLICATION
Read Isaiah 58–66

*"I am the vine; you are the branches. If a man
remains in me and I in him, he will bear much fruit;
apart from me you can do nothing."*

JOHN 15:5

I heard a speaker at a national convention say that the church is losing ground today because we're *adding* people to the kingdom of God while the population of the world is *multiplying.*

For example, if you were to lead one person to Christ every day for the next thirty-two years, by the end of that period there would be 11,680 people in the kingdom of God as a result of your witness. But, let's say you led one person to Christ and then spent an entire year helping that person grow to maturity. You showed the person how to walk with Christ each day and to lead others to Him. By the end of year one, there would be two of you.

If you each won a person to Christ and trained him or her to be disciples, by the end of the second year there would be four of you. By the end of year three, there would be sixteen and so on. Now the staggering thing is this: If this process continued with no broken links in the chain, at the end of thirty-two years, there would be 4,294,967,296 of you.

What kind of person is a spiritual multiplier? From our human perspective, we would look to the person who is good in front of a crowd—a person with a lot of charisma, leadership ability, and organizational skill. But the Lord gives us the answer in Isaiah 66:2: "This is the one I esteem: he who is humble and contrite in spirit, and trembles at my word." The keys to becoming a spiritual multiplier are *humility* and *faith in the Word of God.* The Lord hasn't given any other plan for getting the job done.

Lord, help me to abide humbly in You and Your Word. Amen.

To Ponder: Making a difference for the kingdom of God begins on our knees with an open Bible and a humble heart.

WALKING IN THE WAY
Read Jeremiah 4–6

But I am afraid that just as Eve was deceived by the serpent's cunning, your minds may somehow be led astray from your sincere and pure devotion to Christ.

2 CORINTHIANS 11:3

If you want to be an effective communicator of the gospel, take a close look at the prophet Jeremiah. Three factors about his life made him a dynamic spokesman for the Lord.

First, Jeremiah heard the voice of God with his soul. In Jeremiah 4:19, he says, "Oh, my anguish, my anguish! I writhe in pain. Oh, the agony of my heart! My heart pounds within me, I cannot keep silent. For I have heard the sound of the trumpet; I have heard the battle cry."

Christian, when we read the Bible, we need to ask God to speak to our hearts and our souls. It is not our ears that need changing, but our hearts.

The second factor was that Jeremiah was affected by what he heard. Jeremiah's heart was deeply moved by the Word of God and by the consequences that faced the people of his day as they ignored the Lord. Because he was moved by God's warning of judgment, he spoke with sincerity and conviction.

The third factor in Jeremiah's effectiveness was the clarity and simplicity of his message: "This is what the LORD says, 'Stand at the crossroads and look; ask for the ancient paths, ask where the good way is, and walk in it, and you will find rest for your souls" (6:16). There was nothing complicated or obscure about Jeremiah's message.

Christian, if we will hear God's Word with our souls, be deeply moved by what He says, and speak a simple message of the gospel of Christ to others, God will use us, too. You can count on it.

Lord, as I read Your Word, speak to my heart and give me the desire to follow Your will. Amen.

To Ponder: When your heart is deeply moved by God's Word, you will be deeply moved about the spiritual state of others.

THIS LITTLE LIGHT OF MINE
Read Jeremiah 7–10

"I will surely bless you and give you many descendants."

HEBREWS 6:14

A lot of people look around today and feel like Jeremiah did nearly three thousand years ago. As he watched the moral and spiritual decline of his country, Jeremiah wondered if anything could be done to heal the sin of his people and prevent the judgment of God. Had the darkness become so great that it could not be overcome? Could the condition of the people be set right? The answer to the latter question was yes, and that's the answer for us today. Something can be done about the darkness if we're willing to let the work begin in and through us.

Every year a few weeks before Christmas, we have a candle-lighting service in our church. The entire sanctuary is dark except for one candle at the front. As a few people light their candles from that one, and then pass the flame to the candles around them, the entire sanctuary is lighted. To me, it's a beautiful picture of God's plan for conquering the spiritual darkness of the world.

In Jeremiah 9:24, we read: "'But let him who boasts boast about this: that he understands and knows me, that I am the LORD, who exercises kindness, justice and righteousness on earth, for in these I delight,' declares the LORD."

You see, we get the light for our candle from knowing the Lord Himself. And the greatest thing we can do for our world is to share that light with others, one at a time. So don't be discouraged or frustrated by the darkness of the world around you. Thank God that He has given you the light, and pass it on.

Lord, help me to realize my influence on the darkness around me. Amen.

To Ponder: One of the most deadly attitudes among Christians today is that their little flame of light doesn't matter.

FOR THE COMMON GOOD
Read Jeremiah 11–15

*"But you will receive power when the Holy Spirit comes on you;
and you will be my witnesses in Jerusalem, and in all Judea and
Samaria, and to the ends of the earth."*

ACTS 1:8

———

Thousands of prayer breakfast gatherings are held in towns and cities across the United States. Perhaps you've even attended one. But do you know where the whole thing began? Back in the late 1940s, a man named Abraham Veradi organized a prayer breakfast for the leaders of Seattle. As he saw the positive, continuing results from that outreach, he became concerned about the spiritual welfare of our national leaders in Washington, D.C. In the early 1950s, Veradi moved to D.C. and began to reach out to various members of Congress and others in government. It didn't look like much at first, but out of it grew what we know today as the National Prayer Breakfast. And from that small beginning, the concept has spread across America and literally around the world. It all began with the vision of one man who saw a need and took it to heart.

What a contrast to the situation we find in today's passage. In Jeremiah 12:11, the Lord says of His land and His people: "They have made it desolate and, being desolate, it mourneth unto me; the whole land is made desolate, because no man layeth it to heart" (KJV). How often we see this desolation of spiritual neglect today. It happens when people are not on their knees before God, pleading for Him to intervene and bring healing and health to the land and its people.

Christian, have you seen that kind of need right where you are? It may be among a group of young people or neighbors or business colleagues. Reach out to someone today in Jesus' name.

*Lord, please help me to reach out to someone today and end
their "desolation of spiritual neglect." Amen.*

To Ponder: If God is speaking to you about launching a prayer ministry for the spiritual health of those around you, take it to heart, no matter how hard it may seem.

WE'RE IN THIS TOGETHER
Read 2 Corinthians 1–5

*It was he who gave some to be apostles, some to be
prophets, some to be evangelists, and some to be
pastors and teachers, to prepare God's people for works
of service, so that the body of Christ may be built up.*

EPHESIANS 4:11-12

I know some people who feel that Christian ministry is the job of the
pastor and the paid church staff. The rest of us are like spectators in
the bleachers. We cheer on the team, but we don't play the game.

How do you think the apostle Paul viewed the Christian ministry?
Here are his words from 2 Corinthians 4:1: "Therefore, since through
God's mercy we have this ministry, we do not lose heart." Then in
verse 7, "But we have this treasure in jars of clay to show that this all-
surpassing power is from God and not from us."

Paul does not say, "I," but "we." He speaks of "our" gospel. He
refers to God's power using "us." The apostle knew that he and a few
other full-time workers would never get the job done by themselves,
nor was that ever God's intention. Paul relied on the members of various churches to pray for him, to support him financially, and to
encourage him, but he saw himself as one member of the total
team—a great witnessing brotherhood in which everyone had a
part. Paul would never endorse the idea of a pastor doing all the work
of witnessing and training, while the congregation did nothing but
cheer him on.

That's not the picture of the church we get from 2 Corinthians.
Thank God for your pastor, and then make sure you get into the
battle, too.

*Lord, thank You that You have left the Great Commission to
every one of us. Amen.*

To Ponder: Are you wholeheartedly supporting your fellow believers
in the Lord's work?

THE WORK OF OUR HANDS
Exodus 28–31

And God is able to make all grace abound to you,
so that in all things at all times, having all that
you need, you will abound in every good work.

2 CORINTHIANS 9:8

Today's passage shows Moses demonstrating humility in what could have been a very sticky situation. His brother, Aaron, is appointed high priest, and his descendants after him will fill that role. At the same time, the descendants of Moses are assigned the menial work of the Levite. They carried the Tabernacle about from place to place. They became janitors. They put up the tent. They assisted the priests in their various responsibilities, yet Moses didn't balk at this arrangement. It is clear evidence of his humble spirit and sincere commitment to the glory of God.

Aaron's promotion after he had been in the shadow of Moses is a clear picture of the principle that God will exalt those who abase themselves. We are told that Aaron had on his forehead a plate of pure gold engraved with the words, *Holiness to the Lord.* He was consecrated to God.

Aaron and his sons had no time to fritter away their days. They were involved in a great work; they were set aside to live lives of holiness unto the Lord and give the full measure of their energies to the work of God.

As priests unto God, our lives must be lived in holiness and humility—unspoiled by the lust of the flesh, disdaining the glitter and glamour of the things of this world. Let's live life with our hands full of whatever God has given us to do, whether it is visible leadership or playing second fiddle.

Lord, whatever You call me to do, help me to do it with my whole heart. Amen.

To Ponder: As priests unto God, our lives must be lived in both holiness and humility.

148

A WORTHY LEADER
Read Leviticus 21–23

In a large house there are articles not only of gold and silver, but also of wood and clay; some are for noble purposes, and some for ignoble. If a man cleanses himself from the latter, he will be an instrument for noble purposes, made holy, useful to the Master and prepared to do any good work.

2 TIMOTHY 2:20-21

———

Leadership is a high calling, and in today's passage we see that along with position and authority come great demands on those who hold those positions and provide leadership for others.

First of all, the Lord speaks to the character of the leaders. They shall not defile themselves, being chief men among their people. They shall be holy and not profane the name of their God. They must lead by example — in their personal lives, in their marriages, and in their work. They must draw nearer to God in their devotion; they must have a deep knowledge of the meaning of certain rituals in their religion; and they must keep a great distance from everything that would defile.

Second, they must never get involved in anything that would hinder their availability to help the people in their walk with God. Leadership requires a certain temperament — a steadiness in times of turmoil, a calmness under pressure. Their faith and confidence in the Word of God must be so clear and deep that it could be observed by everyone.

Does God have a leadership role for you? Let me encourage you to accept the challenge to discover what it is, and say to the Lord, "Help me to be the kind of person who can lead others along Your path of life."

Lord, keep me from making personal choices that hinder my testimony before others. Amen.

To Ponder: Spiritual leadership of others requires humility, constant prayer, and a daily decision to follow Christ.

SERVANT LEADERS
Read Numbers 17–20

*[He] made himself nothing, taking the very nature of a servant,
being made in human likeness. And being found in appearance as
a man, he humbled himself and became obedient to death—even
death on a cross! Therefore God exalted him to the highest place
and gave him the name that is above every name.*

PHILIPPIANS 2:7-9

How do you react when someone challenges your leadership and authority? In Numbers 17, the Lord did something out of the ordinary to address the grumbling attitudes of certain heads of the tribes of Israel, who began to ask why the priests had to come only from the tribe of Levi.

He told them to collect the staves they ordinarily used as emblems of their authority—old dry staves with no sap in them, carved with the name of the leader to identify which rod belonged to which man—and lay them in the tabernacle overnight. The rod that budded and blossomed would signify who was to be the priest. Aaron's rod—an ordinary dry stick—budded and blossomed and produced almonds. Aaron was chosen, and no other.

There is a lesson here to the Christian leader whose leadership may be under a challenge. Don't fight back. Let God vindicate His choice. Commit the matter to God and let Him settle the matter in His own way.

Once again, Aaron was reminded of his essential duty. God said, "Aaron, you and your sons with you shall serve." Not rule, not exercise dominion, but *serve* God and the people of God. Leaders must remember that they are servants and that they are to be humble, diligent, and faithful in all they do.

When someone challenges your authority, the Bible says the proper response is to serve and allow the Lord to establish your authority to lead.

Lord, mold me into the kind of leader You want me to be. Amen.

To Ponder: When you get frustrated with leading, read John 13, which describes how Jesus washed the disciples' feet and then told them to do the same for one another.

COMMITMENT
Read Deuteronomy 8

"Don't urge me to leave you or to turn back from you. Where you go I will go, and where you stay I will stay. Your people will be my people and your God my God."

RUTH 1:16

The bride and groom were laughing and enjoying the company of their friends. The groom was snickering about the way they'd changed the traditional wedding vows. These two had vowed to stay married not for as long as they both shall live but for as long as they both shall love. If they got bored, they would just walk out and call it quits.

Now think with me for a moment. What kind of security would either of them feel if, after a few years and a couple of kids, each knew that the other was likely to just walk out? They would live each day in uncertainty.

God planned marriage to begin with a bedrock of commitment by one man and one woman. Their life together was to be as long as they both should live—through sickness and health, good times and lean times, till death parted them. Genuine love is to be understood in the context of commitment.

Early in the life of God's people, God set forth the concept of His unshakable commitment to them. He identified Himself as the faithful God who keeps His covenant to a thousand generations (Deuteronomy 7:9).

Moses told the people: "The eternal god is thy refuge, and underneath are the everlasting arms" (Deuteronomy 33:27, KJV). What a picture of love made secure by commitment. And that's what is desperately needed in a world where there is heartbreak caused by marriages torn apart—the heartbreak of kids confused by Mom and Dad living by the standards of the world and self-interest. Real love is to be understood in the context of commitment.

Lord, help me to be faithful to the people You have put in my life. Amen.

To Ponder: God's faithfulness to us compels our faithfulness to others.

THE PERSONAL TOUCH
Read 2 Samuel 1–4

But we were gentle among you, like a mother caring for her little children. We loved you so much that we were delighted to share with you not only the gospel of God but our lives as well, because you had become so dear to us.

1 THESSALONIANS 2:7-8

—————

The book of Second Samuel gives us a first look at the reign of King David. The first thing that strikes us is David's remarkable reaction upon hearing of the death of Saul, the man he most feared, and of Jonathan, the man he most loved.

Although this meant the path was now wide open to the throne, David's heart was broken by the news of Saul's death. In his eulogy, he found the best in Saul to dwell on and made no mention of his faults.

After paying respect to the memory of Saul, his king, and Jonathan, his friend, David turned to the Lord for guidance, and the Lord sent him to Hebron, where the men of Judah anointed him king over their tribe.

David could have resented that. He could have sent messengers far and wide to summon all the people to come and swear allegiance to him, but in modesty and humility he accepted the scepter to rule over his own tribe.

He rose to power gradually, knowing it would take time for his kingship over all Israel to be confirmed. David manifested a tender heart and a willingness to wait for God's timing—two indispensable ingredients in God's training program for all who would lead others and serve Him.

It's so easy for a leader to have his mind on big, important things and to get too caught up in them. But a big part of leadership is ministering to the heartache that grips the soul of a colaborer or friend. If there is one thing that commends a leader to his people, it is a tender heart.

Lord, help me not to lose touch with the concerns of my friends. Amen.

To Ponder: A great person will never be too overloaded or busy to have compassion.

GOD'S ESTEEM FOR HIS WORD
Read Luke 3–6

*"For my thoughts are not your thoughts, neither
are your ways my ways. . . . As the heavens are higher
than the earth, so are my ways higher than your ways
and my thoughts than your thoughts."*

ISAIAH 55:8-9

If you ask the man on the street where the really important things are happening today, he might say the Oval Office, the House and the Senate, or Number 10, Downing Street, in London. In one sense, that's right. But God doesn't evaluate events by the same measure we do.

How clearly we see this truth in Luke 3:1-2: "In the fifteenth year of the reign of Tiberius Caesar—when Pontius Pilate was governor of Judea, Herod tetrarch of Galilee, his brother Philip tetrarch of Iturea and Traconitis, and Lysanias tetrarch of Abilene—during the high priesthood of Annas and Caiaphas, the word of God came to John son of Zechariah in the [wilderness]."

Now, if you had asked the man on the street in those days where the really important things were happening, he would probably have said Rome or in the palaces of the tetrarchs or in the courts of the high priests. But in this passage, God calls our attention to seven very important men in the eyes of the world, simply to mark the time in history when the Word of God came to an unknown nobody in the wilderness.

You don't have to be important in the eyes of the world for the Word of God to come to you and to come alive in your heart. It can happen at your kitchen table or at a little desk, where you set aside time each day to read the Bible and pray.

*Lord, give me Your perspective on my day, and help me to
daily study, memorize, and obey Your Word. Amen.*

To Ponder: From God's perspective, the most important thing you can do today is meet with Him in His Word and let it change you.

LOVING OTHERS
Read 1 Thessalonians 2:6-12

"A new command I give you: Love one another. As I have loved you, so you must love one another. By this all men will know that you are my disciples, if you love one another."

JOHN 13:34-35

———

Suppose a missionary ministered in one of the college campuses, telling students of the love of God as revealed in Jesus Christ. There he meets a few young men and women who are eager to join him in his ministry. So they team up.

But their lack of maturity and their conduct do not match up with his expectations. So one day he meets with them and gives them this lecture: "I'm not here playing games. I'm here to make an impact for Christ, and you guys had better shape up or ship out. I don't have time to fool around."

If you were one of the new Christians wanting to serve, you'd probably start thinking, "He's not interested in me at all. All he wants to do is use me to get a job done."

Read the apostle Paul's words to the Christians in Thessalonica: "But we were gentle among you, like a mother caring for her little children. We loved you so much that we were delighted to share with you not only the gospel of God but our lives as well, because you had become so dear to us" (1 Thessalonians 2:7-8).

Paul continued to think of the Thessalonians' welfare, and he encouraged them with the words, "We always thank God for all of you, mentioning you in our prayers. We continually remember before our God and Father your work produced by faith, your labor prompted by love, and your endurance inspired by hope in our Lord Jesus Christ" (1:2-3).

If you have the heart of a servant, you have love and concern for others. You will be willing to invest yourself in them and will see fruit produced in God's timing.

Lord, fill me with Your love until it overflows toward others and considers them above my own welfare. Amen.

To Ponder: In His commandment, Christ set a new measure for our love: "As I have loved you."

SAVIOR OF THE WORLD
Read Isaiah 9–12

The first thing Andrew did was to find his brother Simon and tell him, "We have found the Messiah" (that is, the Christ). And he brought him to Jesus.

JOHN 1:41-42

In Isaiah 9, we find a prophecy portrait of the coming Messiah, painted more than seven hundred years before Jesus was born. Let's compare Isaiah's prophecies and their fulfillment.

Isaiah 9:2 says, "The people walking in darkness have seen a great light." When Jesus came, He said, "I am the light of the world. Whoever follows me will never walk in darkness, but will have the light of life" (John 8:12).

Isaiah referred to the coming Messiah as the mighty God (Isaiah 1:24). When Jesus came, He lived a life of power in the things He said, the miracles He performed, and most of all, in His resurrection from the dead. The New Testament says that the Spirit that raised up Christ from the dead shall also give life to your mortal bodies by his Spirit that dwells in you (Romans 8:11, KJV).

Isaiah's portrait of the Messiah also shows Him as the Prince of Peace (Isaiah 9:6). Jesus said, "Peace I leave with you; . . . Do not let your hearts be troubled and do not be afraid" (John 14:27).

Isaiah 26:3 speaks of the perfect peace of the one whose mind is stayed on the Lord. Paul wrote that we have peace with God through our Lord Jesus Christ (Romans 5:1).

The portrait of the coming Messiah still hangs in the gallery of Isaiah. But the Lord Himself is here to bring light to see, power to live, and peace within.

Lord, I want to grow in the grace and knowledge of You, so that the world will catch glimpses of my likeness to You. Amen.

To Ponder: From this side of the Cross, we see Jesus as the perfect man, our Redeemer and our Lord.

WATCHMEN ON THE WALL
Read Isaiah 21–23

"When I say to a wicked man, 'You will surely die,' and you
do not warn him or speak out to dissuade him from his evil
ways in order to save his life, that wicked man will die for
his sin, and I will hold you accountable for his blood."

EZEKIEL 3:18

In Isaiah's time, watchmen were posted on the city walls or on the hilltops near the city. Their purpose was to stay awake, stay alert, and warn the people of danger. In Isaiah 21:11, we read of a man approaching a watchman and inquiring about the current state of things, "Watchman," he asks, "what of the night?" And the watchman gives him an answer.

As Christians, this may happen to us. In 1 Peter 3:15, the apostle Peter said, "But sanctify the Lord God in your hearts, and be ready always to give an answer to every man that asketh you a reason of the hope that is in you" (KJV). If you are walking in fellowship with Christ each day, you'll find people coming to you wanting to know why you can cope with things that are dragging them down.

A watchman had another responsibility. If a watchman spotted an enemy approaching, he didn't sit on the wall drinking coffee and waiting for someone to walk up and ask what was happening. It was the watchman's responsibility to sound the alarm.

Today, most people seem content to go through life engrossed in the affairs of this world. Even though their eternal welfare is hanging in the balance, most of them will not take the initiative to seek spiritual things. So, it is our job to warn them about their separation from God and the judgment to come, and to give them the good news of salvation.

When the question comes to us, "Watchman, what of the night?" let's be awake, alert, and ready to sound the warning to lead the way to safety.

Lord, keep me alert to the needs of others so that I can point
them to You. Amen.

To Ponder: If I look for opportunities to help people, I will be a witness to them.

THE SACRIFICE FOR OUR SINS
Read Isaiah 52–57

*Then Philip began with that very passage of Scripture
and told him the good news about Jesus.*

ACTS 8:35

Isaiah 53 is one of the clearest Old Testament prophecies of the coming Messiah, depicting Him as the suffering servant who endured the punishment we deserve. Perhaps you can quote verses 5-6 from memory: "But he was pierced for our transgressions, he was crushed for our iniquities; the punishment that brought us peace was upon him, and by his wounds we are healed. We all, like sheep, have gone astray, each of us has turned to his own way, and the LORD has laid on him the iniquity of us all."

Years ago, I was holding some evangelistic meetings with college students in Halifax, Nova Scotia. One night after I had shared the gospel and a word of personal testimony with some students in a dorm, a young woman told me how she had recently come to faith in Christ. She was of Jewish descent and had been a vocal opponent of the Christians on her campus. But as she read her Old Testament one day, she came to Isaiah 53. For the first time, she saw what the Christians in her dorm had been trying to tell her. The Messiah had come—and died for her. Through the reading of this passage and through the witness and prayers of Christians on her campus, she gave her life to Christ and became an outspoken witness for Him.

Sometimes we read the book of Acts and wonder why miraculous things like that don't seem to happen today. Friend, they do! Just like the official from Ethiopia, whom Philip led to Christ after he read from Isaiah 53, this young college woman found her Messiah and Savior by reading the very same passage.

Lord, thank You for dying for my sin. By Your wounds, I have been healed. Amen.

To Ponder: Jesus Christ is the Messiah. He died in my place so that I can live eternally.

THE IMPERISHABLE WORD
Read Jeremiah 21–25

*See to it that no one takes you captive through hollow and
deceptive philosophy, which depends on human tradition
and the basic principles of this world rather than on Christ.
For in Christ all the fullness of the Deity lives in bodily form.*

COLOSSIANS 2:8-9

When I was growing up on the farm, we ran grain through a threshing machine. I can remember watching the wind carry the chaff away,
and no one cared. Why? Because chaff is worthless.

God says that human opinion is like chaff, while His Word is like
grain. The Lord said this because there were false prophets who
claimed to have a message from God. In reality, what they spoke was
nothing more than their own foolish dreams.

Sounds like today, doesn't it? People speaking visions from their
own minds, not from the mouth of the Lord. In Jeremiah 23:28, we
find these words from God: " 'Let the prophet who has a dream tell his
dream, but let the one who has my word speak it faithfully. For what
has straw to do with grain?' declares the LORD."

If you plant a bushel of straw, will you get a crop? No, there is no
life in straw. But if you plant a bushel of wheat, you get a harvest many
times greater than the amount of grain you put in the ground. When
it comes to speaking the message of God, human philosophy and reason is like chaff. But the Word of God has spiritual food value. One is
weightless and has no convicting power. But calling a person's attention to the Word of God is like sending grain to people in famine.

As you talk to people about Christ today, don't trust in your own
arguments, remember that "[we] have been born again, not of perishable seed, but of imperishable, through the living and enduring
word of God" (1 Peter 1:23).

*Lord, Your Word is truth. Let me never speak to others about
You from my own reasoning, but only from what Your Word
tells me. Amen.*

To Ponder: God's Word has life within it and the power to bring
people to faith in God.

BY GOD'S SPIRIT
Read Micah 3–5

They asked each other, "Were not our hearts burning within us
while he talked with us on the road and opened
the Scriptures to us?"

LUKE 24:32

The prophet Micah had a love for God, a burden for the souls of men, and a flaming zeal against sin. And he had the boldness to speak out. Now, where did Micah get that boldness? And where can you and I find the boldness we need to witness to the people with whom we rub shoulders every day? Micah 3:8 gives us the answer: "But as for me, I am filled with power, with the Spirit of the LORD, and with justice and might, to declare to Jacob his transgression, to Israel his sin."

Christian, there it is. Micah was full of power by the Spirit of the Lord. And if you and I would experience that same power, we must acknowledge our need and pray for boldness to meet the witnessing opportunities we have each day.

In Acts 4:29-31, we find a situation in which the religious leaders and the people opposed the followers of Christ. So the Christians prayed, and "they were all filled with the Holy Spirit and spoke the word of God boldly."

When the word *boldness* appears in the Bible, it most often means "unashamed freedom of speech." Under His control, we are to walk in obedience to the Lord. Throughout the New Testament, we find the followers of Christ speaking out in obedience to God's command, just as the Old Testament prophets had done centuries before.

If you and I would witness boldly for the Lord, we must be people who are learning the discipline and power of prayer.

Lord, help me to be faithful in prayer and to ask for Your fill-
ing, so that I may speak freely about You. Amen.

To Ponder: "Be filled with the Spirit" (Ephesians 5:18). The word *filled* means "controlled."

SPIRITUAL FERVOR
Read the book of Zephaniah

Then I heard the voice of the Lord saying,
"Whom shall I send? And who will go for us?"

ISAIAH 6:8

It used to be common for people to refer to a committed Christian as being "on fire for the Lord." I don't hear that phrase much anymore. Perhaps it's because a lot of the emphasis today is on knowledge, not on fervor and zeal for God.

The book of Zephaniah points out our need to recapture passion for the Lord in our walk of daily discipleship. In Zephaniah 1:12, the Lord says: "I will search Jerusalem with lamps and punish those who are complacent, who are like wine left on its dregs, who think, 'The LORD will do nothing, either good or bad.'"

This kind of lukewarm, half-hearted attitude is deadly, because the kingdom of God is advanced in this world by people who are on fire for the Lord, whose hearts burn within them to see others brought to Christ through repentance and faith and to see them begin to walk with Him each day.

Paul's spiritual fervor can be seen throughout his life and his writings. When he wrote to the Romans, he said, "I am so eager to preach the gospel also to you who are at Rome" (Romans 1:15). Paul was not just willing to come, to preach, to serve; he was eager. Paul's word for *eager* is the Greek word *prothumos,* which conveys the idea of breathing hard, being set on fire.

Pilgrim, do you want your life to count for Christ? Why not ask God today to rekindle your spirit and make you a member of the fellowship of the burning heart.

Lord, give me a spirit that is on fire for You. Amen.

To Ponder: The person who is convinced that Jesus Christ is the only hope for the world will live unreservedly for Him.

GOD KNOWS OUR FRAME
Read Psalm 103:13-14

And now these three remain: faith, hope and love.
But the greatest of these is love.

1 CORINTHIANS 13:13.

Many years ago I took my family to Disneyland. We'd had a great day visiting the Magic Kingdom, and it was time to leave. At the front gate, I suggested that everyone visit the restroom before the drive home. Randy, our youngest son, refused. He assured me he was ready to get into the car. We were on the freeway when I heard a little voice from the backseat.

"Dad . . . Daddy . . ."

"What is it, son?"

"Dad, I have to go to the restroom."

I could tell by his tone of voice that he knew he'd done something foolish and didn't need a lecture. "Well," I said, "that's no problem. There are lots of gasoline stations along the way. Look, right there. We'll stop there." On the way back to the car, as we walked along hand in hand, Randy looked up at me and said, "Dad, I love you."

Once in a while you do the right thing. And when you do, it makes you feel so good! Oh sure, he delayed the trip, he caused some inconvenience, but it was no big problem.

You and I often do the same thing in our walk with God. Just like children, we do something we know we shouldn't have done, but the Lord understands. He knows we aren't perfect. He knows that sometimes we're going to be silly and childlike. But the Bible says the Lord is gracious, slow to anger, and plenteous in mercy. We can count on His loving patience and understanding.

Lord, may Your Spirit prompt me to be patient, kind, and loving to those who may inconvenience me today. Amen.

To Ponder: God knows me inside and out; He has compassion for my weaknesses and doesn't treat me as I deserve.

CONDEMNED NO MORE
Read Ezekiel 24–28

*"I tell you the truth, whoever hears my word and believes
him who sent me has eternal life and will not be condemned;
he has crossed over from death to life."*

JOHN 5:24

———

I was set to speak at a university campus my wife and I had been told
was the most unresponsive to the gospel of any school in California.
When we got there, the organizers of the meeting were pulling open
a large folding door to enlarge the meeting space. Even then, the place
was packed, and students were standing in the back. I gave a thirty-
minute message explaining the gospel of Christ, and when I opened
the meeting for questions, one student asked, "Are you saying, sir, that
if I come to Christ in the manner you suggested, I would never face
judgment?"

"Yes, that's what I'm saying," I replied. "Christ died to pay the entire
penalty for our sin. When we come to Him in repentance and faith, we
have His assurance that if we hear and have faith, we will not be judged."

The meeting went on for another hour or two, and periodically the
matter of judgment came up. After the meeting, a student asked me
about it one more time.

The judgment of God is not a pleasant topic, yet Scripture is filled
with references to it. In Ezekiel 24–28, the phrase "this is what the
sovereign LORD says" occurs twenty-eight times, followed by a message of judgment.

When you and I came to Christ, we settled that issue once and for
all. But many people are still struggling with it. I didn't think a group
of freewheeling college kids in California would be interested in the
judgment of God. Could there be someone you know who is longing
for the peace of knowing "there is [therefore] now no condemnation
for those who are in Christ Jesus" (Romans 8.1)?

*Lord, help me to represent Your love to those You place within
my sphere of influence. Amen.*

To Ponder: The peace that passes understanding is the legacy of those
who are no longer under condemnation.

FINDING OUR STRENGTH
Read Ezekiel 29–32

It is God who arms me with strength and makes my way perfect.

2 SAMUEL 22:33

Not long ago, I saw an ad for a cassette tape series that promised to dramatically improve my memory in just a few hours; it sounded intriguing. Our mailboxes are filled with ads like that because people are interested in quick fixes and overnight miracles.

The Israelites were no exception. Many times in the history of ancient Israel, we see them turning to Egypt for security instead of trusting God. But through the prophet Ezekiel, the Lord clearly declared just where the power lay. In Ezekiel 29:6-7, God said to Egypt: "You have been a staff of reed for the house of Israel. When they grasped you with their hands, you splintered and you tore open their shoulders; when they leaned on you, you broke and their backs were wrenched."

The Lord was telling them that if God's people were looking for a strong ally to protect them from their enemies, they should look to God Himself.

Christian, you and I need the same warning today. All too often we're attracted to the promise of gimmicks, programs, and schemes. We need to be reminded that the latest book, tape, or method will not equip us to witness for Christ. It is first and foremost personal fellowship with the Lord that prepares us. Without that, nothing counts.

E. M. Bounds wrote in his book *Power Through Prayer,* "The church is looking for better methods, God is looking for better men; men and women who will trust Him, follow Him, and look to Him and Him alone for the advancement of His kingdom."

Lord, empower me by Your Holy Spirit to carry out Your purpose for me today. Amen.

To Ponder: Those who hear the Word of God and respond to Him through faith are the people He uses to build His kingdom.

DRY BONES
Read Ezekiel 37–39

And [Christ] died for all, that those who live should
no longer live for themselves but for him who
died for them and was raised again.

2 CORINTHIANS 5:15

In Ezekiel 37:1, the prophet is carried in the spirit of the Lord to a valley filled with dry bones. In fact, the Bible says the bones were very dry. In verse 2, the Lord asks a surprising question: "Son of man, can these bones live?" I'm sure Ezekiel's first reaction was to think, *No way*. But Ezekiel was used to surprises from the Lord, so his response was, "Lord, only you know." And the lesson that comes ringing through this passage is that all things are possible with God.

In the 1960s, we were ministering in Boulder, Colorado, trying to reach out to young people there. I recall one young man who was hooked on drugs. A lot of people told us we were wasting our time trying to help him, because his drug addiction was too great. I remember one night, trying to keep him moving as he was going through withdrawal.

Over a period of time, we kept talking to him about the Lord, and finally he became a Christian. God not only saved his soul, but He completely delivered him from drugs. Later, he and another guy went off to Bible school for training so they could serve the Lord. This was the young man everyone had said was too far gone.

In Ezekiel's vision, when he prophesied over the dry bones, breath came into them and they stood on their feet, a great army brought to life from the dead. Christian, that's our mission from God. As you and I pray for those who are dead in trespasses and sin, and as we share the life-giving gospel of Christ with them, the power of God can bring life to people who are spiritually dead.

Lord, who breathes life into dry old bones, use me to bring
Your life-giving message to those who are dead in their sin.
Amen.

To Ponder: With God, *all* things are possible.

SOMETHING BEAUTIFUL
Read Ezekiel 40–43

Therefore, if anyone is in Christ, he is a new creation;
the old has gone, the new has come!

2 CORINTHIANS 5:17

Ezekiel was taken in a vision to a high mountain overlooking
Jerusalem, a city that had been demolished and plundered. From this
mountain, God gave Ezekiel a vision of what was to come as recorded
in Ezekiel 40. "Son of man, look with your eyes and hear with your
ears and pay attention to everything I am going to show you, for that
is why you have been brought here. Tell the house of Israel everything
you see" (40:4). A temple, grand and glorious, would rise out of the
rubble, and once again God would be glorified in that place.

Is your Christian life all that you want it to be? Are you as close to
God as you would like to be in your walk of daily discipleship? God can
breathe in a freshness of new life and bring a new beauty to your soul.
But it will take some effort on your part. Begin the day with morning
prayer and Bible reading. Get into a good Bible study designed to get
your roots down into Christ and give your spiritual life a solid footing.
Take some of the most meaningful verses from your Bible study and
commit them to memory. Put them in your heart so God can continue to use them to encourage you and transform your life.

God gave Ezekiel two visions of how His power could bring
beauty out of tragedy. Is there a relationship that was once like a beautiful city that has been destroyed and plundered? We are called to
cooperate with the power of God in Jesus Christ, by which old things
are taken away and all things are made new.

Lord, bring glory to Yourself as You transform the rubble areas
of my life. Amen.

To Ponder: By God's power, life and beauty can emerge from death
and destruction. Where is that happening around you?

AN ANTIDOTE FOR PRIDE
Jeremiah 46–49

When pride comes, then comes disgrace,
but with humility comes wisdom.

PROVERBS 11:2

Not long ago, I was standing in line at the airport. The service was not as fast as the two men in front of me would have liked, so they made their displeasure known to anyone within earshot. They felt they were important people and weren't used to this kind of shoddy treatment.

As I watched these men, I was reminded of some people mentioned in the book of Jeremiah. During Jeremiah's day, the Moabites were a proud and arrogant people who looked down from their location on a high plateau and thought themselves secure. Who would dare attack them? Who could be successful if they tried? They considered themselves the absolute masters of their fate.

I guess we all know people who consider themselves superior to others and demand that they be treated differently. The Bible clearly teaches that God hates pride, because it keeps people from depending on Him. Pride produces a false sense of security that tells a person he's doing just fine without God.

Listen to the Lord's surprising reaction to the proud people of Moab. In Jeremiah 48:31, the Lord said, "I wail over Moab, for all Moab I cry out." In spite of Moab's arrogance and insolence, God looked at her with tender compassion. In the final analysis, there is only one antidote for our pride, and that is the compassion of God. Yes, God hates pride, but He loves the people who are being destroyed by it.

None of us are immune to the spiritual disease of pride. When arrogance threatens to poison our lives, it is God's tender mercy and compassion that draws us to Him.

Lord, help me to have regard for other people and to keep their welfare in mind as I struggle for my place in the world. Amen.

To Ponder: God shows me kindness, not punishment, to lead me to repentance and fellowship with Him.

AUTHENTIC WORDS
Read Isaiah 24–27

I remember your ancient laws, O LORD,
and I find comfort in them.

PSALM 119:52

One time when I was buying a pair of shoes, the salesman wanted to see my driver's license and two major credit cards before he would take my personal check. After I produced all the identification he wanted, I asked if he knew why he needed all this. "It's store policy," he said.

I told him that wasn't the real reason, and when he asked me what I meant, I told him, "The real reason you need all this identification is Romans 3:23: 'For all have sinned and fall short of the glory of God.' If man wasn't sinful, you wouldn't need all this."

Our society is built around the premise that a person's word cannot be trusted. But that's never an issue when we deal with God and His Word. God always speaks the truth, and He is faithful to His truthful word. This is where the Devil has achieved a masterstroke. He has deluded people into thinking the Bible is a bunch of myths, passed down from generation to generation in the most haphazard fashion. Though God has staked His very character and reputation on the fact that His Word is true and trustworthy, millions have been led to mistrust it and thereby are kept from the gates of heaven.

The Old Testament prophets did not fritter away their time on peripheral issues. When they spoke of God, they focused on His integrity and trustworthiness. Listen to the words of Isaiah: "Trust in the LORD forever, for the LORD, the LORD is the Rock eternal" (26:4).

Our eternal Rock has the power to bring His Word to pass.

Lord, Your Word is truth, and I can trust it for all eternity.
Amen.

To Ponder: God is ready, willing, and able to fulfill His Word in our lives.

LIVING OUT HIS WORD
Read Daniel 7–12

All your words are true; all your righteous laws are eternal.

PSALM 119:160

It is clear from the Bible and from the experience of God's people, that as we seek God through His Word, our lives are changed. Of course our purpose in getting into the Word is not to become walking information booths with an answer for every question that comes along. We come to God's Word to become people who are more like Christ. We can see this influence of God's Word in the life of Daniel.

In Daniel 9:2 we read, "In the first year of [Darius the king], I, Daniel, understood from the Scriptures, according to the word of the LORD given to Jeremiah the prophet, that the desolation of Jerusalem would last seventy years." Here is Daniel, having his daily devotions in the writings of Jeremiah, when he discovered something that dramatically altered the course of his life. He believed what he read, he acted on it, and his life was changed.

Notice Daniel 9:3: "I turned to the Lord God and pleaded with him in prayer and petition." Communication from God was immediately followed by communion with God.

Through the Word and prayer, our spiritual life is strengthened. This leads to the result we find in Daniel 11:32: "The people who know their God will firmly resist [the enemy]."

To know the Lord is to love Him, and to love Him is to serve Him. So it begins with time in His Word, continues with time on our knees, and results in effective service in His kingdom.

Lord, I am Yours. Make my life count for Your kingdom. Amen.

To Ponder: When faith and obedience accompany our study of the Bible, our lives will never be the same.

THUS SAITH THE LORD
Read Ezekiel 1–6

I have more insight than all my teachers,
for I meditate on your statutes.

PSALM 119:99

———

Many Bible scholars believe that the prophet Ezekiel was an exceptionally brilliant man. If their conclusions are correct, that may explain why God told Ezekiel over and over, "Speak my words to the people." God made it plain that the prophet was to say to the people, "Thus saith the LORD," not "Thus saith Ezekiel."

We find the heart of God's commission in Ezekiel 3:3-4: "Then he said to me, 'Son of man, eat this scroll I am giving you and fill your stomach with it.' So I ate it, and it tasted as sweet as honey in my mouth. He then said to me: 'Son of man, go now to the house of Israel and speak my words to them.'"

During our days of campus ministry, we invited a Christian professor to debate the leading atheist professor on our campus. The Christian professor was clearly the victor in this debate. As we analyzed it later, it was because he gave a simple, clear, and understandable presentation of the gospel of Christ. He spoke the Word of God.

A couple of years later, we invited a different Christian professor. The atheist wiped him out. This Christian professor had not quoted one verse of Scripture, and he'd kept the whole debate on a plane of philosophical, human argument.

God has commissioned us to take His message to those around us. To do this we must fill our lives with His Word. Like Ezekiel we must eat it, digest it, and make it part of our lives. Then we must share it with others in all its simplicity and power. God uses brilliant people, but only when they speak His Word.

Lord, give me Your words to speak to those around me. Amen.

To Ponder: You are a channel for God's message to the world.

FIRE IN THE BONES
Read Jeremiah 16–20

*Preach the Word; be prepared in season and out of
season; correct, rebuke and encourage—with great
patience and careful instruction.*

2 TIMOTHY 4:2

Have you ever felt as tough there's no point in sharing the gospel any
more because people are so secularized in their thinking, and their
understanding of God is so limited?

I would imagine Jeremiah the prophet could have come to the
same conclusion three thousand years ago. The people's understanding of God was so fouled up they couldn't tell the difference
between a broken cistern and a fountain. He had been giving his
people the message of God, pleading with them and praying for
them, but nothing seemed to do any good. Their hearts were like
stone, hard and unchanging.

There comes a point when even good men get fed up. Notice his
words in Jeremiah 20:9: "If I say, 'I will not mention Him or speak any
more in His name . . .'" But when he stifled and suppressed the message of God, he was like a container filled with hot steam, ready to
explode.

Next, we find these words: "His Word is in my heart like a fire, a
fire shut up in my bones. I am weary of holding it in; indeed, I cannot." It was the Word of God within Jeremiah that wouldn't stay put.

In every generation there are doomsayers who say the world is so
bad nothing can be done about it. Sometimes these are people who
know the Lord but have become so discouraged with a lack of
response that they give up. But inside us, the Word of God should
burn like a fire whose warmth we just have to share.

The key to effective witnessing is not a responsive audience but
the Word of God burning within us.

*Lord, make Your Word burn in my heart so hot that I just have
to let it out or else be consumed. Amen.*

To Ponder: Does your heart burn with the desire to share God's
Word?

REPAIRING A SPIRITUAL LEAK
Read Hosea 7–8

*Make your face shine upon your servant
and teach me your decrees.*

PSALM 119:135

If you've ever had a slow leak in a tire, you probably didn't notice it until the tire was completely flat.

In Hosea 7–8 we have the description of a slow spiritual leak. Over a period of time, the people of God gradually drifted away from Him. It probably started just as it does with us—a small sin, an act that looked quite harmless. But it resulted in disorder and eventually in God's judgment. One stage in the people's downward spiral is noted in Hosea 8:12, where God says: "I wrote for them the many things of my law, but they regarded them as something alien." God had become a stranger among His own people, and they treated His words as something remote and unrelated to their lives.

A phrase I've heard a lot of people use at one time or another is, "I don't want to hear it." That's how Hosea records the reaction of the people to the Word of God. The Word did not fit their lifestyle, so they closed their ears and went their own way. During the days of Hosea the prophet, God pleaded with His people, year after year, to repent and turn to Him. His love and compassion are clearly seen in these pages from the Old Testament. But His people refused to listen and brought judgment on themselves.

To read the Bible, to hear the voice of God, to believe and to obey—that way leads to life. Christian, if there's a slow spiritual leak in your life, why not stop and get it repaired? If the Lord is speaking to you, open your heart to Him and get back on the road of daily discipleship.

Lord, I've been toying with something that I know displeases You and blocks my hearing. I want to turn from my way and listen to Your voice once more. Amen.

To Ponder: Are you open to God's voice, or is there something you don't want to hear from Him?

WONDERFUL WORDS OF LIFE
Read Amos 8–9

I have not departed from the commands of his lips;
I have treasured the words of his mouth
more than my daily bread.

JOB 23:12

———————

I was traveling in a part of the world where I saw people out searching for food every day. I would see grandmother, big brother, and baby sister, along with scores of others, scrounging through what we would call trash, hoping to find enough to eat for that day.

In Amos 8:11-12, the Lord speaks of a spiritual famine every bit as devastating as those that cause physical hunger and death. "'The days are coming,' declares the Sovereign LORD, 'when I will send a famine through the land—not a famine of food or a thirst for water, but a famine of hearing the words of the LORD. Men will stagger from sea to sea and wander from north to east, searching for the word of the LORD, but they will not find it.'" Christian, let those words sink into your heart.

At a missions conference in Canada, I heard the story of a Russian preacher who spent seven years in a labor camp in Siberia. One day, two men and a woman came to the camp and asked to speak to this preacher. Their questions were direct: Is there a God? And if there is, is there a book that tells about Him? The preacher told them there was such a book, but it was very scarce. He gave them his copy of the Bible and the three people fell to their knees and wept tears of thanksgiving.

Is it our familiarity with abundance that causes our lack of appreciation? It would be tragic for us to starve to death spiritually when there is no famine in our land. Let's thank God that we have a Bible and seek the Lord today through His Word.

Lord, feed me with Your words of life that I may share my abundance with a spiritually starving world. Amen.

To Ponder: Have you ever wept in thanksgiving for the opportunity to read God's Word?

RESPONDING TO THE WORD
Read Mark 4–7

Teach me, O LORD, to follow your decrees;
then I will keep them to the end.

PSALM 119:33

I have a friend who keeps threatening to write a book titled *How to Have a Terrible Lawn in Colorado.* He said all the pages would be blank because all you have to do is "nothing." Don't water, don't fertilize, don't do anything about the dandelions and the crabgrass, and by summer your once-beautiful lawn will be a mass of weeds.

Jesus always spoke to the people of His day in terms they could clearly understand. So when He spoke of the different ways people respond to the Word of God, He told the story of sowing seeds in a "field."

In Mark 4:14, Jesus said the sower sows the Word in people's hearts. Some hearts are as hard as an interstate highway, and the seed finds no home at all. Other hearts are fertile ground in which the seed germinates and produces as much as a hundred times what was planted. In between is a group of great interest to me. Mark 4:18-19 says, "Still others, like seed sown among thorns, hear the word; but the worries of this life, the deceitfulness of wealth and the desires for other things come in and choke the word, making it unfruitful."

One man I ministered with was an outstanding evangelist and Bible teacher. But occasionally he would startle me with some reference to wanting a life of luxury and ease. One day those thoughts took over, and now he has all the material things his heart desired, but he's miserable, as well as unfruitful in the cause of Christ.

Christian, I urge you to pray over this parable and ask God to keep the thorns cleared out of your life, so that you might remain fruitful for Him.

Lord, please show me if there are any thorns in my life, sapping my spiritual vigor. Amen.

To Ponder: Even the most growing, fruitful Christian must occasionally spray for weeds.

THINGS AS THEY REALLY ARE
Read 2 Kings 4–8

Be strong in the Lord and in his mighty power.

EPHESIANS 6:10

I was in a South American country shortly after an American missionary was killed by terrorists. When the government raided the headquarters of this terrorist organization, they found detailed battle plans for the capture of one of the mission's main jungle training centers.

When the government asked why they hadn't carried out their plan, the terrorists replied that it was because of the army they saw surrounding the mission camp. They knew they were no match for this large army.

The incredible thing is, there was no army surrounding the mission camp, no human army at least. It was much like the miracle of protection we see in 2 Kings 6. The king of Syria was out to destroy the prophet Elisha and had sent his horses and chariots to surround the city of Dothan and prevent Elisha's escape.

When Elisha's young servant saw the army surrounding them, he cried out, "What shall we do?" He had given up. He thought it was all over. But the prophet answered calmly, "Don't be afraid. Those who are with us are more than those who are with them." And then he prayed that the Lord might open the servant's eyes so he could see things as they really were (2 Kings 6:15-20).

The hills were full of horses and chariots of fire. God had sent His angels to protect Elisha. The young servant saw danger only with his physical eyes, but when his spiritual eyes were opened, he saw God's deliverance.

If you're feeling overwhelmed by circumstances, and there seems to be no provision, ask the Lord to give you a fresh vision of things as they really are.

Lord, give me eyes to see Your army of angels around me and to see Your hand at work in my life. Amen.

To Ponder: The times when it appears we are hopelessly surrounded and outnumbered by enemy forces, God is still in control.

WHEN WE SUFFER
Read Job 1–3

And the God of all grace, who called you to his eternal glory in Christ, after you have suffered a little while, will himself restore you and make you strong, firm and steadfast.

1 PETER 5:10

Thousands of books have been written about human suffering. Most of them grapple with the problem of why good people suffer. Some try to find some meaning in our experience of pain. In their study of suffering, many authors find their way back to the book of Job.

The Bible describes Job as perfect and upright, a man who feared God and shunned evil. He was also well known and wealthy, a man who gave generously to the needs of the less fortunate. Yet neither his godly life nor his great wealth shielded him from the calamities of life.

From Job's experience, we discover that it is possible to undergo intense suffering and loss without coming apart at the seams. When things fall apart, the presence and the power of God are enough to carry us through. After losing all his material possessions and his ten children, Job "got up and tore his robe and shaved his head. Then he fell to the ground in worship and said . . . 'The LORD gave and the LORD has taken away. May the name of the LORD be praised'" (Job 1:20). How could he say that? The same way you and I can—by learning to trust God in every circumstance and to walk with Him one day at a time.

In our walk of daily discipleship, hard times will come. Yet from the book of Job, we are assured that our suffering is known to God, that Satan cannot touch our lives beyond the limits of God's permission, and that God wants to use every circumstance of our lives for His glory and our good.

Lord, thank you for Your sustaining presence, not only in the good times, but also in the bad. Amen.

To Ponder: If we are to identify with Christ, then suffering is part of the package.

A SEVERE MERCY
Read Job 4–7

*For our light and momentary troubles are achieving for
us an eternal glory that far outweighs them all.*

2 CORINTHIANS 4:17

The word *correct* means "to make something right." The word *discipline* conveys the idea of instruction or restraint. When we put those words together, we get a clear picture that God instructs us and disciplines us to help us walk in the right way, within the protective boundaries of His Word.

It's folly to argue with God, the fountain of all wisdom, and it's useless to look for a better path than the one He has selected for us. So how should we react when we suffer? We must trust God for the grace to let Him lead us through the dark and difficult times of life.

I have a friend whose young son was diagnosed with leukemia. When he heard the doctor's report, he went to a park and walked and cried and prayed for hours, seeking to know the mind of God in this devastating situation. He asked God to search his heart and expose any sin or rebellion that might be there. After many days of seeking the Lord, he concluded that he didn't know why God had allowed this and he might never know. But every day he wanted to trust the Lord and walk with Him and witness of His love.

We may never figure out why we suffer. But if we can live a life of thankfulness to God through it, someday we will realize how these momentary troubles have achieved for us an eternal glory that far outweighs them all.

Lord, thank You that You never leave us. Because of this, I know I'm Your dearly loved child. Amen.

To Ponder: God allows a ton of difficulty to come into our lives to teach us one ounce of wisdom.

DOING THE IMPOSSIBLE
Read Nehemiah 1–2

The LORD delights in those who fear him,
who put their hope in his unfailing love.

PSALM 147:11

God has a way of unexpectedly breaking into our lives. Sometimes it comes as a new revelation of Himself. Or it may come as something He wants us to do.

Such was the case with Nehemiah. Everything in his life was just fine until the day he asked one of his fellow Jews how things were going in Jerusalem. That's when God set him on an entirely new course and led him to rebuild the wall of Jerusalem.

When I became a Christian, I got hooked up with The Navigators to learn the basics of the Christian life. One summer at The Navigators' conference center in Colorado, I had a job buffing and waxing the floors. One day the conference director asked me to preach the next morning on the subject of the quiet time.

Now, this was a serious conference and these people were used to hearing good speakers. I prayed and studied the Bible and went through all the notes I had on the subject in preparation for the next morning. I didn't sleep that night.

I guess it went okay because they asked me to speak again, and that was the beginning of my preaching with The Navigators. But it wasn't my idea, and it wasn't a subtle change. The experience hit me like a Mack truck, and I knew it was way beyond my abilities.

Is God breaking into your life in a new way? If so, take Him at His word and accept the challenge by faith. Sure it's frightening, but God will work in you. And you could be on the threshold of a great new experience in your walk of daily discipleship.

Lord, too many times I remain comfortable at the expense of growth. Thank You for breaking into my life in surprising ways and asking me to join Your plans for me. Amen.

To Ponder: When God calls us to do the seemingly impossible, He'll also give us the power to do it.

177

DOWN IN THE DEPTHS OF THE DEEPEST SEA
Read Psalms 50–54

*For I know my transgressions, and my sin is
always before me. Against you, you only, have
I sinned and done what is evil in your sight.*

PSALM 51:3-4

If you've ever studied the rings of a tree, you might discover a time when there was absolutely no growth at all.

I had an entire year like that in my Christian life. As I began my third year as a Christian, I developed a bitter spirit against a brother in Christ. I knew it was a sin to harbor this bitterness, so I went to the Lord and confessed it. On the basis of my earnest confession and God's promises in His Word, I knew He had forgiven me. He buried my sin in the depths of the sea and remembered it no more.

Yes, God had forgotten all about it. But there were two persons who didn't forget—the Devil and me. So the Devil would remind me of my sin and accuse me of being an insincere Christian. After all, if I were a true follower of Christ, I wouldn't have done such a thing. I would agree, and bring it up to the Lord again. This cycle was repeated for a whole year.

Finally the Lord made clear to me that I was truly forgiven, and the pattern was broken. I was able to go to my brother and work it out with him as well.

Psalm 51 is the sinner's guide to restored fellowship. In it the psalmist prays that God will blot out his transgressions, wash him thoroughly from his iniquity, and cleanse him from his sin.

Is your walk of daily discipleship hindered either by unconfessed sin or unacceptance of God's forgiveness? I lost a year of Christian growth because of my failure to believe God's Word.

*Lord, I believe Your promise that if I confess my sin, You are
faithful and just and will forgive me my sin and cleanse me
from all unrighteousness (from 1 John 1:9). Amen.*

To Ponder: When God forgives your sin, to Him it is as if you'd never sinned.

TRUSTING GOD
Read Psalms 111–118

*Delight yourself in the LORD and he will
give you the desires of your heart.*

PSALM 37:4

Psalm 118:8 is the middle verse in the Bible. There are 31,174 verses in all, and this verse is number 15,587. It will probably come as no surprise to many of you that it has a powerful message. It says, "It is better to take refuge in the LORD than to trust in man."

This same theme is stated in Jeremiah 17:5-6: "Cursed is the one who trusts in man, who depends on flesh for his strength and whose heart turns away from the LORD." The prophet here is talking about the person who thinks man is more reliable and has greater wisdom, greater power, and greater compassion in dealing with his problems than God.

What is the outcome of such thinking? Where will it lead? What will the person's life be like who thinks that way? Here's what the Bible says in Jeremiah 17:6: "He will be like a bush in the wastelands; he will not see prosperity when it comes. He will dwell in the parched places of the desert, in a salt land where no one lives."

By way of contrast, the next verses say, "Blessed is the man who trusts in the LORD. . . . He will be like a tree planted by the water that sends out its roots by the stream. . . . Its leaves are always green and it never fails to bear fruit" (17:7-8).

Christian, would you rather be like a scrawny bush in a desert wasteland or a bountiful, fruitful tree beside a stream? The difference depends on where you put your trust—in yourself or in God.

Lord, I confess it's often easier to trust what I can control than what I cannot. Help me to see more clearly that only You can satisfy my heart's desires.

To Ponder: "Faith is being sure of what we hope for and certain of what we do not see" (Hebrews 11:1).

TOO BUSY TO PRAY
Read Psalm 5:1-3

Then Jesus told his disciples a parable to show them
that they should always pray and not give up.

LUKE 18:1

He ran a veterinary hospital and was one of the busiest men I'd ever met. He and his wife had seven children, and he was very involved with the PTA, and was a member of a service club as well.

Here I was, trying to get him to establish a daily time of prayer and Bible reading. He looked at it as just one more activity. I knew he was an Eisenhower fan and was politically involved in Ike's campaign for the presidency. So one day I asked him, "If General Eisenhower came to this city and passed the word that he wanted to meet with you tomorrow morning for breakfast, would you make the time?"

"Of course," he said, "I'd love it."

"Bob," I replied, "someone far greater than General Eisenhower wants to meet with you tomorrow morning. In fact, the Lord Jesus Christ would like to have that fellowship with you every day of your life." I don't think the guy has missed his daily prayer and Bible reading since then. But like every one of us, it hasn't always been easy to show up.

I've found two common problems that can keep us from praying. One is a wandering mind and the other is falling asleep. What can you do to corral a wandering mind? Pray out loud. Try praying over a prayer list or through a chapter of the Bible. To avoid going to sleep, go to bed earlier. And when you get up, wake up.

You can't afford to miss this most important appointment of your day.

Lord, meeting with You sets the tone of my day, and I wouldn't miss this most important standing appointment. Amen.

To Ponder: There's Someone who wants to meet with us each day, and that appointment is far more important than meeting with any person on this earth.

PICTURE THIS!
Read Psalms 107–110

But God demonstrates his own love for us in this:
While we were still sinners, Christ died for us.

ROMANS 5:8

When you got your high school yearbook, whose picture did you look for first? Why, yours of course! It's a pretty natural reaction and one that can serve a good purpose as we consider Psalm 107. Different groups of people are described throughout this psalm.

Verses 4-8 describe people who were tired and lost, but the Lord brought them safely home. Verses 10-16 describe people who sat in darkness, in the deepest gloom, bound in suffering and chains. Then they cried to the Lord in their trouble, and He brought them out of the darkness and broke their chains. Verses 17-22 tell of fools who were suffering because of their own rebellion against God. They hated food and were close to death. Then they cried to the Lord, and He saved them out of their distress.

You may be saying, "I see myself in one of those pictures, but only in the first part. I'm still lost on the journey, trapped in the dungeon, or suffering in my rebellion against God. How do I get out?" The answer is right in the psalm: "They cried out to the LORD in their trouble, and he brought them out of their distress" (verse 28). Prayer to the God of the universe is the way out.

You may know a lot about Jesus Christ or very little about Him, but all you have to know is that Jesus died so you could be forgiven of your sin and live a new life in Him.

Psalm 107 concludes, "Whoever is wise, let him heed these things and consider the great love of the LORD." Can you find yourself in that picture, rescued by the love of God?

Lord, thank You for setting me free from the bondage of sin and death. Amen.

To Ponder: Oh that men would give thanks to the Lord for His goodness and for His wonderful works to the children of men (from Psalm 107).

FROM THE HAND OF GOD
Read Psalms 104–106

Let us then approach the throne of grace with
confidence, so that we may receive mercy and find
grace to help us in our time of need.

HEBREWS 4:16

Did you hear the one about the old Iowa farmer who got sick and tired of farming, so he left the farm and opened a hardware business? His best-selling item was a hammer that sold like hot cakes. He bought them for fifty cents apiece and sold them for a quarter. When a friend questioned the man's wisdom and told him he'd lose money, he said, "Oh, I know I'll lose money. But it sure beats farming."

Maybe so, but his hammer sales were a bad bargain. And that's the lesson we see in Psalm 106:14-15. Speaking of the children of Israel, it says, "In the desert they gave in to their craving; in the wasteland they put God to the test. So he gave them what they asked for, but sent a wasting disease upon them."

Any time we purchase physical pleasure at the expense of spiritual health, it is a poor bargain. Our temporal lives are but a breath, but our souls are eternal.

Notice how the people felt when they finally got what they wanted. They had cried and complained about their boring diet of manna, and they pestered the Lord for meat. Finally He said, "I'm going to give you enough meat to last a month, so much it will come out of your nostrils and become loathsome to you." And that's exactly what happened.

The lesson: If we badger the Lord day and night with selfish prayers for something, He may just give it to us. But there will be no satisfaction with it.

Lord, Your will be done in my life. Amen.

To Ponder: When we pray selfishly, neglecting to seek God's will, what we get may not be what we really wanted.

CLAIMING GOD'S PROMISES
Read Isaiah 40–43

He has given us his very great and precious promises, so that through them you may participate in the divine nature and escape the corruption in the world caused by evil desires.

2 PETER 1:4

Today's passage contains a promise: "Every valley shall be raised up, every mountain and hill made low; the rough ground shall become level, the rugged places a plain. And the glory of the LORD will be revealed, and all mankind together will see it. For the mouth of the LORD has spoken" (Isaiah 40:4-5).

For several years I have claimed that promise for Harvard University and Camp Pendleton, the U.S. Marine base on the West Coast. Why those two places? I know men in both places who are sharing the gospel and working to produce disciples of Jesus Christ. A second reason is that these two places are almost exact opposites, but they're both part of the harvest field in which Christ has called us to labor.

Here's how I claim this promise in prayer: In the margin of my Bible next to Isaiah 40:4, I've written the names of several spiritual mountains that keep people from turning to God—conceit, pride, prejudice against the Bible, stubbornness, rebellion, indifference, apathy, ignorance of the true nature of the gospel, love of sin, and fear of commitment—and I pray that these "mountains" will be made low. I ask the Lord to overcome these obstacles in the hearts of the people who are hearing the gospel. Then I take the monthly prayer letters I receive from my friends and pray for people by name.

Have you ever prayed in this way for your own city, neighborhood, relatives, friends, and coworkers? I challenge you to start today. The Lord calls us to cooperate with Him through our personal witness and prayer.

Lord, I want to help someone find the way into Your kingdom. Would You please bring down the spiritual mountain that prevents him from seeing my love and concern for him? Amen.

To Ponder: God delights in blessing our prayers in a mighty way.

PRAYING BEYOND OURSELVES
Read Jeremiah 30–33

He will call upon me, and I will answer him;
I will be with him and honor him. With long life will
I satisfy him and show him my salvation.

PSALM 91:15-16

"Call to me and I will answer you and tell you great and unsearchable things you do not know." I can never read Jeremiah 33:3 without thinking of Dawson Trotman, founder of The Navigators. Early in his Christian life, he read that verse and discussed it with a friend. They believed the verse and agreed to meet every morning and pray together for two hours before they went to work.

The first morning, they hiked up into the Palos Verdes hills, not far from where they lived in southern California, and by 5 A.M. they had built a little fire and were in prayer. They prayed for family, friends, and coworkers, then began to ask God to raise up laborers for His harvest in other cities in California, and then in other states.

After a few weeks, they bought a map of the world and kept it at their little prayer site in the hills. They asked God to use them in the lives of people in Germany, Japan, India, and countries around the world. Dawson and his friend continued their early morning prayer meetings for forty-two consecutive days, and then they felt the burden lift.

Several years later, Dawson ran across several slips of paper with the names of Navy men he'd been helping in their Christian walk. World War II had brought young men from every state in the union to California, and scores of them had received discipleship training from The Navigators. It was the beginning of God's answer to Dawson's prayers. The "great and unsearchable things" had come in a slow but spectacular way. The same promise is available to you and me, and the same mighty God stands waiting to fulfill it.

Lord, increase my faith to believe You will bring about great
and mighty things as I diligently pray. Amen.

To Ponder: Our responsibility is to call. And when we call, God says, "I will answer."

IN THE CLEFT OF THE ROCK
Read Jeremiah 34–39

*You will keep in perfect peace him whose
mind is steadfast, because he trusts in you.*

ISAIAH 26:3

Jeremiah wasn't a popular man. In fact, there were many unenviable aspects of his life. But there's something about the prophet's experience to which each of us can aspire.

Notice the words in Jeremiah 34:1: "While Nebuchadnezzar king of Babylon and all his army . . . were fighting against Jerusalem and all its surrounding towns, this word came to Jeremiah from the LORD." Think of it! Here is an entire nation under siege from its enemies—facing death, destruction, and slavery— and one man among them is in communication with God. One man hears a voice no one else heard. This happened on at least eight different occasions in this book, where we read that "the word of the LORD came to Jeremiah."

Our pastor once told the story of a painting that was named "Peace." It showed two birds. One had built its nest in a meadow, while the other lived in the rocks above the seashore. The bird in the meadow lived in calm, tranquil surroundings. The bird in the rocks along the shore faced the wild winds and high surf, but her nest was dry and safe because it was nestled in the cleft of the rock. The pastor asked which setting most clearly reflected the peace of God for the Christian. As I thought about it, I chose the bird in the cleft of the rock. When tough times come, God gives us peace.

So don't pity Jeremiah's life. Instead, ask the Lord to help you keep in close communion with Him as the winds of adversity blow about your life. And like Jeremiah, you will have a word from God for the people in need around you.

Lord, thank You for Your supernatural peace available to me when I'm under attack. Amen.

To Ponder: Our "word from the Lord" comes to us from the Bible, giving us a unique perspective on adversity.

ANSWERED PRAYER
Read 2 Thessalonians

You have committed a great sin. But now I will go up to the LORD; perhaps I can make atonement for your sin.

EXODUS 32:30

Did the apostle Paul ever receive an answer to prayer? I'm sure you're thinking, *Of course he did!* But do you have proof? Throughout the New Testament we read Paul's admonitions to pray, and we even have several recorded examples of his petitions and praise to God. But what about answers?

Look at 1 Thessalonians 3:10. Paul says that night and day he has been praying earnestly that God would allow him to see them again, to help them in their life of faith. He goes on to tell them in verse 12 that he has been praying that God would give them a greater, ever-increasing, overflowing love for each other. So there we have a record of Paul's specific request for two needs in the lives of the Thessalonians.

Now look in today's passage at 2 Thessalonians 1:3: "We ought always to thank God for you, brothers, and rightly so, because your faith is growing more and more, and the love every one of you has for each other is increasing." How about that! When Paul wrote his first letter to the Thessalonians, he was praying for their faith and love to grow. Now, he begins his second letter by thanking God for these two graces that are abounding in their lives.

Friend, if you're praying for God's work in the life of someone, take heart. God does answer prayer. Keep at it, and let your prayer life grow. As you pray earnestly, fervently, even night and day as Paul prayed, you will know the joy of answered prayer.

Lord, help me to be faithful to pray for others. Amen.

To Ponder: Scripture gives overwhelming testimony that God hears our prayers, and He answers.

WORDS OF LIFE
Read Luke 22–24

*A wicked man listens to evil lips; a liar pays
attention to a malicious tongue.*

PROVERBS 17:4

———

A few years ago, my friend Walt Henrichsen and I visited several colleges in Colorado and Wyoming, giving lectures on the Christian faith.

One night, a student rose to his feet and said, "I suppose you guys actually believe the Bible is a supernatural book, the Word of God."

I smiled and said, "Yes, we do."

"Then you are fools!" he shouted, and stomped out of the room. That sort of livened up the discussion, and we had a great evening with that large group of young men and women. By the end of the meeting, many of them gave their lives to Christ.

During the next few days, the young student's words rang in my ears, troubling me. As I read my Bible I came to the story of the resurrection and Jesus' words in Luke 24:25: "How foolish you are, and how slow of heart to believe all that the prophets have spoken!" His words brought things back into perspective. Would I rather be called a fool by a college sophomore or by Jesus Christ?

You and I can choose whose judgment we value and whose teachings we will follow. There are a number of modern philosophers, theologians even, who deny the inspiration and authority of Scripture. But Jesus said we should believe all that the prophets have written. Jesus is never wrong, and we can trust Him and His word as the final authority in our life of daily discipleship.

*Lord, when I'm tempted to follow a voice other than Yours,
remind me that "the foolishness of God is wiser than man's
wisdom." Amen.*

To Ponder: Jesus said His sheep know His voice, and they won't follow any other.

ENTRUSTED WITH THE GOSPEL
Read Acts 10:1-33

*To which of the angels did God ever say, "Sit at my
right hand until I make your enemies a footstool
for your feet?" Are not all angels ministering spirits
sent to serve those who will inherit salvation?*

HEBREWS 1:13-14

Before I trusted in Christ, all I knew about heavenly angels was that
they were the ornament on top of a Christmas tree! As I study the
Scriptures now, I see angels much differently. They can do supernatural things—like scare off entire armies or appear miraculously in
bright light. But did you know there is one thing angels aren't allowed
to do that only you and I can do? Angels may not communicate the
message of the gospel of Christ. That has been reserved for us alone.
Paul said that we—you and I—have been entrusted with the gospel.

You may recall the story of Cornelius, a centurion described as a
devout man—one who feared God, gave alms, and prayed. One day
an angel of God came to him and assured him his prayers had been
heard. Now, here was a man who was ready to repent and believe the
gospel. Yet the angel didn't tell him how to trust Christ! The only thing
the angel was allowed to do was tell the man how to get in touch with
the apostle Peter, who could then tell him what he must do to be
saved.

Think of it! The heavenly messengers of God—those beings
whose only desire is to do God's will—are not able to call men and
women to follow Christ and turn to Him in repentance and faith. That
task has been given to you and me.

Friend, I urge you to share Christ where you live, work, and play,
by setting a Christlike example and being willing to talk to others
about Jesus Christ.

*Lord, what a privilege to share in Your plan of redemption for
the world! Help me to boldly proclaim the way of salvation.
Amen.*

To Ponder: Are you carrying out the work God has assigned you?

TRANSFORMING POWER
Read Romans 6

And we, who with unveiled faces all reflect the Lord's glory, are being transformed into his likeness with ever-increasing glory, which comes from the Lord, who is the Spirit.

2 CORINTHIANS 3:18

The closer we got to the airport in Monrovia, West Africa, the more agitated the man became. He was sitting in the row in front of my wife and me. When we landed in Sierra Leone—the last stop before Monrovia—he went to the flight attendant and asked if she had any rubber bands.

"No," she said, "we have no use for them." So during our short stop in Sierra Leone, he went up and down the aisle asking people if they had a rubber band. I had no idea why he wanted one, but I looked in my briefcase, and found two.

When the man returned to his seat, I handed the rubber bands to him. Boy, did that light up his face! He told us that on his trip to Europe he had bought a shirt but had forgotten to check the sleeve length. He feared what his wife would say if he stepped off the plane with shirt sleeves hanging down over his fingers. We watched him take off his suit coat, adjust the sleeves using the rubber band, and put the coat back on with a look of satisfaction on his face.

"Now I am a well-dressed gentleman," he said in broken English. Amazing! Moments before, the man had been ashamed of himself, standing there as a poorly-dressed klutz. But with a slight "rubber band" adjustment, he was transformed into a well-dressed gentleman.

That's a picture of what happens when we become Christians. One moment we are lost sinners on our way to hell. The next moment—when we receive Christ and the Holy Spirit comes to live in us—we become a child of God and joint heir with Christ.

Lord, thank You for Your amazing transformation in my life, based on my faith in the atoning work of the Lord Jesus Christ for my sins. Amen.

To Ponder: How has the Holy Spirit living in you transformed your life?

189

MAN'S NATURE
Read 2 Corinthians 5

You made him a little lower than the angels;
you crowned him with glory and honor
and put everything under his feet.

HEBREWS 2:7

What does the Bible say is the basic nature of man? He was created in the image and likeness of God, God breathed into him the breath of life, and man became a living soul. Put it all together and you find a person with a moral nature, intellect, and the ability to make decisions—a will that enables him to say yes and no.

When God created man, He used both visible and invisible material. He used both dust and the breath of life. The New Testament refers to this in 2 Corinthians 4:16: "Though outwardly we are wasting away, yet inwardly we are being renewed day by day." Earlier in the same chapter, Paul spoke of the glory of God, "a treasure in jars of clay" (4:7). The material part of man—the jars of clay—house the treasure of the life of God. While the body quickly returns to dust, man's soul and spirit is immortal. The awesome thing about this is that you and I are called upon by the Lord to help bring the immortal souls of others back to God who made them. We are to help direct our friends and neighbors back to the arms of a loving God who, in turn, yearns for their love.

God has done His part. He sent His Son to die on the cross to redeem the lost. Now He turns to us and charges us with the commission to help people find the way home, that their souls might find eternal rest.

Lord, help me live with eternity in view by telling as many people as possible how they can live forever in Your presence. Amen.

To Ponder: Who has God impressed on your heart today?

NEW LIFE
Read John 3:1-21

Jesus declared, "I tell you the truth, no one can see the kingdom of God unless he is born again."

JOHN 3:3

One Saturday night when I was about twelve years old, my dad gave me fifteen cents to go to the motion picture show — ten cents to get in and five cents for a sack of popcorn. They weren't showing the usual Tom Mix, Hoot Gibson, or Buck Jones cowboy show. It was some movie called *Frankenstein*. I had no idea what it was about, but I got my sack of popcorn and went in and sat down.

The show began in an old castle on a stormy night. In the tower lay a great big monster of a man into whom the doctor was shooting thousands of volts of electricity to try to bring him to life. All of a sudden there was the biggest bolt of lightning and a thunderclap that shook the whole theater, and lo and behold this dead thing moved its arm and opened its eyes. It was alive! As I left the theater that night, I walked pretty fast and kept looking over my shoulder all the way home.

Of course the story was pure fantasy, because all the lightning in the world can't bring the dead to life. But there's an amazing fact revealed in the Bible: God can. This teaching is called the doctrine of regeneration. It happens when God imparts to us His divine nature and we are born again.

The Bible says that when we receive Christ into our lives we are born not of blood — you cannot inherit it from your parents or of the will of the flesh. Someone else can't do it for you; you are born of God.

Lord, thank You for giving me eternal life. Amen.

To Ponder: Through the new birth, God imparts to us a new life — the life of God Himself.

BAPTISM AND THE FULLNESS OF THE HOLY SPIRIT
Read Galatians 3:26-27 and Ephesians 5:18

*We are witnesses of these things, and so is the Holy Spirit, whom
God has given to those who obey him.*

ACTS 5:32

I was walking in downtown Colorado Springs when I saw a car going
the wrong way on a one-way street. People on the sidewalk were waving and shouting; people in cars were honking their horns. But the
most interesting sight of all was the look of wild panic and confusion
on the driver's face.

Many aspects of our walk as disciples can be confusing, especially
if we're heading the wrong way! For instance, there are two words
relating to the ministry of the Holy Spirit. One is *baptism,* and the
other is *fullness.* Is the baptism of the Holy Spirit the same as the fullness of the Holy Spirit? In 1 Corinthians 12:13, Paul writes, "For we
were all baptized by one Spirit into one body." And to the Galatians, he
wrote, "You are all sons of God through faith in Christ Jesus, for all of
you who were baptized into Christ have clothed yourselves with
Christ" (3:26-27). The teaching is clear. The baptism of the Holy Spirit
is a once-for-all event and occurs when a person invites Christ into his
or her heart and becomes part of the body of Christ.

The filling of the Holy Spirit is another matter entirely. Paul says
in Ephesians 5:18, "Do not get drunk on wine. . . . Instead, be filled
with the Spirit." When a person is drunk with wine, he is under the
control of that wine. Paul says to be filled with the Spirit, so we can
be controlled by the Spirit. As we walk in obedience to the Word of
God—submitting ourselves to the Spirit's control and yielding our
will to Him day by day—we are walking by the Spirit's power.

*Lord, I want to honor You by walking in the fullness of the
Holy Spirit. Amen.*

To Ponder: Today, are you walking under your own steam or by the
power of the Holy Spirit?

THE MINISTRY OF ANGELS
Read Hebrews 1–2

"See, I am sending an angel ahead of you to guard you along the way and to bring you to the place I have prepared."

EXODUS 23:20

I know a young man who lives in the city of Monrovia in Liberia, West Africa. A few years ago, he was involved in a terrible accident. He fell off a truck going at high speed down a crowded road. When he hit the ground, he was struck in the head by another vehicle, and his scalp was peeled back by the force of the blow.

The emergency team at the hospital was convinced he would die in a matter of minutes. Nevertheless, they sewed his scalp back, cleaned him up as best they could, and placed him in a bed in a crowded room.

In the middle of the night, the young man regained consciousness. His relatives were sitting near his bed asleep. And in the corner stood two men in white. They glowed with a shining white brightness. They came over to his bed, and without waking his family, told him they were angels who had been given charge over him to guard him and to minister to his needs. They then left, but not before assuring him they would always be near—that he could count on their help.

To the astonishment of the hospital staff, the young man made a complete recovery and regained his full strength. Today he suffers no effects from the accident, and of course his faith in God has been greatly strengthened.

Before you conclude this young man was hallucinating, look up the word *angel* in a Bible concordance and do a short study on these beings. You might start with Hebrews 1:14: "Are not all angels ministering spirits sent to serve those who will inherit salvation?" By the way, have you considered that angels are watching over you right now?

Lord, thank You for Your Word that says the angels protect us and minister to our needs. Amen.

To Ponder: Do you believe angels really exist?

ANGELS IN DISGUISE
Read Genesis 18:1-19

Offer hospitality to one another without grumbling.

1 PETER 4:9

Do you remember the fairy tale of the king who wanted to find out if his people really loved him? He traveled as a homeless beggar and was taken into homes and given food and lodging. But there were some who turned him away and would not show kindness and hospitality to this ragged old man. Later, when he returned to his throne, he summoned those who had shown compassion to him and publicly rewarded them for their deeds. Try to imagine the disappointment of those who suddenly realized they had been given the opportunity to entertain the king but had turned it down!

There's a Bible verse that speaks clearly of this: "Do not forget to entertain strangers, for by so doing some people have entertained angels without knowing it" (Hebrews 13:2). One such person was Abraham. He was sitting in his tent door when three men approached. His immediate response was to help them—to show kindness and hospitality to them.

Water was brought to wash their feet; they were given a morsel of bread with some butter and milk to satisfy their hunger, as well as a young calf. It was soon revealed to Abraham that these were not mere men but a visitation from the Lord. Abraham had the privilege of entertaining God's holy angels!

Friend, hospitality is becoming a lost art. Our homes today have become a hiding place instead of a sharing place. Yet thousands of people have been launched on the road to salvation when they were invited into a Christian home and saw faith in action. Open your home today, and who knows, you might entertain an angel!

Lord, help me to show loving hospitality to others so they can see Christ in me. Amen.

To Ponder: What keeps you from opening your home—and life—to others?

OBEYING GOD'S VOICE
Read 2 Chronicles 33–36

So he gave them what they asked for,
but sent a wasting disease upon them.

PSALM 106:15

Reading the story of the people of God is often like reading the biography of a yo-yo. Finally the string of the yo-yo breaks, and we watch the nation plunge to the bottom and stay there.

Second Chronicles 36 tells us that Zedekiah was twenty-one when he became king, and he did evil in the sight of the Lord. He stiffened his neck and hardened his heart against the Lord God of Israel. And the people and the priests followed his leadership. The record says they transgressed after all the abominations of the heathen and defiled the house of the Lord. When God continued to call them back to Himself, they mocked His messengers and despised His words till there was no remedy. And so we see the destruction of the kingdom of Judah and the city of Jerusalem by the Chaldeans.

If Zedekiah had simply made the Lord his friend, he could have prevented the ruin and saved the land. Because he would not humble himself and make himself the servant of God, he became the slave of his enemies. Multitudes were put to the sword, even in the sanctuary where they fled for refuge. But the sanctuary was ransacked, its treasures seized and carried to Babylon. The temple was burned, the walls of Jerusalem were demolished, and the stately palaces lay in ashes. The people who survived were carried to Babylon, enslaved, impoverished, insulted, and exposed to much misery in the enemy's land.

What a picture of the person whose heart becomes hard and unyielding toward God. By the Lord's grace, may we respond to His voice today, break out of the yo-yo syndrome, and walk with Him in daily discipleship.

Lord, speak to me today and I will listen to Your voice and obey it. Amen.

To Ponder: The Lord calls to us through His Word, through our conscience, and through providential circumstances. What might He be saying to you today?

195

THE GRACE IN WHICH WE STAND
Read 1 Kings 12–16

To him who is able to keep you from falling and to present you before his glorious presence without fault and with great joy.

JUDE 24

The tragedy revealed in 1 Kings 12–16 is that although it took Israel many years to achieve its place of power and grandeur, it took but a little while for them to sink in the mire of sin.

So it is with our spiritual lives. Growth is slow. It takes a long time to get our spiritual roots anchored firmly into the person of Christ. But it doesn't take long to slide back into a place of rebellion and cold-heartedness.

I have a friend who showed great promise in his Christian growth. Year by year he took steps of faith that led to his becoming an established, mature, dedicated disciple of Christ. He went on to become an equipped spiritual laborer in the harvest fields of the world and was mightily used by God to bring many others to a personal faith in Christ. Then one day it happened. He met a woman to whom he was attracted, and today he is living in sin. Compared to the time required to mature in his faith, his decline was almost overnight.

That's the warning from today's passage. One after the other, we learn of the decline and fall of the leaders of the people. We see it in Solomon, in his son Rehoboam, in Jeroboam, Abijah, Nadab, Baasha—the list goes on.

You might be thinking, *If I'm going to hit the skids spiritually someday, why not fall into sin today and get it over with?* But the warning of Scripture is that while spiritual failure is always possible, it is never inevitable. Our challenge is to stand by the grace of God, recognize that we are vulnerable, and take heed lest we fall.

Lord, may I never take for granted the Holy Spirit's work in my life. Amen.

To Ponder: When was the last time you chose to stand by the grace of God against temptation?

WHO WILL YOU FOLLOW?
Read 2 Kings 18–21

*But if serving the Lord seems undesirable to you, then
choose for yourselves this day whom you will serve. . . .
But as for me and my household, we will serve the Lord.*

JOSHUA 24:15

When a child rebels against the Lord, the parents often turn the situation inward on themselves. "Where did we go wrong? How did I fail? Why couldn't I have done better?" While it is true that we have a great influence on our children, there's another side to the issue.

Hezekiah was a good king who did what was right in the sight of the Lord. Yet in 2 Kings 16, we read that Hezekiah's father, Ahaz, lived according to the abominations of the heathen and sacrificed and burned incense to the pagan gods. In spite of having an evil father, Hezekiah was a good king because he made the right choices.

Now let's look ahead to Hezekiah's son, Manasseh. Because Hezekiah was such a godly man, we would expect his children to live in the fear of God. But when Manasseh became king, he did evil in the sight of the Lord. And while Manasseh's son Amon also did evil, Amon's son, Josiah, became a godly king.

How do we account for this strange pattern? Did the parents of those who did evil fail, or was it a problem of environment? Why did these children of godly kings turn their backs on God? Because God gives everyone a choice. He opens the way for each of us to follow Him, but He leaves the choice with us.

As Christian parents, we should love our children, set a godly example for them, pray for them, and do all we can to lead them along the path of obedience to the Lord. But if they choose another direction, even though it causes us tremendous grief, we should not spend the rest of our lives condemning ourselves for their choices.

Lord, I want to follow You and do Your will for the rest of my life. Amen.

To Ponder: In the grace, mercy, and sovereignty of God, He has made us free to choose.

BE ON GUARD
Read Joshua 9–12

For such men are false apostles, deceitful workmen,
masquerading as apostles of Christ. And no wonder,
for Satan himself masquerades as an angel of light.

2 CORINTHIANS 11:13-14

A jewelry store vault in a fashionable section of London was adver-
tised as one of the world's safest. It had armed security guards, steel
walls two feet thick, bulletproof glass, infrared detectors, and sound
detectors. How could anyone rob a vault like that?

It happened when two well-dressed men came in posing as
prospective customers and convinced the manager to show them
around. While a third man posed as a guard and turned other customers away from the front door, the two men put a gun to the
manager's head and robbed the vault of an estimated $32 million in
jewelry and cash. Where brute force would have failed, they succeeded
by trickery and deception.

This was the strategy of the men of Gibeon, recorded in Joshua 9.
They pretended to come from a far country, seeking a treaty of peace
and mutual alliance. It certainly seemed the Gibeonites were telling
the truth. It looked like they had come from a far country. Their bread
was moldy, their wineskins were torn, their shoes were worn out. But
it was all a hoax, and Joshua was taken in. While he was victorious in
open warfare, he was defeated by trickery. We can learn an important
lesson from Joshua's failure. Did he ask counsel of God? No. Did he
seek the Lord? No. Did he counsel with the priests and elders? No. He
acted on his own.

We must always remember that the enemy of our souls is not only
a roaring lion going about seeking whom he may devour, he is also a
subtle serpent.

Lord, remind me to seek Your counsel in everything, great or
small. And give me the discernment to resist Satan's subtle
ploys. Amen.

To Ponder: If you made a list of the five most dangerous temptations
facing you today, what would they be?

HASTY CONCLUSIONS
Read Joshua 22–24

*Hannah was praying in her heart, and her lips were
moving but her voice was not heard. Eli thought she
was drunk and said to her, "How long will you keep
on getting drunk? Get rid of your wine."*

1 SAMUEL 1:13-14

The war in the land of Canaan had ended. They had rest according to
all that God had promised, and every man had a clear title to his farm.
Joshua dismissed those whose inheritance was on the east side of
Jordan, so they started for their homes. And then they did something
that almost led to tragedy. When they came to the borders of Jordan,
they built an altar.

When the children of Israel in the west heard about what they had
done, they gathered together at Shiloh to go to war against their eastern brothers! But before the army marched off to battle, they did a
very wise thing. They sent Phineas the priest and ten leaders to
Gilead to talk to their brothers and find out why they had built an
altar. They found that the eastern tribes had not built an altar for sacrifice, but as a witness to the present and future generations of their
vow to worship the Lord in His sanctuary.

Here is a tremendous lesson for us today. Hasty suspicion leads to
false accusation and division. It is so easy to jump to conclusions and
go off half-cocked and say things or do things that we will regret
later—things Satan can use to bring reproach on the cause of Christ.

Are you in the midst of making some battle plans today? Your
cause may be just, and the sin you are opposing may be serious. But
are you sure the fellow Christians you're getting ready to fight have
actually done what you think they did? Do you know the motive
behind their apparently wrong action?

*Lord, as Your Word says in James 1:19-20, teach me to be "slow
to speak and slow to become angry, for man's anger does not
bring about the righteous life that God desires." Amen.*

To Ponder: "He who answers before listening—that is his folly and
his shame" (Proverbs 18:13).

BEYOND THE BEACHHEAD
Read Judges 1–5

Dear children, keep yourselves from idols.

1 JOHN 5:21

When the children of Israel took possession of their respective areas in the Promised Land, it was a lot like establishing a beachhead. This was not the end but the beginning. They were to move on from there and rid the land of idolatry, blasphemy, occult practices, and sin of every kind. But they didn't. We are told Judah didn't drive them out; neither did Manassah, Zebulun, Asher, and so on. Why? Basically, they failed to move out from their beachhead.

I recall the day our Marine outfit invaded an enemy-held island during World War II. We weren't ten feet out of the water when a Marine right next to me had his left arm blown off, and another man had his upper lip shot off. It took a lot of work to establish that beachhead, but that was only the beginning. From there we had to move inland and capture the airfield, one of our major objectives.

The people of God had done a lot of work to possess the Promised Land, yet they failed to follow through and finish the job. Why? It seems to me there were three reasons: fear, slothfulness, and tolerance for idolatry.

These same traits—fear, sloth, idolatry—can defeat us as well. In our saner moments, we know we're not to be controlled by fear but by the Holy Spirit of God. If we're not careful, our sloth can keep us from our morning prayers and Bible reading. And if we don't have a deep and abiding hatred of idolatry, we can soon find ourselves becoming idolators.

Lord, protect me from idolizing the things I love. Amen.

To Ponder: Are you growing in the Lord, or have you been content merely to establish a spiritual beachhead?

THE PEOPLE GOD USES
Read Ezekiel 20–23

I will listen to what God the LORD will say;
he promises peace to his people, his saints—
but let them not return to folly.

PSALM 85:8

Although it has been almost forty years, it seems like only yesterday that I heard Dawson Trotman preach to us about God's search for a certain kind of person. We were at a conference at Lake Iduhapi in Minnesota.

One of Dawson's recurring themes was the value of one person who is fully committed to God, and he always challenged us to be that person. Dawson's text there at Lake Iduhapi, and on many other occasions, was Ezekiel 22:30: "I looked for a man among them who would build up the wall and stand before me in the gap on behalf of the land, so I would not have to destroy it, but I found none."

Here is the all-knowing, all-seeing God searching the landscape for a person He could trust to intercede and plead for the people, and He searched in vain. Something of the intensity of His search is revealed in a cross-reference to 2 Chronicles 16:9: "For the eyes of the LORD range throughout the earth to strengthen those whose hearts are fully committed to him."

As a young man, D. L. Moody once heard a preacher say, "The world has yet to see what God can do with a man who is fully yielded to Him." So Moody resolved in his heart, "By the grace of God, I will be that man." In spite of all of Moody's educational and physical limitations, God used him to bring thousands into the kingdom.

God is still looking for that man or woman with a heart to do His will and with a commitment to His work. Will you tell Him today that you're available?

Lord, I'm available to do Your work and Your will. Amen.

To Ponder: Who does God want you to share the gospel with today?

SERVING GOD
Read Ezekiel 33–36

I planted the seed, Apollos watered it, but God made it grow.

1 CORINTHIANS 3:6

In 1956, Dawson Trotman asked my wife and me to move to the Midwest and begin the Navigator ministry there. We invited a young mechanical engineer named Ron Rorabaugh to join us, rented a U-Haul trailer, and moved to Omaha, Nebraska.

As I searched the Scriptures for a plan of attack, the Lord led me to Ezekiel 36:37-38 which said the Lord would fill the ruined cities with flocks of people, and they would know that He is the Lord.

Ron and I began praying every morning that God would raise up a flock of men to join us in starting a disciple-making ministry throughout those Midwestern states. God soon put us in touch with a young insurance executive in Des Moines, a veterinarian in Sioux City, and a manager of an electrical firm in Omaha. As Ron and I continued to pray, I met with these men to teach them how to have a walk of daily discipleship with Christ, and we began to see people come to Christ through their witness. Gradually, there were little flocks of people all over the place. When we had our first weekend conference about a year later, 125 people came.

Years later, when I asked a staff worker for The Navigators how many people in the Midwest were being touched by all aspects of Navigator ministries, including our publications and church training courses, he thought for a minute and said, "Oh, I suppose around 50,000." Now, I didn't make that happen and neither did Ron. God did it, just as He promised He would. God can do the same through you as you claim His promises by faith and make yourself available to Him.

Lord, use me to help increase Your flock in my neighborhood and the surrounding areas. Amen.

To Ponder: If our testimony is faithful, God will take care of the multiplication.

SPIRITUAL CRUISE CONTROL
Read the book of Malachi

We love because he first loved us.

1 JOHN 4:19

I've heard it said that in the Christian life you are either moving forward or going backward. But I know people who seem to be on a kind of spiritual plateau. They aren't in rebellion against God nor are they living in open or secret sin. But they aren't making any progress either. They haven't led anyone to Christ in years, and they aren't excited about anything related to the kingdom of God. They seem to have leveled out — just cruising on some kind of spiritual automatic pilot.

During the time of the prophet Malachi, God's people were existing on a plateau of lukewarm mediocrity. The fifty thousand Jews who returned to Jerusalem from their captivity in Babylon had been settled in Judah for over seventy years, but the Messiah spoken of by Haggai and Zechariah had not yet come. All excitement about a genuine and intimate relationship with God seemed to have drained away. Even the worship of God had become an empty chore.

This is the background against which Malachi speaks, calling this lukewarm community of believers to return to a living and vital relationship with God. It's fascinating to note that in forty-seven of the fifty-five verses in this book, God speaks with first-person directness to His people. The book of Malachi is God's call to His lukewarm people to be faithful during a time when heaven seemed silent. Notice how God begins in Malachi 1:2: "'I have loved you,' says the LORD."

It is love that binds God to His own. And it is love that God seeks from His own. He wants to walk with you in the devotion and commitment of your first love.

Lord, I confess that my spiritual life is often on automatic pilot. Rekindle the fervor of my first love for You and Your purposes in this world. Amen.

To Ponder: If the joy is gone from your walk with God, how hard are you looking for it?

THE FOCUS OF LIFE
Read Matthew 8–11

So I tell you this, and insist on it in the Lord, that you must no longer live as the Gentiles do, in the futility of their thinking.

EPHESIANS 4:17

What do we do when our lives get out of focus and we're no longer doing what God has called us to do? Too often, nothing! Sometimes the blurring occurs so gradually that we don't even know we're out of focus. All the more reason to keep our eyes on Jesus. You see, He was a very focused person, and He stuck with His mission.

Notice Jesus' words in Matthew 9:12-13: "It is not the healthy who need a doctor, but the sick. . . . For I have not come to call the righteous, but sinners." Throughout the Gospels, we see Jesus healing, teaching, and preaching—all part of revealing His kingdom. And everything He did was focused on His goal of calling people to repent and believe.

Can you imagine everything Jesus could have talked to people about? After all, He was the eternal Son of God who knew everything about everything. He could have explained all the scientific wonders of the universe or warned against the various manmade philosophies that would arise over the years—how each of them would lead down a blind alley and leave the followers of those teachings confused and frustrated. But Jesus didn't deal with any of those things. Instead, He focused on what people need most—the good news of salvation. Why? Because unless people hear and respond to the gospel, they are lost and going to a Christless grave.

There are hundreds of good activities you can be involved in as a Christian, but what is most important? What is worth giving your life to? Jesus' primary objective was to help people walk in the light of God's Word and experience the salvation He offered. Shouldn't that be our focus, too?

Lord, You are the way, the truth, and the life. Empower me each day, as I meet and talk with people, to point them in Your direction. Amen.

To Ponder: What goals are most important to you?

CHRIST IN YOU
Read Mark 11–13

"Why do you call me, 'Lord, Lord,' and do not do what I say?"

LUKE 6:46

Jesus was a man of action, and His actions never failed to communicate the great desire and heart of God toward His people.

There is no greater example of this than in Mark 11:15-17: On reaching Jerusalem, Jesus entered the temple area and began driving out those who were buying and selling there. He overturned the tables of the money changers and the benches of those selling doves, and would not allow anyone to carry merchandise through the temple courts. And as he taught them, He said, "Is it not written: 'My house will be called a house of prayer for all nations'? But you have made it 'a den of robbers.'"

Can you picture the scene? The house of God had actually become a hindrance to those seeking God. Jesus came in and started turning over tables and cash registers, and told people to get out. He took drastic action, because anything that would keep people from finding salvation in the true and living God must be dealt with.

This is true of our lives as well. God wants us to be like salt, making people thirsty for God. And He wants us to be channels through which His living water can flow and quench the spiritual thirst of others.

Christian, does your life attract others to Christ, or have you become like the temple of Jesus' day, full of commerce and religious activity, but void of any spiritual dimension and appeal? If some major housecleaning needs to be done, why not invite the Lord of action to take over and get started on it today?

Lord, if there's anything in my life right now that is hindering Your witness, please sweep it away. Amen.

To Ponder: When was the last time someone sought you out to talk about spiritual things?

THE LORD'S RETURN
Read Matthew 24–25

[God's grace] teaches us to say "No" to ungodliness and worldly passions, and to live self-controlled, upright and godly lives in this present age, while we wait for the blessed hope—the glorious appearing of our great God and Savior, Jesus Christ.

TITUS 2:12-13

I remember the day I walked into a college class to take a final exam, only to discover I had studied for the wrong subject. I broke out in a clammy sweat, and I had a sinking feeling in the pit of my stomach. Needless to say, I did poorly on the exam. I wasn't prepared, and it was my own fault.

Jesus told a parable recorded in Matthew 25:13 that ended with these words: "Therefore keep watch, because you do not know the day or the hour." Whenever Jesus mentioned His return, He usually ended His remarks with the admonition to be prepared.

The Bible teaches that one way we can prepare for the Lord's return is by living a life of purity. First John 3:3 says, "Everyone who has this hope in him purifies himself, just as he is pure." We also are to be doing the work Jesus left us to do. A big part of that is telling others about Him.

I knew someone who was passing out tracts on the streets of Chicago when, much to his surprise, a man asked how he could be saved. My buddy experienced a feeling similar to mine when I sat unprepared for my exam. He didn't know how to lead a person to Christ. He apologized to the man and left him standing there on the street with his need unmet.

What are you doing to prepare for Christ's return? Are you living a pure life? Can you present the gospel to the lost? Are you praying for friends, that God might open the door for you to witness to them? As we pray, "Even so, come, Lord Jesus," let us be ready.

Lord, keep me mindful of Your imminent return, and help me to put my energies in the things that count for eternity. Amen.

To Ponder: If Jesus should return today, would He find you doing the work He's given you to do?

A TRUE DISCIPLE
Read 2 Corinthians 6:14-18

*Perseverance must finish its work so that you
may be mature and complete, not lacking anything.*

JAMES 1:4

———

When my hair began to turn gray, and it was evident I'd been around a long time, people began asking me, "How are Christians today different from Christians when you came to Christ?" My answer is always the same: Today's Christians are far better trained to serve the Lord. There are conferences, seminars, and workshops available today that were unheard of in my early years. There's also one thing lacking: the intense hunger for holiness that was in the lives of Christians a few decades ago.

Paul told the Romans, "I would have you wise unto that which is good, and simple concerning evil" (Romans 16:19, KJV). The word translated *simple* also is translated *guileless* and *innocent*! The word doesn't come from the field of religion but from the study of metal. There are pure metals — gold, iron — and there are mixed metals — steel, bronze. And that's the word Paul uses to mean unmixed regarding evil.

To the Greeks in Corinth, he spelled it out by asking them five questions recorded in 2 Corinthians 6:14-16: What do righteousness and wickedness have in common? Or what fellowship can light have with darkness? What harmony is there between Christ and [Satan]? What does a believer have in common with an unbeliever? What agreement is there between the temple of God and idols?

It's clear, isn't it? You can't mix light with darkness, or Christ with Satan. And to make this point, Paul never hesitated to go head-on against the culture in which these new converts were living. He warned them that God had called them to holiness in a culture where chastity was an absolutely unknown virtue. Christian, take your stand. Abstain from fleshly lusts that war against the soul.

Lord, create in me a hunger for holiness in my life. Amen.

To Ponder: Is the light of Christ in you so bright that it's like a beacon in this dark world?

THE LIKENESS OF CHRIST
Read 2 Corinthians 7:17-18

"He who speaks on his own does so to gain honor for himself, but he who works for the honor of the one who sent him is a man of truth; there is nothing false about him."

JOHN 7:18

———

Most things that are taken to extreme can be harmful. For example, if you read on a medicine bottle that one tablet a day will make you well in ten days, and then foolishly reason that ten pills will make you well in one day, you will harm yourself.

The same thing can be true of our application of Scripture. Now, one of the clear teachings of Scripture is that you and I should live separated unto the Lord and separated from sin. The apostle Paul's words recorded in 2 Corinthians 6:17-18 say, "'Therefore come out from among them and be separate,' says the Lord. 'Touch no unclean thing, and I will receive you. I will be a Father to you, and you will be my sons and daughters,' says the Lord Almighty." If you and I are to serve the Lord, our lives must be clean.

"Fair enough," you say. "But how is it possible to carry to extreme such a simple teaching of Scripture as this?" Let me give you an example. When my wife became a Christian, she stopped using any sort of makeup. Dawson Trotman, founder of The Navigators, encouraged her and other women to try using some. His reasoning? All they were accomplishing by being pale-faced was to draw attention to themselves. They stood out in a crowd.

As far as we know, Jesus never did that. He did nothing to draw attention to Himself in the way He dressed or combed His hair. As Christ's people we must come out from among the worldly by our attitude toward sin and by our love for Christ, but not through excessive outward practices that draw attention to ourselves.

Lord, keep me from getting caught up in equating godliness or ungodliness with outward appearances. Amen.

To Ponder: To draw attention to self through either excess or restraint can interfere with our witness.

THE WAR THAT NEVER ENDS
Read Galatians 5:16-25

*But among you there must not be even a hint of sexual
immorality, or of any kind of impurity, or of greed,
because these are improper for God's holy people.*

EPHESIANS 5:3

Some years ago I became acquainted with a young man who lived on the West Coast. He had become a Christian and was showing great promise in his life of daily discipleship. Scripture memory came easy to him; he soon became consistent in his morning prayer and Bible reading; he joined a Bible study group; and he enjoyed going to church. His witness to fellow students at the university was clear and effective.

Gradually I began to notice a change. Although he continued to be involved in discipleship activities, the sparkle was gone. Then one day we happened to meet, and I asked if there was anything he wanted to talk over. He didn't answer for a few minutes, and then finally said yes, there was. He had gotten to know a group of students on campus and had begun to hang around them so he might witness to them concerning faith in Christ.

He began to adopt their lifestyle, drinking with them, laughing at their crude jokes—all for a good purpose. Then it happened. He went with them to X-rated movies, and the war that never ends began to rage in his soul. The Bible describes it this way: "The flesh lusteth against the Spirit, and the Spirit against the flesh: and these are contrary the one to the other, so that ye cannot do the things that ye would" (Galatians 5:17, KJV). It wasn't long before his walk with God became a shambles and his witness ineffective.

Fortunately, through the prayers and loving care of some friends, he was restored. He came back to the Lord in true repentance, and today he is walking with God. But it was a very costly lesson.

*Lord, as I live among the lost and witness to them, keep me
from crossing the line into their lifestyle. Amen.*

To Ponder: Never underestimate the power of the lust of the flesh.

CHRIST IN US
Read Ephesians 4:21-24

*How can a young man keep his way pure? By living
according to your word. . . . I have hidden your word in my
heart that I might not sin against you.*

PSALM 119:9,11

The people who were instrumental in my coming to Christ didn't find
their pleasure in the usual places or the usual ways. For instance, I was
a gambler, and every Sunday afternoon a few of us would gather to
play poker. They didn't gamble. When something upset me, my usual
response was a string of swear words that would peel the hide off a
donkey. They would pray and commit the matter to the Lord. I
enjoyed hanging out in bars. They enjoyed going to church. And
frankly, folks, I was intrigued.

It was through the lives of these people that God put it in my heart
to buy a Bible and investigate the person of Jesus Christ for myself.
After I turned to Christ in repentance and faith, I wanted my life to
reflect the life of Christ as theirs did. Fellowship with God on a daily
basis was foundational, and I learned that morning prayer and Bible
reading were a solid way to start the day. My wife and I began attend-
ing church services and participating in a young couples' Sunday
school class.

After a year or so, the Lord called us to serve Him on a full-time
basis. We moved to Minneapolis and attended Northwestern College,
where we met up with The Navigators. They reinforced my Bible reading and church attendance with practical instruction in Scripture
memory, personal Bible study, and the consistent practice of meditation on the Word of God.

This combination had a profound effect on my life. Old habits began
to melt away under the spotlight of God's Word as I learned to apply the
Word to my life. Sin was replaced with a desire for a holy life.

*Lord, I rejoice that the old me is gone and that You have made
me a new creation, empowered to follow Your will as a true
disciple. Amen.*

To Ponder: The Lord Jesus Christ is revealed in all His truth and
beauty through yielded and caring disciples.

210

A CONTENTED LIFE
Read Philippians 4:11-13

But who are you, O man, to talk back to God?
"Shall what is formed say to him who formed it,
'Why did you make me like this?'"

ROMANS 9:20

The year my son Randy and his wife installed a wood-burning stove in their home, they were afraid their two-year-old boy might burn himself. So they spent a lot of time warning him about the dangers of the stove. One day Randy fired it up and let the lad feel the heat. He not only wanted his little boy to know what not to do, but also why he shouldn't get too close to the stove.

That is what the Lord does with you and me. He not only warns us to keep away from various dangers that can hurt us spiritually and damage our daily walk of discipleship, but He also tells us why. Take, for instance, the problem of greed and covetousness. This is one of the Ten Commandments God gave to Moses: "You shall not set your desire on . . . anything that belongs to your neighbor" (Deuteronomy 5:21).

Why shouldn't I covet what someone else has? The overriding reason is that when I inwardly complain that my neighbor has a new lawnmower and I have to use an old one, I am accusing God of mismanagement of His resources. He owns everything; if He has seen fit to give something to my neighbor and overlooks me in the process, that's His business.

So it's not only an accusation of mismanagement, it's a lack of faith in the wisdom of God! I am actually telling the Lord that I have a better plan for my life than He does. I am proclaiming myself smarter than God and more loving than God. Let's learn to keep things in proper perspective.

Lord, create in me a grateful heart for my life and all it comprises. Amen.

To Ponder: How long is your list of God's blessings?

211

OUR FIRST PRIORITY
Read Colossians 3:1-4

For the LORD God is a sun and shield; the LORD
bestows favor and honor; no good thing does he
withhold from those whose walk is blameless.

PSALM 84:11

Several years ago, our local paper reported a car accident on U.S. Highway 24 near Green Mountain Falls, Colorado. The car had plummeted 323 feet down an embankment, rolling over twice, according to the state patrol. Our son Randy was admitted to Penrose Hospital with a broken foot and shoulder injuries.

As soon as we were notified, we left for the hospital emergency room. After they set the bone in his foot and got his foot in a cast, we all went home. None of us slept very well that night. We were a bit shaken over the ordeal, but our number-one inclination was to praise the Lord that no one was seriously hurt. The foot healed, the cast came off, and our household returned to normal. Well, almost normal.

That winter Randy, who loved to ski, hung up his skis, poles, and boots and didn't touch them again that entire ski season. Finally, he talked about it. Skiing had become his life. He had put it first above anything else. Time on the slopes meant far more to him than time with the Lord. Through the accident, the Lord had reminded him of this. He accepted the rebuke and recommitted his life to the Lord and decided for that year, at least, skiing had to go.

It is so easy to get wrapped up in some activity, possession, or person, and thereby squeeze the Lord out of our lives. How about it? Are you putting anything before God? If so, deal with it now. Confess it to the Lord, turn to Him with a repentant spirit, and recommit your life to Him.

Lord, fill my life with Yourself. Amen.

To Ponder: Is anything crowding the Lord out of first place in your life?

RELATIONSHIP VERSUS FELLOWSHIP
Read Mark 1–3

*God, who has called you into fellowship
with his Son Jesus Christ our Lord, is faithful.*

1 CORINTHIANS 1:9

It is essential for every Christian to understand the difference between relationship and fellowship. Relationship is fixed and cannot be broken. Once we come to God through repentance and faith in Jesus Christ, we are His sons and daughters, and nothing can change that.

I remember talking to a businessman who was bowled over by this truth. He couldn't fathom the depth of the grace of God. He was convinced there was something he had to do, some work that would buy him a ticket to heaven. I told him it was too late, Jesus Christ had died on the cross to pay the penalty for his sins, and nothing more was needed.

Fellowship, on the other hand, is fluid and must be constantly renewed. We do it by confessing our sins and asking His forgiveness. Once restored, we must maintain our fellowship with God. In Mark 1:35, we read these words about our Lord Jesus Christ: "Very early in the morning, while it was still dark, Jesus got up, left the house and went off to a solitary place, where he prayed." The previous verses tell us that the evening before, the whole town had gathered at Jesus' door after sundown, and He had healed many. No doubt He had been up late. But long before sunrise, He left His bed and went to prayer.

Have you come to God through faith in Jesus Christ? If so, nothing can change your relationship with Him. But are you spending time with Him each day in prayer and reading the Word? Relationship and fellowship—one depends on God's action, the other depends on our own.

Lord, it is beyond my understanding that You have made me Your child—forever. Please give me the faithfulness to come to You every day in fellowship. Amen.

To Ponder: Relationship has to do with our standing in Christ while fellowship concerns our walk with God.

JUST DO IT
Read Luke 13–16

*In Joppa there was a disciple named [Dorcas], who was
always doing good and helping the poor.*

ACTS 9:36

One of the first things we seem to learn in life is to make excuses for not doing what we should. It reminds me of the three people the Lord talked about in Luke 14:16-20.

A certain man was preparing a great banquet and invited many guests. At the time of the banquet he sent his servant to tell those who had been invited, "Come, for everything is now ready." But they all alike began to make excuses. The first said, "I have just bought a field, and I must go and see it. Please excuse me." Another said, "I have just bought five yoke of oxen, and I'm on my way to try them out. Please excuse me." Still another said, "I just got married, so I can't come."

One lame excuse after another. What good businessman would buy land he had not seen? Who would test oxen after buying them instead of before?

Now, Christian, let me ask you, what have you been putting off for one excuse or another? Have you decided to be more diligent in memorizing the Word of God, but you keep putting it off? Have you vowed to witness to your neighbors and invite them to church? Have you talked about establishing the practice of morning prayer and Bible reading? It's so easy to get sidetracked with other things and never finish what we set out to do. And whenever we talk about it, we always have a new excuse why we haven't done it yet.

The truth here is, when God issues the invitation, there is no good excuse for refusing to accept. Whatever God is calling you to do, do it.

Lord, I want to start a schedule of spending more time with You. Help me to take the first step today. Amen.

To Ponder: What spiritual discipline have you been telling the Lord you would get back to soon, but you haven't yet found the time?

THE ABUNDANT LIFE
Read John 15

*"You did not choose me, but I chose you and appointed
you to go and bear fruit—fruit that will last."*

JOHN 15:16

Let's begin today with a little absurdity. Let's say an investment firm phones a wealthy person and asks him to let them invest all his money for him. I'm sure the rich man would ask, "And what would be the return on my investment?"

Here comes the shocker. "Based on our research, we can guarantee that you will lose no more that $50,000 a year. Yes, sir, you can count on it. Let us take control of your money, and in a few years you will be broke."

The man would decline the offer, wouldn't he?

Now, Christian, if we have only one life to invest, we'd better ask about the bottom line. What does God promise in John 15 to those who follow Christ? First, Jesus says, "If a man remains in me and I in him, he will bear much fruit" (verse 5). Second, "If you remain in me and my words remain in you, ask whatever you wish, and it will be given you" (verse 7). Third, "I have told you this so that my joy may be in you and that your joy may be complete" (verse 11). Fourth, "If you obey my commands, you will remain in my love" (verse 10). Think of it! A life enveloped in the love of God. Then He summarizes: "You did not choose me, but I chose you and appointed you to go and bear fruit. . . . Then the Father will give you whatever you ask in my name" (verse 16).

Friend, how do you like those dividends!

Lord, may I seek my all in You. Amen.

To Ponder: The world tries to buy joy, love, and lasting fruit. But those things only come to us one way—by abiding in Christ!

FRUIT-BEARING FAITH
Read John 15

*"I have told you this so that my joy may be in you
and that your joy may be complete."*

JOHN 15:11

Oftentimes people worry about the wrong things. I have a friend who built a new supermarket. It carried all the name brands, plus a complete line of generic foods. It had computerized checkout stands, a pharmacy, a fish market, and an ice-cream parlor.

On grand opening day, my friend's primary concern was the computerized electronic gear that was supposed to help people get checked out in a hurry. So, while clowns entertained the kids with free balloons, he watched over the checkout stands. And out front everything went smoothly. What he didn't know was that back in the warehouse everything was bogged down to the extent that it would soon cripple his business. This man was concerned about the wrong thing!

Christians can be like that, especially about a passage of Scripture such as we have today in John 15:2: "He cuts off every branch in me that bears no fruit. . . ."

Later He talks about those who do not abide in Him being cast out as a branch and thrown into the fire to be burned. Remember, He's talking about fruit-bearing faith, not saving faith. So in this passage, when Jesus talks about taking away a branch, He's not talking about throwing away Christians! For heaven's sake, He's talking about making more Christians! And that's what we should be concerned about.

Are you abiding in Christ? Are you spending enough time in the Word of God to have something to share with others? Are you thinking about the Lord through the day and seeing answers to prayer? Begin to practice the abiding life and God will give you a fruitful life.

Lord, thank You for my life in You—a place of joy and purpose. Amen.

To Ponder: Pruning may pain us, but it will never harm us.

THE FRUITFUL BRANCH
Read John 15:1-8

But the fruit of the Spirit is love, joy, peace, patience, kindness, goodness, faithfulness, gentleness and self-control.

GALATIANS 5:22-23

My dad was a gardening genius. He knew just when and how to plant to get the maximum yield. But one year he did something that astounded me, and I've never forgotten it. He surrounded the entire garden with nasturtiums. I wondered why he'd planted those flowers around the perimeter of the garden, and toward the end of summer I found out. A plague of millions of grasshoppers came through, demolishing gardens and crops. They gobbled up those nasturtiums that surrounded our garden and moved on to the next one, leaving our garden intact.

In John 15, we are introduced to the greatest gardener of all. Every good gardener knows you have to prune your plants and trees to get maximum yield. And so with God. Jesus said, "My father is the gardener. He cuts off every branch in me that bears no fruit, while every branch that does bear fruit he prunes so that it will be even more fruitful" (15:1-2).

Notice two things here. First, there is a severity in this picture of God. And second, there is a single-mindedness in this picture of God. As a gardener, He has one interest—that the branches bear lots of fruit. If He doesn't find any, Jesus says He takes that branch away. And every branch that bears fruit He prunes to bring more fruit. God takes whatever action is necessary to cleanse His people so they will produce fruit for His glory. The key to it all is that the people of God must abide in—live in close, day-by-day fellowship with—Jesus Christ.

Lord, may this connection and this dependency thrill my soul forever. Amen.

To Ponder: If God is pruning your life, you can rejoice that you're a fruitful branch, and He wants your life to be even more fruitful for His glory.

ABUNDANT LIFE
Read John 15:9-17

"I have come that they may have life, and have it to the full."

JOHN 10:10

Why do you think Jesus told us to abide in Him? In the first verse of John 15, called the "abiding chapter," Jesus begins His message to us by reminding us that He is the true vine . . . the real vine . . . the genuine vine. He goes on to say, "You are the branches."

Now, what does the vine do for the branches? First of all, the vine gives the branches life. Second, the vine gives the branches stability. The vine provides an anchor for the branch. Now, those two things—life and stability—tell us why we must abide in Christ. You see, if Jesus is the true vine, it naturally follows that there must be some counterfeits furnished by the Devil. And there are many.

I'm sure you know people who believe they can find life and stability in their profession, in economic security, in some form of religion, through the right political party being in control, through drugs and alcohol, through education, by having a new home or a second home in Florida. You name it, I've heard it all, and so have you.

The Bible says there is one genuine source of life and stability, and that is Jesus Christ. That is why Jesus says in contradiction to anyone or anything else, "I am the true vine." He and He alone can give us life. And He and He alone is the one who can produce the life of the vine in the branches. When the wind and floods come, it will not be shaken as we abide in Him.

Lord, You provide the only life I want to live. Thank You for giving me life to the full. Amen.

To Ponder: If you cut yourself off from the Source of nourishment, you will soon wither away.

YOUR SPIRITUAL CHILDREN
Read the book of Joel

But you are a chosen people, a royal priesthood, a holy nation, a people belonging to God, that you may declare the praises of him who called you out of darkness into his wonderful light.

1 PETER 2:9

Have you ever stopped to think what would happen if people stopped having children? I don't mean a few people in some parts of the world, I mean everyone, everywhere. There would certainly be less joy, laughter, and unselfishness. But the ultimate result, within less than a century, would be the extinction of the human race. And the same is true of the church of Jesus Christ. If we fail to have spiritual children, to lead others to Christ and help them grow, then the Christian church is only one generation away from extinction.

During the days of the prophet Joel, a great plague of locusts came on the people of Israel as a judgment from God. It was not meant to destroy them but to bring them back to God. Here is the command Joel gave the people after the plague: "Hear this, you elders; listen, all who live in the land. Has anything like this ever happened in your days or in the days of your forefathers? Tell it to your children, and let your children tell it to their children, and their children to the next generation" (1:2-3).

Our responsibility toward God is twofold: We are to obey Him today and to teach His truth to the next generation. I'm talking about spiritual great-great-grandchildren. And we don't have to wait seventy or eighty years to see it happen. From the prophet Joel to the apostle Paul, from the Old Testament to the New, we are commanded to be spiritually fruitful. We are to be God's witnesses, to raise up new generations of men and women who will love and follow Him.

Lord, I want to be spiritually fruitful and multiply Your children. Guide me as I share the good news of eternal life with another person today. Amen.

To Ponder: When we lead just one person to Christ, we've had a part in leading untold future numbers to salvation.

THE LOST SHEEP
Read Amos 1–2

When he saw the crowds, he had compassion on them, because they were harassed and helpless, like sheep without a shepherd.

MATTHEW 9:36

———

How do we get a burden for the lost? We must be in contact with people who need Christ; we must feel their anguish and spiritual need. But we must also pray that God will burden our hearts for these people.

A few years ago, we were living in a condominium where the walls were so thin I could hear the alarm clock of the people next to us. And sadly, those people were in constant conflict. I think their dog was the only thing holding them together.

And it made me mad. I told Virginia I was about ready to go over there and tell them to shut up. Virginia said, "Well, it's sure evident that they need the Lord." You see, we were both exposed to people who needed Christ. But I got mad at them while Virginia prayed for them.

One of the most important elements in being an effective witness for Christ is to have a burden for people who don't know Him. We see it in Amos 1–2, and even in the prophet's name, which in Hebrew is related to a verb meaning "to bear a load, to be burdened."

It takes exposure plus the compassion of Christ to produce a burden for the lost. Christian, where are you in this process today? Are you getting mad at the lost or getting burdened for them? May God give each of us a burden, like Amos, to share His word with the people around us who so desperately need Him.

Lord, give me eyes of compassion to see the lost as You see them. Amen.

To Ponder: A burdened heart is the beginning of a burning witness.

HIS POWER IN OUR WEAKNESS
Read Amos 6–7

For the LORD your God is the one who goes with you to fight for you against your enemies to give you victory.

DEUTERONOMY 20:4

What does it take to be used by God in a special way? Read the prophet Amos's description of his background: "I was neither a prophet nor a prophet's son, but I was a shepherd, and I also took care of sycamore-fig trees. But the LORD took me from tending the flock and said to me, 'Go, prophesy to my people Israel'" (7:14-15).

Amos was a plain country boy engaged in country work, gathering figs and following the flocks. In spite of his humble background, God had a job for Amos to do. And when God told Amos what it was, he got right at it. He didn't waste time complaining about his lack of training in the art of prophesying. He trusted the Lord to give him the ability and wisdom he needed for the task.

Many years ago, I attended a weekend Navigator conference and heard Dawson Trotman speak on vision. He stressed the fact that God could use any Christian to make a serious impact on this world.

Daws had been driving a truck for a lumberyard when God touched his life through some Bible verses he'd memorized. From that point on, Daws obeyed the Lord and moved ahead. He never sat around bemoaning the fact that he'd never attended college or seminary. He studied hard, learned from others, and put into practice what he learned.

What kind of background does it take to serve God effectively? Whatever kind you have. Christian, if God is calling you to serve Him, then say yes, and get started right where you are today.

Lord, with the Holy Spirit's help, may I exercise my gifts and talents for Your glory. Amen.

To Ponder: The Holy Spirit strengthens our weaknesses.

KINGDOM WITHOUT END
Read Matthew 26–28

"And this gospel of the kingdom will be preached in the whole world as a testimony to all nations, and then the end will come."

MATTHEW 24:14

In the sixteenth century, a man named Suleiman ruled the Ottoman Empire in Eastern Europe. To the world, he was known simply as "the magnificent." His goal was to set up a worldwide kingdom that would be known for its justice and humanity. But then Suleiman died, his son who ruled after him was a drunken and immoral man, and the kingdom that Suleiman had worked so hard to build began to collapse.

How different it is with Jesus Christ and the kingdom of God. When Jesus was crucified, it appeared that all hope for the coming kingdom of God had been destroyed. The faith of the disciples burned at a low ebb. They had followed Jesus and believed Him, but had seen Him die on the cross.

And then with heart-stopping joy, Jesus came to them, alive forevermore, with these words: "All authority in heaven and on earth has been given to me." He had defeated even death itself. And while the disciples looked at Him in awe and wonder, He gave them a command that would change the course of their lives, and of the world. "Therefore go and make disciples of all nations, baptizing them in the name of the Father and of the Son and of the Holy Spirit, and teaching them to obey everything I have commanded you. And surely I am with you always, to the very end of the age" (Matthew 28:18-20).

These are the words of a king who has given a royal commission. It begins with a royal claim, proceeds to a royal command, and ends with a royal covenant to His followers.

Lord, by Your power and presence I want to help fulfill the Great Commission. Amen.

To Ponder: We have been commissioned by a King whose kingdom will come, and it will have no end.

FAITHFUL, NOT FAMOUS
Read Luke 10–12

"Therefore go and make disciples of nations, baptizing them in the name of the Father and of the Son and of the Holy Spirit, and teaching them to obey everything I have commanded you. And surely I am with you always, to the very end of the age."

MATTHEW 28:19-20

God's plan isn't to win the war against the forces of evil through a few Christian superstars, but through multiplied thousands of believers working behind the scene—people like you and me.

Notice what Jesus did in Luke 10:1-2: "After this the Lord appointed seventy-two others and sent them two by two ahead of him to every town and place where he was about to go. He told them, 'The harvest is plentiful, but the workers are few. Ask the Lord of the harvest, therefore, to send out workers into his harvest field.'"

Now who were these men? Nobody knows. But what we do know of them speaks volumes about the Great Commission of Christ. They were unknown, ordinary disciples, but they were certainly well trained for their mission.

How do we know that? Because if we compare the mission of the Twelve in Matthew 10 with the mission of the seventy-two here in Luke 10, the job description is practically identical. And when they returned, they rejoiced in their successes. Their names are not known like the names of the Twelve, but they had been trained to be effective in carrying out the commands of Christ.

Now what do you think would happen in our world if every person who turned to Jesus Christ in true repentance and faith went on to become a strong, mature, fruitful disciple? This would fulfill the ministry of evangelizing the lost and establishing the new believer, just as Jesus commissioned.

Lord, help me to be faithful in sharing the gospel with my neighbors and friends. Amen.

To Ponder: As you pray to the Lord of the harvest to send forth laborers, are you including yourself in the process of spiritual reproduction and multiplication?

LIVING FOR THE GOAL
Read John 1–2

We proclaim to you what we have seen and heard, so that you also may have fellowship with us. And our fellowship is with the Father and with his Son, Jesus Christ.

1 JOHN 1:3

I always enjoy traveling with someone who knows where he's going, don't you?

John the Baptist knew exactly where he was going. He had a definite purpose in mind and knew exactly how to reach his goal. The message in the book of John is that he wants you and me to find life in Jesus Christ. Everything in his gospel points us to the saving grace of the Lord Jesus.

In John 1:7, we are introduced to John the Baptist and told that "he came as a witness to testify concerning that light, so that through him all men might believe." The focus is not on the baptismal ministry of John the Baptist or his call to the nation of Israel to repent. He is presented primarily as a witness to Jesus Christ, the Lamb of God who would take away the sin of the world.

Christian, when people observe your life, what do they see? A person frantically busy doing Christian activities? A person who says one thing and does another? Or do they see a person who knows where he's going? Make it your goal today to point people to the Savior.

Lord, today I need You to refocus my sight on the task You've given me to do. Amen.

To Ponder: Witnessing involves all that we are and all that we do.

SOMETHING FOR GOD
Read 2 Samuel 5–7

*"Don't be afraid," David said to him, "for I will surely show you
kindness for the sake of your father Jonathan. I will restore to you
all the land that belonged to your grandfather Saul, and you will
always eat at my table."*

2 SAMUEL 9:7

For many years, I worked closely with a man who saw his primary
function of leadership in terms of what he could do for others. He was
never a person to put himself first, but was consistently figuring out
ways to push me, or someone else, to the front. The thing that got
him excited about the Christian life was seeing others become something for God.

Whenever I think of this man, I see that little plaque with the letters J O Y on it—Jesus first, others second, yourself last.

When David was crowned king over all Israel, the Bible says he
understood that the Lord had exalted him for the sake of His people,
Israel. It was not to make David rich or powerful or famous, but that
he might provide godly leadership, guidance, and protection.

What is your desire for the people over whom God has given you
leadership? You see, I believe everyone is a leader to someone. It may
be your children, the people who work for you, the members of your
Sunday school class, a neighbor, a young person who looks up to you.

And what is on your heart for them? Let me encourage you to take
a few minutes today to write one or two specific things you want to
help that person do or a quality you want to see them develop.
Determine to pray for that person every day.

Lord, help me to encourage someone today. Amen.

To Ponder: What God is doing in our lives is of greatest value when
it is expressed in the life of another person.

MIRRORING GOD'S EXAMPLE
Read 2 Samuel 8–10

Be kind and compassionate to one another, forgiving each other,
just as in Christ God forgave you.

EPHESIANS 4:32

———

David had such a diverse life and ministry. He was a shepherd, a musician, a composer, a military hero, and a king. And that's not all. He kept an eye on the future. Whenever he conquered a foe, he took all the bounty and tribute, and dedicated it to the Lord. Why? His eye was on the temple that his son would build. David secured two blessings for Israel—he won peace in the land, giving Solomon time to build the temple, and he dedicated an unbelievable amount of wealth, so that Solomon might have the resources to do the job right.

Today's portion of Scripture reveals yet another side of David. He asked, "Is there anyone still left of the house of Saul to whom I can show kindness for Jonathan's sake?" With all David has on his mind, still he desires to show concern for the household of Saul.

When David learned there was one person, he invited him to the palace and made provision for his needs. The record states, "When Mephibosheth son of Jonathan, the son of Saul, came to David, he bowed down to pay him honor." David received him with all kindness and spoke to him by name.

Like David, perhaps you can take the initiative to show compassion to someone in need.

Lord, make me aware today that I represent You in my kindness shown to others. Amen.

To Ponder: "Whoever is kind to the needy honors God" (Proverbs 14:31).

WORKING BEHIND THE SCENES
Read 1 Chronicles 10–16

"He leaves his house and puts his servants in charge, each with his assigned task, and tells the one at the door to keep watch."

MARK 13:34

A lot of Christians feel discouraged because they can't preach or sing or stand up in front of a group. Sometimes they begin to think their gifts and abilities don't count for much in the kingdom of God.

Nothing could be further from the truth. Over the years, I've been involved in hundreds of Christian conferences and church meetings. And while the speaker often gets the most attention, it is usually someone else who deserves the most credit. Someone sent invitations, handled the registration, prepared the room, and prayed for the Lord's blessing. The speaker stands on a platform of service provided by those who work unnoticed and out of sight.

In 1 Chronicles 12, we see that thousands of men, with a wide variety of gifts and abilities followed David and swore allegiance to him. Some were advisors and some were warriors. In the midst of their celebration of turning Saul's kingdom over to David, the Bible tells us that people came bringing provisions—flour, cakes of figs and raisins, wine, oil, cattle, sheep. And we read that there was joy in Israel.

Those who work behind the scenes have a ministry just as important as those who stand up front and lead. Perhaps God has given you a gift of ministry behind the scenes. If so, thank God for it and for its importance in the building of His kingdom.

Lord, thank You for giving me a gift for service. Amen.

To Ponder: Whatever your gift, exercise it, rejoice in it, and the Lord will reward you in a wonderful way.

MOTIVATING OTHERS
Read 1 Chronicles 28–29

Finally, brothers, we instructed you how to live in order to please God, as in fact you are living. Now we ask you and urge you in the Lord Jesus to do this more and more.

1 THESSALONIANS 4:1

One of the most difficult tasks of any leader is motivating others. How does the leader stimulate people to love and good works?

In 1 Chronicles 28 and 29, we are given a clue. With his eye of faith and vision, in his final days as king, David saw the magnitude of the task Solomon would face when he took over the throne of Israel. Solomon would need the dedicated help of hundreds of people to build the temple. He would need materials of all kinds, and he would need a lot of money.

So David assembled all the representatives of the people and challenged them to give themselves unreservedly to the task before them. He followed Moses' example and reminded the people that God had chosen Solomon to do this job, so to back Solomon was to fulfill the will of God.

He told them he had given out of his personal treasures of gold and silver in abundance, then said, "Now, who is willing to consecrate himself today to the LORD?" (1 Chronicles 29:5).

God used David's personal example and his words of challenge to fire the people up, and the people offered willingly and gave in abundance.

These same principles apply today. Do you want your kids, your family, to love the Lord . . . to pray . . . to study the Scriptures? Then challenge them with biblical principles, and set the example in your own life. God will use it for His glory.

Lord, may I be an example of a good steward. Amen.

To Ponder: If we manifest costly, self-sacrificial love within our families, it will have a spiritual impact upon the world.

SUPPORTING A NEW LEADER
Read 2 Chronicles 1–5

*Now we ask you, brothers, to respect those who work hard
among you, who are over you in the Lord and who
admonish you. Hold them in the highest regard in love
because of their work. Live in peace with each other.*

1 THESSALONIANS 5:12-13

A change in leadership can be disastrous or, with balance and wisdom, it can be a growing experience for everyone involved.

In 2 Chronicles 1, Solomon assumes the throne after the death of David. Solomon was a man of peace; David was a man of war. Solomon engaged in building; David engaged in battle. David was concerned primarily with the ark of God; Solomon with the temple. David and Solomon were different in approach and style, but shared the same heart and purpose before the Lord.

Second Chronicles 1:8 records that Solomon prayed: "You have shown great kindness to David my father and have made me king in his place." He was saying there would be a new emphasis now, but with a clear endorsement of what had gone before.

In 1956, Dawson Trotman drowned in a boating accident at Schroon Lake, New York. The Navigators was a young, growing organization, and suddenly we had a new leader in the person of Lorne Sanny. Now that could have thrown us, but for two things. First, we knew that Lorne was Dawson's clear choice as a successor. Although they were different in temperament and style, their heart and vision were the same. Second, Lorne, in wisdom, brought about change slowly. While building on the past, he planted seeds of new ideas and methods, and let them mature in the minds of his coworkers.

When God calls a leader, he also is calling followers. Both have the responsibility to trust God for the strength, wisdom, and grace to fulfill their calling. When that happens, the Lord is honored and the work goes on.

*Lord, help me to be a good follower behind the leaders You've
placed over me. Amen.*

To Ponder: In what ways can you support the leaders God has placed
in authority over you?

No Place for Pride
Read 2 Chronicles 26–28

Pride goes before destruction, a haughty spirit before a fall.

PROVERBS 16:18

———————

In our city, the police cars all bear the slogan "Serve with pride." Now I think that's a positive thing, because it deals with dignity and self-respect. As Christians, we need to cultivate pride and self-esteem while avoiding the cost of egotism and conceit.

Much of my life has been spent in working with young men and women in a discipleship ministry. All along this narrow pathway lurk hazards to their growth and development. And one of them is the deadly sin of arrogant pride. Whenever I spot the warning signs of this kind of pride in the life of a person with whom I'm working, we stop everything and do a Bible study on 2 Chronicles 26.

Here we are introduced to King Uzziah, who was sixteen years old when he became king. As long as he sought the Lord, God caused him to prosper. He had victory in the battle against the Philistines, their ancient foe. He built mighty towers and fortified the city of Jerusalem. He had a great, well-equipped, standing army, along with war machines to shoot arrows and hurl large stones.

With all that going for him, you'd think he would be safe. But he wasn't. The Bible says, "When he was strong, his heart was lifted up to his destruction." He fell, through the sin of pride. When he had grown great in power, popularity, and wealth, he did not lift up the name of God in gratitude. His prosperity puffed him up, and down he went.

I have seen this sin of pride, more than any other, take its toll in people's lives.

Lord, help me to see the warning signs of pride so that I can walk humbly with You. Amen.

To Ponder: Pride is one of the most subtle sins Satan uses to bring us down.

LEADING BY OBJECTIVE
Read 1 Timothy 1–3

Not that I have already obtained all this, or have already
been made perfect, but I press on to take hold of that
for which Christ Jesus took hold of me.

PHILIPPIANS 3:12

Mention the great leaders of this century and Winston Churchill immediately comes to mind. During World War II, the people of England were blasted night after night by Nazi bomber planes. Yet Churchill was able to rally them to the cause of winning the war in spite of overwhelming odds.

You see, one thing a good leader does is help his people stay on target, so they give their lives for what really matters. That's what the apostle Paul did in his relationship with churches, and with many individuals, especially Timothy, his son in the faith. Paul trained Timothy for a significant leadership role in the first-century church. In Paul's first letter to Timothy, he gave him a clear picture of the goal: "The goal of this command is love, which comes from a pure heart and a good conscience and a sincere faith" (1 Timothy 1:5).

Paul reminded Timothy that when teachers wander from this central issue of love, their ministry soon degenerates into vain arguments and meaningless talk. His advice was to give no importance to those people who occupy themselves with useless speculations that promote controversies.

Paul's instruction and modeling clearly has given all of us God's standard for evaluating the direction and effectiveness of our lives. Christian, are you on target today? Are you growing in love, as Christ commanded?

Let's make sure our lives are on target for Christ and that we love and lead others along the right way.

Lord, help me to keep my focus on You and Your objectives
detailed in the Word. Amen.

To Ponder: We can only help others hit the mark when we have taken correct aim ourselves.

A HOPE AND A FUTURE
Read Jeremiah 26–29

*"For God so loved the world that he gave
his one and only Son, that whoever believes
in him shall not perish but have eternal life."*

JOHN 3:16

———

There are millions of people in the world who believe God is out to get them, that His thoughts toward them are not thoughts of love and peace, but thoughts of evil and destruction.

I recall going into a beautiful temple in one of the most magnificent cities in Asia. Inside there were about two hundred people staring blankly at the huge statue of their god as they sat cross-legged on the floor, moaning and crying out in fear. They were convinced that their god was intent on destroying their crops. They knew nothing of our gracious God.

Some of the most encouraging words ever written are found in Jeremiah 29:11-14: "'For I know the plans I have for you,' declares the LORD, 'plans to prosper you and not to harm you, plans to give you hope and a future. Then you will call upon me and come and pray to me, and I will listen to you. You will seek me . . . and I will be found by you,' declares the LORD."

When we know that God's plans for us are good, we will call on Him in faith, not in fear. When we seek Him, He will reveal Himself to us in all His gracious love. Now Christian, the blinded masses cringing in fear before a pagan idol aren't the only ones who need to hear about God. There are people in your neighborhood and your place of work who don't know the Lord. Many of them feel they have no future and no hope. But we have the gospel of Christ, a message that can turn their lives completely around.

Lord, prompt me to speak words of persuasion to people for whom You died. Amen.

To Ponder: God's ways are revealed to me if I pray and seek His will.

IN CHRIST ALONE
Read Jeremiah 40–45

*"Many will say to me on that day, 'Lord, Lord, did we not prophesy
in your name, and in your name drive out demons and perform
many miracles?' Then I will tell them plainly, 'I never knew you.
Away from me, you evildoers!'"*

MATTHEW 7:22-23

As I have talked with people over the years, I've noticed a great deal
of confusion over the assurance of salvation. There are multiplied
thousands of people who have never received Christ as their Savior
and Lord, yet they feel confident they will go to heaven—if there is
a heaven. They have a false assurance that everything is right between
themselves and God.

In Jeremiah 43, we are told that a group of Jews had left the land
of Judah and gone to live in Egypt in direct disobedience of God's
command. They thought that in Egypt they would be safe from all the
calamity of their homeland. They burned incense and worshiped a
deity called the Queen of Heaven, whom they believed would bring
them health and prosperity. When the prophet Jeremiah warned
them, we find their reply in Jeremiah 44:16-17: "We will not listen to
the message you have spoken to us in the name of the LORD! . . . We
will burn incense to the Queen of Heaven and will pour out drink
offerings to her." The people were convinced that everything would be
all right, even after God's prophet told them otherwise.

Today there are millions of people who have a false assurance
about their eternal destiny. Some trust in the fact that they are
church members or that they've been baptized or confirmed. Some
trust in their good works or a moving experience they once had on a
weekend retreat. But the Bible urges us to place our confidence in
Jesus Christ alone.

*Lord, You are my only source of strength, and my certainty of
eternal life. Amen.*

To Ponder: Jesus said, "I am the way and the truth and the life. No
one comes to the father except through me" (John 14:6).

GOD'S GRACE
Read John 6–8

He saved us, not because of righteous things we had done, but because of his mercy. He saved us through the washing of rebirth and renewal by the Holy Spirit.

TITUS 3:5

All during my growing-up years, what little religious instruction I was given led me to believe that good works was the key to going to heaven. But through a series of events, I did something that turned my life upside-down, or maybe I should say right-side-up. I bought a Bible and read it from cover to cover, and God took hold of my heart.

My wife and I gave our lives to Christ and vowed to follow Him all our days. My mother, although relieved to see me change my behavior, continued to believe that the real key to heaven was good works.

One day I was in the kitchen at my parents' home, reading John 6:28-29, and I came across these words, "Then they asked him, 'What must we do to do the works God requires?' Jesus answered, 'The work of God is this: to believe in the one He has sent.'"

I ran into the living room shouting, "Ma, Ma, look at this!" She read it, reread it, and believed it. From that moment on, she placed her faith in Jesus Christ.

The person depending on good works never knows where he or she stands with God. How many good works are necessary? People who do not understand the grace of God will go to great lengths to try to please God. I met a lady in an oriental temple who had burned off her index finger to show God she would do anything to gain His favor.

Christian, what a message we have for people burdened by their efforts to please God!

Lord, thank You for Your grace in which I stand. Amen.

To Ponder: "For it is by grace you have been saved, through faith—and this not from yourselves, it is the gift of God—not by works, so that no one can boast" (Ephesians 2:8-9).

YOUR KINGDOM COME
Read Acts 1–4

For the Lord himself will come down from heaven, with a loud command, with the voice of the archangel and with the trumpet call of God, and the dead in Christ will rise first.

1 THESSALONIANS 4:16-17

Sometimes it's tough to get our minds off one thing and onto another. We tend to come back to what we want to think about, even if those thoughts are not profitable.

This is what we find in the conversation between Jesus and His disciples in Acts 1:6-8.

> So when they met together, they [the disciples] asked him, "Lord, are you at this time going to restore the kingdom to Israel?" He said to them, "It is not for you to know the times or dates the Father has set by his own authority. But you will receive power when the Holy Spirit comes on you; and you will be my witnesses in Jerusalem, and in all Judea and Samaria, and to the ends of the earth."

The disciples had one thing on their minds—the restoration of Israel. To them, the kingdom of God meant a return to the splendor of the days of David and Solomon, a powerful political kingdom for the nation of Israel. If Jesus was the Messiah, wouldn't He overthrow the tyranny of Rome?

Jesus answered His disciples' question by shifting their focus from a kingdom of political power to one of spiritual power. He promised that the Holy Spirit would indwell them, and they would become His witnesses.

The next time you can't get your mind off a troubling issue, look for an opportunity to share Christ with someone. It will change your focus.

Lord, Your kingdom come, Your will be done. Amen.

To Ponder: The call of Jesus is to tell others what He has already done for us, and trust Him with what He will do in the future.

235

STAR WITNESSES
Read Acts 5–7

*For since in the wisdom of God the world through its wisdom did
not know him, God was pleased through the foolishness of what
was preached to save those who believe.*

1 CORINTHIANS 1:21

The Bible says that you and I are not called to be spiritual judges or
lawyers, but witnesses. The apostles of Jesus understood this well, and
their actions speak clearly in Acts 5:25: "Then someone came and
said, 'Look! The men you put in jail are standing in the temple courts
teaching the people.'"

The Jewish authorities complained that the apostles had filled
Jerusalem with their teaching, and they were right. But they couldn't
stop them. Even after they were imprisoned, beaten, and threatened,
Acts 5:42 says, "Day after day, in the temple courts and from house to
house, they never stopped teaching and proclaiming the good news
that Jesus is the Christ."

What qualifies a person as a good witness for Christ? The witness
must be familiar with the subject under consideration. The apostles
had not been off in Egypt or Spain during the public ministry of Jesus;
they had been with Him and were eyewitnesses of His life, death, and
resurrection. Because of their actions and their reputations for
courage and integrity, their words were taken seriously. Acts 4:13
sums it up: "When they [the Jewish authorities] saw the courage of
Peter and John and realized that they were unschooled, ordinary men,
they were astonished and they took note that these men had been
with Jesus."

Christian, how do you stack up as a witness for Christ? Are you
willing to speak courageously to others of what you know of Him?
Why not share with a friend today something that you know person-
ally about Jesus Christ. In the drama of life, you have a key role as a
witness for the Lord.

*Lord, help me to speak in such a way that people would be
drawn to You. Amen.*

To Ponder: We are called to be witnesses of the risen Christ.

236

AN UNLIKELY PROSPECT
Read Acts 8:29-35

Devote yourselves to prayer, being watchful and thankful. And pray for us, too, that God may open a door for our message, so that we may proclaim the mystery of Christ, for which I am in chains. Pray that I may proclaim it clearly, as I should.

COLOSSIANS 4:2-4

When I stepped out in the backyard, there was this big, tough, mean-looking guy working on his motorcycle. We were in Auckland, New Zealand, and he was something equivalent of a Hell's Angel here in the States. I walked over to him and said, "What's wrong with your bike?"

"I dunno. I think the people down at the garage ruined it. I took it in to get it tuned up, but now it won't even start."

He asked what I was doing in New Zealand. I told him I was with a Christian group called The Navigators, and I was helping people grow in their knowledge of the Bible. "For instance," I said, "do you know much about the Bible?"

"No," he said, "but I've always wondered what it was all about."

"I'll mention that to the group that lives next door, and maybe one of them can sit down with you and help you get into a study of the Scriptures."

"Man," he said, "I'd like that."

When our group got together that night for Bible study, one of the men asked what I was talking about with the biker who lived next door. When I told them, they almost dropped their teeth. "I told him one of you would help him get started in his search to understand the message of the Bible."

Now friend, you probably don't have a member of the Hell's Angels living next to you, but your neighbor may have that same desire to know what the Bible says. You won't know until you've talked to them.

Lord, keep me from making judgments about a person's interest in spiritual things, and let me see only their soul's need. Amen.

To Ponder: Are you ignoring an "open door" to tell someone about Jesus?

TAKING EVERY OPPORTUNITY
Read Acts 21–23

How, then, can they call on the one they have not believed in? And how can they believe in the one of whom they have not heard? And how can they hear without someone preaching to them?

ROMANS 10:14

In Acts 21–22, Paul was seized by a bloodthirsty mob who tried to kill him. Now how would you view the situation if you were in Paul's shoes? Amazingly, Paul saw it as a witnessing opportunity and asked the Roman commander who rescued him to allow him to speak to the crowd. Most of our opportunities are more routine.

Some years ago my wife and I were in Christchurch, New Zealand, on a preaching mission. A young man came by our motel to take us to the university for a meeting, and as we headed for the car, he said, "I've heard you talk about witnessing, and on the way to the meeting I want to watch you witness to someone."

"To whom?" I asked.

"Oh, we'll just stop in some neighborhood, knock on a door, and I'll watch you witness to the person who answers the door." I admired his creativity, but it seemed like a faulty plan.

"Okay," I said, "but first I need to stop at the desk to see if my laundry is done."

I mentioned to the desk clerk that I was on my way to the university to conduct a Bible study. She seemed interested, so I proceeded to explain how I'd come to Christ, clearly outlining the gospel. Just as I finished, several people came into the lobby, and I couldn't pursue the matter any further.

As we got into the car, I said to the young man, "Well, there it was."

"There what was?" he asked.

"You saw me witness."

It was so simple he had missed it. Most of our witnessing opportunities are just as ordinary, but we won't recognize them unless our eyes are open.

Lord, open my eyes to the witnessing opportunities all around me. Amen.

To Ponder: Most of us miss witnessing opportunities every day.

GOD'S FAITHFULNESS
Read the book of Lamentations

Every word of God is flawless;
he is a shield to those who take refuge in him.

PROVERBS 30:5

As Jeremiah wrote the book of Lamentations, he was standing in the midst of a city that was once the joy of the whole earth, full of people, a queen among the provinces. Now Jerusalem was like a slave wearing her chains in shame and disgrace. Yet against that dark background, we find words that have brightened the lives of believers down through the ages: "Because of the LORD's great love we are not consumed, for his compassions never fail. They are new every morning; great is your faithfulness" (Lamentations 3:22-23).

There is a poem based on these verses from Lamentations, written in the early 1920s by a life insurance agent named Thomas Chisholm. He sent the poem to a friend who set it to music. It has become one of the best-loved hymns of this century—"Great Is Thy Faithfulness." The hymn writer wrote these words about God: "Morning by morning new mercies I see. Thou changest not, Thy compassions they fail not, as Thou hast been Thou forever wilt be." According to Thomas Chisholm, there was no special or dramatic circumstance surrounding the writing of this hymn; he simply penned the lines from his impressions about God's faithfulness gleaned from reading the Bible.

Christian, there's an important lesson here: You and I can fully experience the faithfulness of God in our ordinary, day-to-day circumstances. And when the dark times come, God is still there.

The prophet Jeremiah was surrounded by tragedy, he was touched and moved by it, but he was not overcome. In the midst of a very dark scene, he saw a brilliant ray of hope based on the mercy, compassion, and faithfulness of God.

Lord, help me to keep my eyes on You, who have promised to provide all I need. Amen.

To Ponder: My circumstances may change, but God *never* changes.

LIFE FROM GOD'S PERSPECTIVE
Read Ezekiel 7–11

And we know that in all things God works for the good of those who love him, who have been called according to his purpose.

ROMANS 8:28

———

Two people use the same grass seed and fertilizer in their lawn; one person's lawn is filled with crabgrass while the other's is not. Two people work equally hard at their jobs; one is promoted and the other is not. Two men exercise regularly, eat lowfat yogurt, soybeans, and fish. One has a heart attack and the other does not. And so we may conclude: Life isn't fair.

But no matter how hard we protest, none of us can say that God isn't fair. In Ezekiel 7:3, the Lord describes the basis of His judgment: "I will judge you according to your conduct and repay you for all your detestable practices." And then, as the passage continues, God repeats His reason for judgment three more times! These people will be repaid exactly what they have earned—nothing more, nothing less. God won't make up a list of things that aren't true.

But God's actions may not always appear fair, and there's a very good reason for that. *His great purpose for His people is to conform them to the image of His Son.* This is His primary concern. But if we're not careful, we can fall into the same pitfall that snared the Old Testament people of God. While God wanted them to be a kingdom of priests whose lives would bless the world, they became concerned with their own comfort and complained when their prosperity was disrupted.

Christian, God is not concerned primarily with our comfort, but with our being conformed to the image of Christ. And in whatever way He chooses to bring that about, He will be fair. We can count on that.

Lord, mold and shape me until You make me what You want me to be. Amen.

To Ponder: I have a choice: either I can look at my circumstances and scream, "Unfair!" or I can rejoice in an opportunity to be conformed more closely to the image of Christ.

PRESUMPTUOUS OR PENITENT?
Read the book of Nahum

If we confess our sins, he is faithful and just and will forgive us our sins and purify us from all unrighteousness.

1 JOHN 1:9

There's a saying in business: "It's easier to ask forgiveness than to ask permission." This same attitude seems to be prevalent among some Christians. The problem with this approach is that every time we take God's forgiveness for granted, we are more likely to tolerate what we've done, and less likely to see it as sin that needs to be repented of.

Apparently this is what happened to the city of Nineveh, and the prophet Nahum had a message for them about God's judgment. About a hundred years before, Jonah had gone to the city. The people turned to God and the city was spared. Later, the people of Nineveh turned back to their old ways and became worse than before. In Nahum 3:1, the prophet says, "Woe to the city of blood, full of lies, full of plunder, never without victims!" In the midst of Nineveh's violence and deception, God sent a prophet to tell them He would not always strive with man.

While God is good and merciful, it is dangerous to presume upon His goodness. It is the goodness of God that should lead us to repentance, but if we persist in our sin, God will respond in judgment.

Christian, if you are acting like the people of Nineveh, figuring that you'll get forgiveness later for deliberate wrongs today, there's only one solution. Confession! To confess means to say the same thing about sin that God says. When we agree with the Lord about the sin in our lives, He is faithful and just to forgive our sins and to restore our fellowship with Him

Lord, show me how I take Your goodness for granted, and help me turn from my sin of presumption. Amen.

To Ponder: What does God's goodness mean to me?

OUR APPROACHABLE GOD
Read Hebrews 4:14-16

*"Call to me and I will answer you and tell you
great and unsearchable things you do not know."*

JEREMIAH 33:3

I was at O'Hare airport in Chicago, trying to find the man who was to take me to Trinity College where I would give a series of lectures for the college's spiritual emphasis week.

I saw a gentleman dressed in a red coat—an airport employee. I walked up and said, "Excuse me, sir, but can you tell me how to get to Terminal 1?" He turned to me with a scowl on his face and shouted in a loud booming voice, "You want to know how to get to Terminal 1? Try walking!" He then turned his back on me, indicating that the conversation was over.

As I walked along, still uncertain as to which way I should go, I thought, *What if God treated us like that?* What if when we went to the Lord in prayer with our questions, He shouted in a big booming voice loud enough for all the world to hear, "What a stupid question. Imagine anyone coming to me with a foolish question like that. You are really ignorant!"

And then what if He turned His back on us, indicating the conversation was over. But He never does that. In fact, the Bible says, "If any of you lacks wisdom, he should ask God, who gives generously to all without finding fault, and it will be given to him" (James 1:5). God is so approachable! He never puts you down or makes you look like a fool.

Do you face a situation today that you don't know how to handle—something that is beyond you? Go to the Lord with it. He will never turn you away.

Lord, I'm facing a situation today that is beyond my ability to handle. Give me Your wisdom to know how to deal with it. Amen.

To Ponder: The Lord delights to reveal His will and His Word to those who need His help.

LORD OF ALL
Read Zechariah 5–6

*And beginning with Moses and the Prophets, he explained to them
what was said in all the Scriptures concerning himself.*

LUKE 24:27

One of the primary things to remember as you read God's Word is
that both the Old Testament and the New Testament are basically the
story of Jesus Christ and the life He came to give us.

For instance, we have both a type of Christ and a direct prophecy
regarding Him in Zechariah 6:11-13. Joshua, the high priest, is a type
or a picture of Christ, the coming Messiah, the high priest of our profession. We also have the direct prophecy concerning the Lord Jesus
Christ as the Branch, a title applied to the Messiah or the offspring of
David, son of Jesse, a righteous branch, beautiful and glorious.

Joshua was active in building the temple of Zechariah's day. In like
manner, the Branch, the Messiah of the New Testament, would build
the spiritual temple, the church, the body of Jesus Christ. Now if all
this sounds a little theological and remote, let's think about what it
means to you and me.

If Jesus Christ is the central theme of the Old and New
Testaments, the central figure of the entire Bible, then what place
should He have in our lives? If He is the centerpiece of history, the
Bible, and the Christian faith, where have we placed Him in our hearts
today?

A practical way of looking at what this means is to realize that
every decision we make must involve Christ, His Great Commission,
and His will for our lives.

*Lord, come and take Your rightful place in my heart and my
life as Lord of all. Amen.*

To Ponder: The same Lord who will return in majesty and power to
occupy the place of honor on the stage of human history,
patiently awaits my invitation to take His rightful place in my
heart.

WHO'S IN CHARGE?
Read Revelation 15–16

He is before all things, and in him all things hold together.

COLOSSIANS 1:17

A while back, I was invited to speak at a conference sponsored by The Navigators of San Diego, who ministered to the many servicemen from that area. The conference director and I arrived early, and while he went his way, I wandered over to the meeting hall.

There were half a dozen guys sweeping, straightening chairs, and putting out the hymnbooks, so I asked, "Who's in charge here?"

Ed Gansz, a young naval officer, stopped sweeping, waved to me, and pointed his finger toward heaven. What he was indicating was quite profound. Although he was responsible for the work crew in the auditorium, God was in charge.

Friend, that's the message that comes across loud and clear in Revelation 15:3-4.

Great and marvelous are your deeds, Lord God Almighty.
Just and true are your ways, King of the ages.
Who will not fear you, O Lord, and bring glory to your name?
For you alone are holy.
All nations will come and worship before you,
for your righteous acts have been revealed.

There should be no doubt in anyone's mind who's in charge here. And, Christian, that thought may well be the most important one that enters your mind today. For who knows what the day will hold? For some of us, it may bring joy and delight. For others, sickness and sorrow. But, take heart. No matter what the circumstances, God is in control. You can look to Him for the guidance, comfort, and wisdom you need.

Lord, I yield the circumstances of my day to Your masterful control. Amen.

To Ponder: One day, every living being on the face of the earth will humbly bow before the Lord God Almighty.

LISTENING TO THE WORD
Read Acts 2:42

But the man who looks intently into the perfect law that gives freedom, and continues to do this, not forgetting what he has heard, but doing it—he will be blessed in what he does.

JAMES 1:25

Think about the last airplane flight you took. When it came time for the flight attendant to impart the vital information about oxygen masks, exit doors, and the workings of your seat belt, how closely did you or your fellow travelers pay attention? Most people were probably knitting, reading, chatting—anything but listening to the attendant.

I'm usually just as lackadaisical, but there was one particular flight in which I hung on the flight attendant's every word. I was flying from Bogota, Colombia, over the high, rugged peaks of the Andes Mountains, to Loma Linda, the Wycliffe Bible Translators jungle base. The airplane had gone into service in the 1930s and was not equipped with an automatic oxygen system for high altitude, so all of us on board were instructed in the use of the emergency oxygen system that might keep us alive. I not only listened and paid attention, I asked the steward questions to make sure I had it right.

In many ways, going to church on Sunday morning is like an airplane ride. You've heard it all before. You've sung the hymns a hundred times; the sermon topic is familiar. So your mind drifts, and you don't really listen to the vital information passed along by the minister of Christ, the steward of the mysteries of God. But it doesn't have to be that way.

Ask God to give you the spirit of our early ancestors in the faith, who devoted themselves to the apostles' teaching. Ask the Lord to give you the same hunger God's people exemplified when they gathered together to hear the Word of God expounded and hung on to every word. Be one of those who truly hears the Word.

Lord, only You have the words of life. As I sit in church this Sunday, give me a passion for what I hear, and keep me from taking Your truth for granted. Amen.

To Ponder: "The words of the LORD are flawless, like silver refined in a furnace of clay, purified seven times" (Psalm 12:6).

A MIND FOR THE WORD
Read Acts 16–18

I have hidden your word in my heart
that I might not sin against you.

PSALM 119:11

What made the apostles of Jesus Christ so powerful in their ministry and so effective in their witness? I believe we find one of the keys in Acts 17:1-2: "They came to Thessalonica, where there was a Jewish synagogue. As his custom was, Paul went into the synagogue, and on three Sabbath days he reasoned with them from the Scriptures."

The Bible was absolutely indispensable to Paul's witness for Christ. Now, think with me for a moment. Before you can quote the Bible, what must you do? You must memorize it. If you take the time to discipline yourself to memorize the Word, when the opportunity arises you can quote Scripture and help others understand the gospel.

Among the early apostles, memorizing the Old Testament Scriptures was a standard practice. They knew the Word of God, and when the opportunity arose for witness, they were ready. Remember Peter's great opportunity on the day of Pentecost? There he was, out in the middle of the street with no Bible, no sermon notes—nothing but a heart filled with the Word of God. And he began his sermon by quoting from memory the Old Testament prophet Joel (2:28-32). God used Peter's preaching to bring three thousand souls into the kingdom.

I see a great need today for us to return to this apostolic practice of memorizing the Word of God. I challenge you to get on your knees before God and ask Him to give you a hunger and a thirst for His Word. Then get started in the vital practice of memorizing key portions of the Bible as you prepare your mind and heart to speak to others about Christ.

Lord, create in me a hunger and thirst for Your Word, and I will share it with others. Amen.

To Ponder: When we commit Scripture to memory, we're committing to the transformation of our minds.

THE POWER OF THE WORD
Read Acts 19–20

For you have been born again, not of perishable seed, but of imperishable, through the living and enduring word of God.

1 PETER 1:23

Sports commentators often remind us how difficult it is for a visiting team to play at someone else's home court or field, because the home fans are so fanatical about their team. But any coach will tell you that in order to be successful and win on the road, a team must be able to overcome all the jeers and cheers.

Have you noticed in the book of Acts that Paul rarely had the home field advantage? He was usually preaching the gospel in difficult venues. In Acts 19, we find him in the city of Ephesus. Here stood the great temple to Artemis—a worship built around the practice of immorality. The city reeked with all the pollutions of paganism, while the people were dominated by sorcery, black magic, witchcraft, and demonism.

Paul didn't have the home field advantage, but his message was the power of God unto salvation. The book he carried in his heart was the Word of God. And his life was under the control of the Spirit of God. Soon, many people from this city gripped by Satan's power responded in repentance toward God and faith in the Lord Jesus Christ. Against the backdrop of an evil power that seemed unstoppable, once again the Bible proved to be alive and powerful.

What will it take to change the lives of people we know and to clean up our towns that are in the grip of drugs, alcohol, false religions, materialism, and secularism? In Ephesus, it took the Bible. I'm sure it will take nothing less today. Let's study the Word, live it, share it, and watch God work!

Lord, I am reminded today that Your Word has given me the home field advantage in the war against Satan. I love Your powerful Word. Amen.

To Ponder: The Word of the Lord endures forever.

MARCHING INTO THE ENEMY'S CAMP
Read 2 Corinthians 10–13

But thanks be to God, who always leads us in
triumphal procession in Christ and through us spreads
everywhere the fragrance of the knowledge of him.

2 CORINTHIANS 2:14

During World War II, one of the greatest threats to Marines in the South Pacific was snipers. An enemy soldier, armed with a rifle and a telescopic sight, would hide himself in a tree and pick off our guys one by one. But in all my time in the Pacific, I never saw a sniper armed with a tank. First of all, it would be really tough to get a tank up a tree, and then it would be very difficult to hide it once you got it there. A tank is a powerful weapon, but it's not the right weapon for a sniper.

In today's passage, the apostle Paul pictures the Christian life as a spiritual warfare and says that in order to win, we must use the right weapons. Listen to his words in 2 Corinthians 10:3-5: "For though we live in the world, we do not wage war as the world does. The weapons we fight with are not the weapons of the world. On the contrary, they have divine power to demolish strongholds. We demolish arguments and every pretension that sets itself up against the knowledge of God, and we take captive every thought to make it obedient to Christ."

The strongholds of Satan include ignorance of the Word of God and prejudice against it, indifference to spiritual truth, and the allurements of the world. To overcome these powerful forces, we can't rely on our own strength or wisdom; we must place our confidence in the spiritual weapons God has given us. Christian, we cannot win our spiritual battles with human ingenuity, human wisdom, or human strength. We must call on the mighty name of the Lord and find our strength in Him.

Lord, I call on Your mighty name and the power of Your Word
to fight my spiritual battles. Amen.

To Ponder: Jesus overcame the temptation of the Devil, not by any human effort, but by His total reliance on the Word of God.

PREPARED FOR BATTLE
Read Ephesians 1–6

*So let us put aside the deeds of darkness
and put on the armor of light.*

ROMANS 13:12

Whenever I turn to Ephesians 6:13-18 and read Paul's description of
the whole armor of God, I think back to a day when I went into
another kind of battle without mine. I was part of a Marine invasion
force in the South Pacific, and our landing craft had just reached the
island when it was hit by two enemy shells.

I was not a Christian at the time, and the essence of what I yelled
to the other men was, "Let us depart here speedily." So we ran across
the beach and began making our way toward the airfield, which was
our objective.

Pretty soon, a sergeant came to check up on us. When he saw me,
he said, "Eims, where is your helmet?" "I must have lost it," I said. He
looked again and said, "Eims, where is your duty belt?" My duty belt
had my ammo pouches, my first aid kit, my bayonet, and all kinds of
other things. "It must be in the landing craft." And then the sergeant
got really exasperated and said, "As a matter of fact, Eims, where is
your rifle?"

In my rush to get out of the landing craft, I had left everything
behind. There I was, hopping around from tree to tree, from bush to bush,
with no equipment, no weapon, absolutely worthless to the cause.

Paul said that if we want to avoid that situation in the Christian
life, we are to put on the full armor of God. And we are to pray in the
Spirit, on all occasions, with all kinds of prayers and requests.
Although God has freely provided this armor, you and I have the
responsibility of putting it on. Don't go into battle without it.

*Lord, thank You for providing the armor I need to stand firm
against the Evil One. Amen.*

To Ponder: If the Lord approached you today, would He have to ask,
   "Christian, where is your helmet? What about your belt, shield,
   and sword?"

GOD'S CLEAR VOICE
Read 2 Peter 1–3

I trust in your word.

PSALM 119:42

Picture this: You're up on a high mountain with two of your Christian friends and you hear a voice from heaven saying, "Jesus Christ is the Son of God." The three of you look at each other and say, "Did you hear that?" You all nod your heads and look around to see if anyone else is up there with you, but it's just the three of you.

Would you be more convinced that Jesus Christ is the Son of God through hearing a voice from heaven than by reading the Bible's declaration that Jesus Christ is the Son of God?

While you turn that question around in your mind, let's reflect on 2 Peter 1:16-19.

> We did not follow cleverly invented stories when we told you about the power and coming of our Lord Jesus Christ, but we were eyewitnesses of his majesty. For he received honor and glory from God the Father when the voice came to him from the Majestic Glory, saying, "This is my Son, whom I love; with him I am well pleased." We ourselves heard this voice that came from heaven when we were with him on the sacred mountain. And we have the word of the prophets made more certain, and you will do well to pay attention to it, as to a light shining in a dark place.

In the context of what Peter writes here, the reference to a more sure word of prophecy is obviously the Bible. This is a mind-boggling evaluation of the validity of the Scriptures, which Peter says are more dependable, more reliable than a voice from heaven. And remember, he's the one who heard the voice.

Lord, thank You for Your Word—my permanent record of Your love and promises to me. Amen.

To Ponder: When someone wants to know if you're really serious about something, they usually say, "Put it in writing." God did that for us.

THE GOD WE CAN KNOW
Read Psalms 135–139

*Yours, O LORD is the greatness and the power
and the glory and the majesty and the splendor,
for everything in heaven and earth is yours.*

1 CHRONICLES 29:11

Some years ago I was speaking to a group of university students in Tucson, Arizona. A young man near the front asked if I believed God created the world. When I told him I did, he replied, "Well, if God created this world you and I live in today with all of its pain and sorrow and violence and hatred and misery of every kind, then God must be the Devil."

To understand what God is like, we must turn to the Bible, God's revelation of Himself. Today's passage has a great deal to tell us about God. First, God is omniscient. He knows everything about everything. But notice that this great truth is expressed in a very personal way. David said, "O LORD, you have searched me and you know me" (Psalm 139:1). For the person who loves and trusts God, theology is more than high-sounding phrases.

Second, He's omnipresent. He is exempt from the limitations of space. This attribute of God guarantees His nearness to each of us. It means we can have communion with Him anywhere, anytime. The psalmist said, "Where can I go from your Spirit? Where can I flee from your presence? . . . If I rise on the wings of the dawn, if I settle on the far side of the sea, even there your hand will guide me, your right hand will hold me fast" (Psalm 139:7-10).

Interwoven into the doctrines of omniscience and omnipresence is the doctrine of omnipotence, the idea that God has perfect and absolute power. Today, think about what God is like, and revel in the fact that He's your Father.

Lord, there is nothing too hard for You. Amen.

To Ponder: God knows everything about you, He is always with you, and He has all the power you will ever need.

DO IT NOW
Read Numbers 1–4

In Joppa there was a disciple named [Dorcas],
who was always doing good and helping the poor.

ACTS 9:36

In Numbers 1:2-3, Moses received a rather imposing task from the Lord. "Take a census of the whole Israelite community . . . all the men in Israel twenty years old or more. . . ." Imagine how Moses could have reacted: *I don't have time to do that! I'm already leading all these people across the burning desert. I try to keep them from sin. I set up their various forms of worship. And I'm writing the Bible!*

God gave him the job on the first day of the second month of the second year. Notice when he got around to doing it—on the same day! (verse 18).

This is a great lesson for us. When we're given a job that doesn't really excite us, the best thing to do is get on with it, because if we keep putting it off, it will insist that we give it our attention. Christian, don't waste time trying to figure out ways to get out of something distasteful. Roll up your sleeves, thank the Lord, and get it done.

Moses expended his energy accomplishing things for God, instead of figuring out all the reasons why they couldn't be done. You see, what we're talking about here is more than just success through a positive mental attitude. For a Christian to respond to the command of God requires faith, not just an act of pulling himself up by his spiritual bootstraps.

Genuine faith responds to the call and command of God by saying, "Lord, by your grace and power, I'll do it now." Obedience must be complete, enthusiastic, and immediate.

Lord, thank You for letting me join Your work in this world.
Amen.

To Ponder: Usually, it requires the same amount of energy to get out of doing a task as it does to do it.

RITUAL OR REVERENCE?
Read Isaiah 1–4

*"Yet a time is coming and has now come when the true
worshipers will worship the Father in spirit and truth,
for they are the kind of worshipers the Father seeks."*

JOHN 4:23

There is an old story about two families in the mountains of Kentucky who had been feuding for years. When a young man was asked why he was fighting the other family, he had no idea. It's what his family had always done.

That was exactly the situation in Isaiah's time. When the Lord spoke to His people through the prophet Isaiah, it wasn't good news, because judgment was on the way. The reason? They were going through various rituals and religious activities, but they had forsaken the Lord, spurned the Holy One of Israel, and turned their backs on Him.

Oh, they were bringing offerings, but they were meaningless. They celebrated various convocations—feasts of the new moon and special Sabbaths—but God said, "They have become a burden to me." Isaiah 1:15 records these words of the Lord: "When you spread out your hands in prayer, I will hide my eyes from you; even if you offer many prayers, I will not listen."

They had kept the form but lost the meaning. And the problem is still with us today.

A close pastor friend of mine spent twenty years in Christian work, but all the time he was drifting away from the Lord. He doubled the membership, tripled the budget, and built a 100,000-square-foot building. But today he weeps and says that not one person came to faith in Jesus Christ during that time. He had kept the form but lost the meaning.

Christian, do you read the Bible merely to satisfy a habit? How do you approach your time of worship at church? Take a moment and reflect on Isaiah's words. God longs to restore the meaning to your walk of daily discipleship.

*Lord, I want to be the kind of worshiper You seek. Show me
how to worship You in truth. Amen.*

To Ponder: In our worship of God, what pleases Him most?

GOD, OUR REFUGE
Read the book of Obadiah

*He will be like a bush in the wastelands; he will not see
prosperity when it comes. He will dwell in the parched
places of the desert, in a salt land where no one lives.*

JEREMIAH 17:6

When I was a kid back in Iowa, we played a game called "King of the
Mountain." Someone would get up on a mound of dirt, and everyone
else would try to get him off. There was one big kid we could never get
off the hill. And he stayed on top until he was ready to come down.

In the book of Obadiah, we encounter the Edomites, who thought
they were king of the mountain. But God saw things differently.

"See," [the Lord said], "I will make you small among the
nations; you will be utterly despised. The pride of your heart has
deceived you, you who live in the clefts of the rocks and make
your home on the heights, you who say to yourself, 'Who can
bring me down to the ground?' Though you soar like the eagle
and make your nest among the stars, from there I will bring you
down," declares the LORD. (Obadiah 2-4).

I recall standing at the foot of the ancient Edomite capitol city of
Petra, the stronghold from which the Edomites launched their raids.
They thought they could get away with anything, but their invasion
of Judah in 587 B.C. brought God's judgment.

You don't have to be an arrogant Edomite to trust in the wrong
thing. Even Christians can make the mistake of trusting in hard work,
physical appearance, finances. But all those sources of security and
pride can be gone in an instant. We must keep our eyes on the Lord
and trust in Him as our Rock and high tower.

*Lord, when I put my security in a fortress of my own making,
bring me back to the shelter of God Most High. Amen.*

To Ponder: Blessed is the man or woman who boasts in the Lord's
strength.

WALKING IN THE WORD
Read Micah 1–2

*I pray that out of his glorious riches he may strengthen
you with power through his Spirit in your inner being.*

EPHESIANS 3:16

A recent magazine article dealt with our society's growing trend of making celebrities of people involved in criminal or immoral activity. But it really isn't anything new.

Consider life in the time of the prophet Micah. The Bible tells us the land was filled with idolatry, covetousness, oppression, and contempt for the Word of God. The spiritual and political leaders abused their power, leading the people down the path of destruction. There were also false prophets who enjoyed celebrity status as they said that nothing would come of all the evil in their society (see Micah 2:6).

Micah stepped forward with a clear warning from God. Judgment was coming for all who defied the Lord. He also gave a word of comfort to the faithful people of God. Micah 2:12 records God's promise of restoration: "I will surely gather all of you, O Jacob; I will surely bring together the remnant of Israel. I will bring them together like sheep in a pen, like a flock in its pasture; the place will throng with people."

How we need to give this word of mercy to hurting and helpless people! I have a friend who went through a time of deep disappointment and hurt. She could hardly hold up her head when she walked. At her lowest point, a friend began praying with her and sharing the Scriptures. Weeks passed, and the Word and prayer began to have their effect. She emerged from her ordeal revived in spirit, with a new sparkle in her eye.

Do you know someone who needs comfort—prayer and a thought from the Word of God? Just like Micah, God can use you to speak boldly and compassionately in His name.

Lord, give me a mouth that speaks "only what is helpful for building others up according to their needs." (from Ephesians 4:29) Amen.

To Ponder: No matter how dark our circumstances, God's Word can light our way.

REJOICE IN THE LORD
Read the book of Habakkuk

"Do not grieve, for the joy of the LORD is your strength."

NEHEMIAH 8:10

The book of Habakkuk contains a passage you can cling to when the bottom falls out of everything. "Though the fig tree does not bud and there are no grapes on the vines, though the olive crop fails and the fields produce no food, though there are no sheep in the pen and no cattle in the stalls, yet I will rejoice in the LORD, I will be joyful in God my savior" (Habakkuk 3:17-18.)

I know of a missionary who has labored for twenty-five years with very few people responding to the gospel. Yet he clings to this passage in Habakkuk and finds comfort and encouragement.

I think also of a mother who reared two children in a godly home. When they came of age, both daughters decided to follow the ways of the world. This praying woman continues to trust in the Lord.

I know a man who spent the greater part of his life working for a large corporation. After twenty-five years of faithful service, he was fired without notice. Eventually, he also lost his home and his savings, but not his peace of mind.

Joy is not a matter of good fortune and pleasant circumstances. Joy is a decision, and God is the focus.

Christian, what are your disappointments? What circumstances have gone wrong for you and are sapping your joy? I challenge you to memorize the passage from Habakkuk and claim it each morning.

Finding our joy in the Lord is a matter of will—a decision we can make because of the love and faithfulness of God.

Lord, show me how to fix my inward gaze on You, my hope and my joy. Amen.

To Ponder: Circumstances can defeat us only when we've taken our eyes off the Source of our joy.

THE LIFE OF THE PRAY-ER
Read Micah 6–7

The prayer of a righteous man is powerful and effective.

JAMES 5:16

In Micah 6:6-8, the prophet asks this penetrating question about prayer:

> With what shall I come before the Lord and bow down before the exalted God? Shall I come before him with burnt offerings? . . . Will the Lord be pleased with thousands of rams, with ten thousand rivers of oil? Shall I offer my firstborn for my transgression? . . . He has showed you, O man, what is good. And what does the Lord require of you? To act justly and to love mercy and to walk humbly with your God.

Micah was convinced that true prayer is more than just words. The Bible is clear that God pays as much attention to the life of the one who is praying as He does to the words of the prayer. And He also urges us to persevere in prayer.

One evening I was in a prayer meeting in Council Bluffs, Iowa. I asked for prayer for my father, who never darkened the door of a church. I had prayed for him every day for seven-and-a-half years. After the meeting, two men asked if they could visit my dad and share the gospel with him. On their first visit, my dad threw them out of the house, but a few weeks later they tried again. My dad invited them in and went over to the sofa and knelt down, weeping his way to the foot of the cross. Six weeks later, he died.

Christian, God is not reluctant to answer our prayers. He simply asks that we walk humbly with Him, pray without ceasing, and never lose heart.

Lord, purify my heart, and that will purify my life. Amen.

To Ponder: To be effective, our prayers must be accompanied by a God-honoring life.

TRUE RELIGION
Read Zechariah 7–8

They would flatter him with their mouths, lying to
him with their tongues; their hearts were not loyal to
him, they were not faithful to his covenant.

PSALM 78:36-37

In Zechariah 7:4-6, we read: "Then the word of the LORD Almighty came to me: 'Ask all the people of the land and the priests, When you fasted and mourned in the fifth and seventh months for the past seventy years, was it really for me that you fasted? And when you were eating and drinking, were you not just feasting for yourselves?'"

God questioned the heart motive behind their religious practices. And then in verse 9: "This is what the LORD Almighty says: 'Administer true justice; show mercy and compassion to one another. Do not oppress the widow or the fatherless, the alien or the poor. In your hearts do not think evil of each other.'" You see, the real issue is not fasting or feasting, but a commitment to live in a way that pleases the Lord.

As I studied this passage, I thought of a man I knew in high school and served with in the Marines during World War II. After the war, we returned to our hometown in Iowa and continued to pal around. We were pretty wild in those days. But this guy had a practice I thought was strange. After a wild week of rough living, he went to church on Sunday and made his confessions. Then it was back to another week of drunken brawls and wild parties. Even though I wasn't a Christian at the time, I wondered if his confession was genuine, and I questioned in my heart if it was doing him any good.

The end result of our fasting, confession, Bible study, church attendance, and every other religious practice should be a life that brings honor and glory to God.

Lord, keep me from empty religious ritual, and help me to live
in close relationship with You. Amen.

To Ponder: How has last Sunday's church service affected your life this week?

PRAYING WITH GOD'S PEOPLE
Read Acts 2:42-47

When they heard this, they raised their
voices together in prayer to God.

ACTS 4:24

───────────

There is a great amount of space given in the Bible regarding the fact that individuals should pray. We read of the prayers of Abraham, David, Jacob, Daniel, Solomon, Paul, and others—even Jesus Himself. But there is also a lot of instruction that we should pray together.

When Peter was thrown unjustly into prison, the church was not led to organize a protest but to organize a prayer meeting. The Bible says, "So Peter was kept in prison, but the church was earnestly praying to God for him" (Acts 12:5).

What makes group prayer meaningful and profitable? Here are a few tips that might add new life and spark to your prayer meeting. First, pray loud enough for others to hear so they can pray along with you. Second, don't spend half the time discussing what to pray about. I know it's helpful to list some specific needs, but don't take the bulk of the time doing it. Third, pray about common needs. As a general rule, people get their hearts into those petitions that affect them as well—a missionary the church supports, a need in the Sunday school, a sickness suffered by a member of the class, and so on.

This next "don't" is very important. Don't hang your dirty linen out for all to see. If it involves someone else, go to the individual involved and get right with that person. Jesus taught, "If you are offering your gift at the altar and there remember that your brother has something against you . . . first go and be reconciled to your brother; then come and offer your gift" (Matthew 5:23-24).

Praying with others is a part of worship we must exercise faithfully.

Lord, thank You for the privilege I enjoy of lifting my voice
freely in corporate prayer. Amen.

To Ponder: God delights to see His children gather for prayer.

259

OUR HEART'S DESIRE
Read Romans 9–11

Those who sow in tears will reap with songs of joy. He who goes out weeping, carrying seed to sow, will return with songs of joy, carrying sheaves with him.

PSALM 126:5-6

Years ago, Lorne Sanny, then president of The Navigators, was teaching a seminar on prayer. He told us, "Prayer is not preparation for doing the work of God; prayer is the work of God." I wrote it down at the time and have given it a good deal of thought since. I believe he was right.

The apostle Paul prayed, "Brothers, my heart's desire and prayer to God for the Israelites is that they may be saved" (Romans 10:1). Paul's heart desire led him to pray.

Perhaps you know someone you would like to see come to salvation in Christ. One of the first steps you can take in bringing that desire to reality is to pray. However, there's more to prayer than walking into God's office and dropping a memo into His in-basket. The context of Paul's prayer is that it grew out of a deep inner longing. In Romans 9:2, Paul said of his desire for his people's salvation: "I have great sorrow and unceasing anguish in my heart."

Most of us don't have much trouble coming to God with a heart full of deep personal concerns—work, finances, relationships. But are we just as burdened for others? Does their salvation weigh as heavily on our minds and hearts as the material things we think we need?

How can we get the same kind of heart as the apostle Paul? The only way I know is to spend time with Jesus Christ, who was moved with compassion toward people. When Jesus looked at the city of Jerusalem, He wept. The closer we walk with Christ in our life of daily discipleship, the deeper our desires will grow in prayer for others.

Lord, as I spend time with You in prayer, give me a heart like Yours for the lost. Amen.

To Ponder: Prayer is sharing our hearts with God, not just reciting a list of people and things for Him to bless.

MAINTAINING LIFE SUPPORT
Read 1 Thessalonians 5

Pray continually.

1 THESSALONIANS 5:17

Years ago the only means of going to the bottom of the ocean was in a diving suit. It was made of thick canvas and was complete with weighted shoes, a heavy metal headpiece with a window to look out, a long rope to jerk if something went wrong, and most important of all, an air hose that supplied oxygen.

Everything about the environment into which the diver went was hostile—there were a thousand things that could go wrong and cost the diver his life. For that reason, the crews constantly monitored the air hose to make sure everything was okay.

Friend, that's an exact picture of your situation every day. The environment in which you and I live is hostile to our Christian growth and development. The world is always trying to squeeze us into its mold, the Devil is trying to lure us off track, and the inner corruptions of our own fleshly desires are constantly trying to sap our spiritual strength.

How do you get through this hostile environment? You keep the connection with your life-support system above. I guess you could say, "You keep your air hose connected with heaven"—a strong avenue of prayer by which you keep in constant touch and receive strength and wisdom from God.

The apostle Paul understood this key to an effective Christian life. When he wrote his first letter to the Thessalonians, he ended with an exhortation to pray without ceasing. Why? Because he knew prayer would help these people maintain a daily fellowship with God, and thus, a powerful Christian witness in a hostile world.

Lord, teach me the discipline of praying continually. Amen.

To Ponder: The Christian who fails to keep his prayer connection intact runs the danger of spiritual disaster.

HARVEST TIME
Read Hebrews 11–13

We tell you the good news: What God promised our fathers he has fulfilled for us, their children, by raising up Jesus.

ACTS 13:32

I remember sitting along a river that flowed quietly through a missionary jungle base in South America. A man was telling me about the many opportunities all around his mission that they could not pursue because the laborers were few. It broke his heart. He was a man with a burden for the lost, but with an inadequate labor force to fully reap the harvest.

A few months later I was with two pastors in downtown London. They were surrounded by some of the most powerful corporations in the world, businesses with global influence. These men echoed the lament of the missionary in South America—a lack of laborers to reach out to the spiritually hungry people in these great corporations.

Jesus said, "Ask the Lord of the harvest, therefore, to send out workers into his harvest field" (Matthew 9:38). This is also what the writer of Hebrews prayed: "May the God of peace, who through the blood of the eternal covenant brought back from the dead our Lord Jesus, that great Shepherd of the sheep, equip you with everything good for doing his will, and may he work in us what is pleasing to him, through Jesus Christ, to whom be glory for ever and ever. Amen." (13:20-21).

God calls on us to co-labor with Him to fulfill the Great Commission through evangelism and teaching new Christians how to grow in faith. And He's looking for people who will go to the fields early, work hard, and stay late because they are committed to Christ and to the task at hand. This kind of person cannot be produced by human endeavor alone. Will you make the need for spiritual laborers a matter of prayer today?

Lord, I want to be a spiritual laborer for You. Show me where You're working and how I can join You there. Amen.

To Ponder: The fields are ripe, the laborers are few; the solution begins with prayer.

THE CLAIMS OF CHRIST
Read John 17:1-5

He is the image of the invisible God, the firstborn over all creation.

COLOSSIANS 1:15

What would you do if your dad began to say outlandish things about himself? Like one morning he came to breakfast wearing his hat sideways and claiming to be Napoleon? Or he packed his bags to leave for Carnegie Hall, saying he was going to launch a singing career, and you knew the poor guy couldn't sing a note!

You would probably try to stop him and quickly call a family pow-wow to figure out what to do. But for a person to say he's Napoleon or Pavarotti is nothing compared to what Jesus claimed for Himself.

In His great high priestly prayer to His Father, He said, "And now, Father, glorify me in your presence with the glory I had with you before the world began" (John 17:5). Jesus Christ claimed He was alive and present with God before the creation of the world! That's either one of the most outlandish claims ever made or it is a simple statement by the eternal Son of God.

Jesus also said, "I am the way and the truth and the life. No one comes to the Father except through me" (John 14:6). Now where does that leave those people who claim we're all heading for the same place and there are many ways to God? Obviously it leaves them in conflict with what Jesus said.

Yes, there are other men in history who have been labeled "divine" by their followers. But none of them ever died for the sins of the whole world. None of them rose again from the grave. Jesus fulfilled hundreds of prophecies given many years before His birth. The extreme claims of Jesus sound unbelievable . . . unless they are true.

Lord, I believe every claim You ever made about Yourself, and I worship You as my God and Savior. Amen.

To Ponder: Jesus is God, yet His sacrifice was necessary to satisfy His holiness.

GREAT DELIVERANCE
Read Romans 6:13-14

Then they cried out to the LORD in their trouble,
and he delivered them from their distress.

PSALM 107:6

During the height of the Vietnam War, a young man named Larry
Bleeker spent an evening in our home in Colorado Springs. He was on
his way to Travis Air Force Base the next day. He'd stopped in the
Springs to talk to me about what he should do after the war was over
and he was discharged from the Marines.

I had known Larry for a number of years. He'd been involved in
the ministry of The Navigators at Iowa State University and had
become an outstanding young man of God. I asked him what he
would like to do when he got out of the service. He told me he would
like to spend more time with me and get some further training in the
Christian life.

I assured him I would look forward to that, and he left for Travis
the next morning and off to Vietnam. Very soon I received a letter
from him lamenting the ungodly surroundings in which he was living. He looked forward to being in our home where he could draw
closer to Jesus and enjoy a godly atmosphere.

He had already experienced God's salvation from the penalty of sin
and deliverance from the power of sin, but he longed to be delivered
from the presence of sin. The next news I received was that he had
been killed in action, and I knew he was now delivered from the very
presence of sin itself.

Christian, you have been delivered from the penalty of sin, and
you look forward to deliverance from the presence of sin, in heaven.
But are you experiencing God's deliverance from the power of sin
right now?

Lord, thank You for Your great salvation that delivers me
from the penalty and power of sin in this life and from the
presence of sin in eternity. Amen.

To Ponder: "For sin shall not be your master, because you are not
under law, but under grace" (Romans 6:14).

A NEW STANDING
Read Romans 5:1-11

For we maintain that a man is justified by
faith apart from observing the law.

ROMANS 3:28

On June 21, 1947, my wife and I were married in the Presbyterian Church in Neola, Iowa. Population: 900.

Virginia and her bridesmaids were all decked out in their long flowing gowns, and I was at the front of the church with the best man and the attendants. We repeated our vows, the preacher preached a little sermon, and then he pronounced us man and wife. With that pronouncement, my legal standing was changed. Up until that declaration I had been a single man. But with that declaration, I was now legally married.

In a sense, that is a clear picture of what the apostle Paul said in Romans 5:1: "Therefore, since we have been justified through faith, we have peace with God through our Lord Jesus Christ." The word *justification* is not from the field of religion but from the field of law. Justification can best be defined as the legal act of God by which God declares the sinner righteous on the basis of the perfect righteousness of Jesus Christ.

We are made righteous by a declaration of God. And with that declaration, our legal standing is changed. Before God declared me justified in His sight, and I became clothed in the righteousness of Christ, I was a sinner separated from God. But when I came to Christ, who had died on the cross to pay the penalty for all my sins, I was pronounced righteous in His sight.

Forgiveness is negative—the removal of condemnation. Justification is positive—the bestowing of righteousness based on our standing in Christ.

Lord, I rejoice in Your declaration of my right standing with
You through Jesus Christ. Amen.

To Ponder: Forgiveness and justification are like two sides of a coin. Forgiveness is the cancellation of sin; justification is the transmittal of righteousness.

THE INCARNATION
Read John 3:16-17 and 1 Corinthians 15:1-4

He appeared in a body, was vindicated by the Spirit,
was seen by angels, was preached among the nations,
was believed on in the world, was taken up in glory.

1 TIMOTHY 3:16

One holiday season my wife and I were in Tokyo, Japan. We had been in that city quite a few times over the years, but traffic was never like this! Always bad, but not this bad! So I finally asked the cab driver why there was such a horrendous traffic jam. He smiled and said, "It's the Christmas rush. Christmas is one of the most celebrated holidays in our country."

Later I thought about what he'd said. Had the Asians begun to honor and worship Jesus Christ? No, Christ had very little to do with it. This was simply a nice time to give gifts to people you like. It was good for business and made a happy, festive occasion.

If that's why Jesus Christ came, He could have done it much more easily without going to the cross. You and I both know He didn't come just to create a happy holiday. The only begotten Son of God was given by His loving Father to a world lost in sin and spiritual darkness, that we might have everlasting life in Him.

The Asian culture hadn't caught it, and friend, our culture has almost lost it. Although America grew out of deep, religious roots, there's no question that today the majority of our population knows little or nothing about the Bible or Christianity. In some areas, Christians have even had to defend the use of manger scenes and sacred carols in the celebration of Christ's birthday.

Why not resolve that this year someone in your family, someone in your neighborhood, someone where you work will hear the truth of why Jesus came . . . from your mouth. The message is simple: God gives eternal life through Jesus Christ our Lord. Let's tell it.

Lord, until You return, help us in our homes and in our
churches to proclaim and teach why You came. Amen.

To Ponder: How can you be a light in this dark world?

CHRIST'S DEATH
Read John 19:1-37

He was pierced for our transgressions, he was crushed for our iniquities; the punishment that brought us peace was upon him, and by his wounds we are healed.

ISAIAH 53:5

I've always enjoyed reading the history of the Old West. The days of Custer, Doc Holliday, and Wyatt Earp hold a special fascination for me. I've been to the site of the O.K. Corral, but there is one tragic story in Western history that I can't forget.

It concerns a young woman from Boston who came west in a stagecoach to teach school in a frontier town. Out on the prairie, a gang of drunken outlaws intercepted the stage, killed the drivers, and took the young woman to an abandoned shack, where they raped and beat her throughout the night.

Can you possibly imagine the revulsion, the shame, the pain and agony she went through? Here was an innocent, refined, young woman suddenly thrust into a world so horrifying it defied description. That scene has helped me imagine just a fraction of the agony of Jesus on the cross, where on a tragic day He was made sin for us as He suffered and died for you and me.

The physical agony was great, but it did not compare with the agony that was His when all the sin and moral filth of the world was laid on Him, and His spotless soul—which had known only the purity and glory of His home in heaven—was made sin on our behalf. He died that we might live.

Jesus took our sin and clothed us in the robes of His own eternal righteousness. We can echo the apostle Paul when He wrote, "Therefore, since we have been justified through faith, we have peace with God through our Lord Jesus Christ" (Romans 5:1).

Lord, You are my righteousness. Amen.

To Ponder: We cannot fully comprehend what it meant for Jesus Christ to be made sin for us—to be forsaken by God, when He took on all the filth of the world that ever was and ever would be. But now He is risen to His glory and is sitting at the right hand of the Father.

THE ACCUSER OF THE BRETHREN
Read Job 1:6–2:10

Therefore he is able to save completely those who come to God through him, because he always lives to intercede for them.

HEBREWS 7:25

It all began with a young man needing financial help. His mother was sick and needed a doctor, but they had no money. Now there was an old man who lived down the street who knew of the desperate plight of this young man and his mother. He told the young man of a home in the neighborhood where the people were away, but they kept a large amount of money hidden. All the young man needed to do was climb up to an unlocked window, come downstairs, open the door, and the old man would do the rest—and he would split the money with the young man so he could help his mother.

In a moment of weakness, the young man agreed to do it. All went as planned; the young man got his money, and his mother got well. But one day there was a knock on the door, and the police arrested the young man. At the trial, guess who the primary witness against him turned out to be? The old man down the street. The very person who had led him into sin now stood in the witness box and accused him of being a thief.

Revelation 12:10 calls Satan the accuser of our brothers "who accuses them before our God day and night." Satan, the very one who has led us into sin, now assumes the role of accuser, reminding God that we are sinners.

The good news is that we have an advocate with the Father in Christ Jesus. Scripture tells us that "by one sacrifice he [Christ Jesus] has made perfect forever those who are being made holy" (Hebrews 10:14).

Lord, by Your perfect sacrifice I come boldly into God's presence, no longer fearful of Satan's accusations against me. Amen.

To Ponder: When the Holy Spirit convicts us of sin, we must confess it. When Satan accuses us, we can ignore him.

THE DESTROYER
Read 1 Peter 5:8-9

Your enemy the devil prowls around like a
roaring lion looking for someone to devour.

1 PETER 5:8

I'll never forget the day my dad took me to my first circus in Council Bluffs, Iowa. The whole city was decorated with banners and posters! We found a place to park and walked over to the empty lot with the big top. Three rings, a high wire, clowns, horses, jugglers . . . and right in the middle was a giant cage filled with fierce animals. All of a sudden, one of those big tigers looked directly at me and gave a huge roar that lifted me right off the bleachers.

Then a man wearing a sparkly suit, black boots, and carrying a chair and a whip walked into that cage! He had those animals jumping through fiery hoops, sitting down in rows, rolling over—amazing stuff. Then it happened. One of the cats broke rank and leapt at the guy. The trainer stepped back, lifted his chair and snapped his whip, and for a second, it was a standoff as he and the tiger stared at each other. Finally the big cat went back to his place. Even though I was a young kid, it was clear to me the tiger's goal had not been merely to sniff the trainer's boots.

Christian, never underestimate the goal of your enemy, the Devil. He is out to devour you. Does that mean you must live in fear, wondering if he's lurking behind every bush? No, the apostle Peter said, "Resist him, standing firm in the faith. . . ." You can overcome the Devil by relying on God's Word, just as Jesus did when He faced Satan in the wilderness. Remember, He repeated those powerful words "It is written" as he stood firm against Satan!

Lord, I will hide Your Word in my heart so that I can stand
firm in the faith. Amen.

To Ponder: Satan is defeated by God's Word. Are you giving top priority to memorizing Scripture?

IT'S THE LITTLE THINGS
Read Isaiah 17–20

*Catch for us the foxes, the little foxes that ruin the
vineyards, our vineyards that are in bloom.*

SONG OF SONGS 2:15

Many Christians treat sin as some people treat extreme weather. They feel invincible and don't perceive it as a threat. Consequently, they aren't prepared to meet each day as it comes. Their quiet time takes a back seat to hurried morning preparations and the rush to get to work; they begin to compromise their values here and there. Over a period of time, their spiritual life degenerates into nothing.

In Isaiah 17:4, we read a sobering prophecy: "In that day the glory of Jacob will fade; the fat of his body will waste away." God was saying what would happen to His people because they had turned their backs on Him. The glory of Jacob was numerical strength. But God said this glory was going to fade slowly away like the body of a person with a lingering disease. Little by little, sin would take its toll until finally the nation would be nothing but skin and bones. In Isaiah 17:10, God's assessment of the cause is clear: "You have forgotten God your Savior; you have not remembered the Rock, your fortress."

Are there little things in your life that don't bring honor to God? Are there areas of compromise that have begun to undermine your walk with Him? If so, bring them to the Lord and seek His forgiveness and restoration. The time to deal with it is now. If you wouldn't think of walking in winter without a coat or hiking in the desert without a canteen of water, don't begin your day without a time of personal fellowship with the Lord. It really is a matter of spiritual life or death.

Lord, search me and bring to mind the little things that prevent me from walking with You. Amen.

To Ponder: Is there any "little" thing you are doing, or perhaps some subtle thing you are tolerating in your environment, that has compromised your walk with God?

IDOL WORSHIP
Read Isaiah 44–48

Jesus replied, "Love the Lord your God with all your heart and with all your soul and with all your mind."

MATTHEW 22:37

I was participating in a Christian conference just outside Jakarta, Indonesia, and was walking to breakfast one morning when I saw a young man on his knees bowing down to something hidden from my view. I walked a little farther and saw it was a motorcycle. He had a set of wrenches and screwdrivers nearby. I smiled at my ignorance and felt bad that I had mentally accused the young man of idol worship.

Later that day, when I shared the incident with a friend, he told me I had been right. That young man's god was his motorcycle. He loved it more than anything else in this world.

Notice the words in Isaiah 44:9: "All who make idols are nothing, and the things they treasure are worthless." He goes on to describe a blacksmith and a carpenter who use the tools of their trade to fashion an idol they bow down to, saying, "Save me; you are my God."

Idols take many forms. I've watched a businessman make an idol of the brass nameplate on his office door that indicates his high position. I've seen women make an idol of their kitchens, filling them with the latest gadgets. I've watched young men worship their cars or their new three-finned surfboards. And some of these people are Christians.

If there's an idol in your life, hold it up to the light of God's Word as we find it in Isaiah 45:5. Here God declares, "I am the LORD, and there is no other; apart from me there is no God." It doesn't make sense to worship a motorcycle or a food processor or anything else manmade when the Lord of heaven has staked His claim on our hearts.

Lord, You have first place in my heart. Help me to see when I'm in danger of worshiping something or someone other than You. Amen.

To Ponder: What are you allowing to take the place of God in your heart and affection?

GIVING GOD FIRST PLACE
Read the book of Haggai

Set your minds on things above, not on earthly things.

COLOSSIANS 3:2

———

The Bible clearly teaches that God and His kingdom must have top priority in our lives. Listen to these words from the book of Haggai:

> Then the Word of the LORD came through the prophet Haggai: "Is it a time for you yourselves to be living in your paneled houses, while this house remains a ruin?" Now this is what the LORD almighty says: "Give careful thought to your ways. You have planted much, but have harvested little. You eat, but never have enough. You drink, but never have your fill. You put on clothes, but are not warm. You earn wages, only to put them in a purse with holes in it." (1:3-6)

The people of Haggai's day were so wrapped up in their own concerns that they had completely neglected God, His worship, and His house. Self had marched to the front and commanded their complete attention.

When we neglect God, the very things we seek begin to elude us. Why? Because the things of this world cannot satisfy the hunger of our souls. Both Old and New Testaments testify to this truth. To neglect God and turn our minds and hearts inward and not upward is self-defeating. So Haggai challenged the people to give careful thought to the set of their hearts and the direction of their lives.

Christian, where are your priorities today? Only God can give meaning and ultimate satisfaction in life. And it comes as a by-product as we obey the words of Jesus: "Seek ye first the kingdom of God, and His righteousness; and all these things shall be added unto you"(KJV).

Lord, nothing I can attain in this world can take the place of intimacy with You. I will wait on You to bring the "added things" to my life. Amen.

To Ponder: What gives meaning and satisfaction to your life?

NO MORE STAINS
Read Zechariah 12–14

In him we have redemption through Jesus Christ,
in accordance with his pleasure and will.

EPHESIANS 1:7 (PARAPHRASE MINE)

———————

The next time you go to the grocery store, take a look at all the cleaning products that claim to make even the most stubborn stains disappear. But for the most difficult stain known to man, the stain of sin, there is only one remedy.

In Zechariah 13:1, we read: "On that day a fountain will be opened to the house of David and the inhabitants of Jerusalem, to cleanse them from sin and impurity."

When I read that verse, I always think of Dr. Robert "Dick" Wilson of Princeton Seminary. As the story goes, a student asked, "Dr. Wilson, what is the most profound thought to ever enter your mind?" Without hesitation, Dr. Wilson quoted the words of an old gospel hymn: "There is a fountain filled with blood drawn from Immanuel's veins; and sinners plunged beneath that flood lose all their guilty stains."

This fountain will never lose its power to cleanse people like us from sin. When Jesus died on the cross, He shed His blood that we might receive the gift of eternal life, if we turn to Him in repentance and belief.

And what does it mean to believe? According to the apostle John, it means to open the door of your heart to Christ and welcome Him as your Savior and Lord. To be cleansed from sin is to be free from guilt and free to live a new life of power. Christ Himself is the fountain where you can lose all your guilty stains.

Lord, I can never thank You enough for Your shed blood that cleansed me from my sin and gave me a completely new life, now and forever. Amen.

To Ponder: How would you explain to a nonbeliever the meaning of the terms *repentance, belief,* and *salvation?*

A POWERFUL ENEMY
Read 1 Corinthians 6:15-20

*Flee the evil desires of youth, and pursue
righteousness, faith, love and peace, along with
those who call on the Lord out of a pure heart.*

2 TIMOTHY 2:22

The mistake I made was trying to read in bed by lamplight. We were in the jungles of Colombia, South America, and I should have known better. Within minutes, thousands of tiny bugs were flying in circles around the lamp.

I jumped up, turned on the ceiling light, and turned off the light by the bed. Immediately, these pesky insects flew to the top of the room and began to circle that light. Next, I opened the door to the hallway and turned on the hall light, then turned off the ceiling light in the bedroom. Off they flew into the hallway and began to fly circles around the light in the hall.

I quickly shut the door, kept all lights off in the bedroom, and had a good night's sleep. The next morning when I stepped into the hallway, there they were—thousands of insects dead on the floor directly under the light. They had circled hundreds of times, then got too close and were killed.

Friend, I have seen a similar thing happen to people who play around with sexual lust. Like these insects, they flit around and finally go too far. I watched this happen to a friend of mine who seemed to be a dedicated Christian. He was a handsome guy who easily attracted women. When we ate together in a restaurant, he'd often kid around with the waitress, making some witty remark, and the two of them would laugh and wink and flirt with each other. Then it happened. He got caught up in a sexual sin and today he is not serving God.

Beware! Lust is a powerful enemy.

Lord, Your Word says that my body is the temple of the Holy Spirit. Help me to honor You with my body. Amen.

To Ponder: To continue to play around danger is to end up serving the sin we thought we were master of.

THE FLESH
Read Hebrews 4:14-16

No temptation has seized you except what is common to man. And God is faithful; he will not let you be tempted beyond what you can bear. But when you are tempted, he will also provide a way out so that you can stand up under it.

1 CORINTHIANS 10:13

There isn't a person on earth who doesn't experience temptation with fleshly lust at some time during life.

I recall being on a panel to discuss this in a high school class at a local church. The man who spoke before me was a local pastor, and since I was fairly new in my ministry with The Navigators, I was looking forward to what he would say. But when he began to speak, I couldn't believe my ears. He told these kids, "Sure, it's okay to park in a car on a dark, deserted country road. Just make sure you stay within the bounds of proper behavior." Then it was my turn.

"Okay," I said, "if you follow this man's advice, make sure that when you park that car and turn off the lights on that dark, deserted country road that you both get out of the car, kneel down, and earnestly plead with the Lord in prayer that He will give you the strength and wisdom to stay within the bounds of proper behavior."

The Bible tells the story of Achan, who stole something that didn't belong to him. Listen to his explanation: "When I saw in the plunder a beautiful robe from Babylonia, two hundred shekels of silver and a wedge of gold weighing fifty shekels, I coveted them and took them. They are hidden in the ground inside my tent, with the silver underneath" (Joshua 7:21).

Notice the progression. He saw it, he lusted after it, he took it, and then he tried to cover up his sin. Friend, is there a temptation you're flirting with today that looks innocent on the surface? Yield yourself immediately in prayer to the power of Christ.

Lord, thank You for Your victory over sin and Your saving power in my life. Amen.

To Ponder: God's Word says that we are not controlled by the sinful nature (see Romans 8:9). How does that truth come into play when we are tempted?

FIRST LOVE
Read Revelation 1–3

"I know your deeds, that you are neither cold nor hot. I wish you were either one or the other! So, because you are lukewarm— neither hot nor cold—I am about to spit you out of my mouth."

REVELATION 3:15-16

I was sitting in the Sunday evening service of an evangelical church in the South. The preacher was delivering a sermon that was known in that part of the country as a stem-winder, or barnburner. His Scripture-filled message was fiery—full of compassion and concern for the lost.

About halfway through, I looked around at the congregation and saw that some were responding to the preacher's impassioned plea with a hearty yawn. Eyelids were drooping, and some had even drifted off to sleep.

Don't get me wrong. These were good people. Some had put in years of faithful service for the Lord. Many had shown a zeal for evangelism and a concern for the spiritual growth of new Christians. But somehow they had become spiritually flat. They were comfortable, lethargic, engulfed in spiritual dullness. What happened?

Jesus said in Revelation 2:2-5, "I know your deeds, your hard work and your perseverance. I know that you cannot tolerate wicked men, that you have tested those who claim to be apostles but are not, and have found them false. You have persevered and have endured hardships for my name, and have not grown weary. Yet I hold this against you: You have forsaken your first love. . . . Repent and do the things you did at first."

Christian, has your devotion to Christ cooled? Has your fervency in serving God been replaced by a sense of duty? If there was a time when your heart burned hotter and brighter than it does today, Jesus says it's time to repent and go the other way. Ask Him to rekindle the flame and renew the joy and excitement of your first love for Him.

Lord, renew the flame of my first love—for You and for Your kingdom. Amen.

To Ponder: Do you still experience the same excitement, dedication, and hunger for the Word that you did as a new believer?

SELF-DENIAL
Read Mark 14–16

*"If anyone would come after me, he must deny
himself and take up his cross daily and follow me."*

LUKE 9:23

Some years ago I spent the summer studying the book of Mark. I was reading Mark 15, when I came across these words in verse 31: "The chief priests and the teachers of the law mocked him among themselves. 'He saved others,' they said, 'but he can't save himself!'" I wondered, *Who else mocked Him as He hung on that cross?* I started to find cross-references in other Gospels and discovered that along with the chief priests, Jesus was mocked by the soldiers, the thieves who were crucified with Him, and the people who passed by. This was a microcosm of humanity—the religious leaders, the military, those outside the law, and the general public. They all said essentially the same thing: "He saved others but he can't save himself." And then it hit me. "Right!" I shouted. "That's right!"

To be used of God in the salvation of others requires denying self on behalf of others. The jeering crowd didn't understand this as they hurled abuse at Jesus. They thought they had all their theological bases covered. But in their ignorance, they actually expressed a great truth.

Jesus said that if you're not willing to give up your life for His sake and His kingdom, you will lose it (Luke 9:24). But if we deny self; if we follow the example of Christ and put the welfare of others before our own desires; if we repudiate self and give our lives for the salvation of others, we will find our lives and, in the end, come out winners.

Does your life reflect this Christlike characteristic of self-denial for the sake of others? If not, what stands in your way?

*Lord, give me the grace to give up my life for You and Your
eternal purposes. Amen.*

To Ponder: Leading others to Christ calls for self-denial.

WHEN GOD SPEAKS
Read Luke 1–2

Today, if you hear his voice . . .

PSALM 95:7

———

There were four hundred years of silence between the writing of Malachi, the last book of the Old Testament, and the announcement of the birth of Jesus. I guess that's what makes the Christmas story, and particularly what happened to the shepherds, so amazing.

Listen to the familiar words beginning in Luke 2:8:

> And there were in the same country shepherds abiding in the field, keeping watch over their flock by night. And, lo, an angel of the Lord came upon them, and the glory of the Lord shone round about them; and they were sore afraid. And the angel said unto them, Fear not; for, behold, I bring you good tidings of great joy, which shall be to all people. For unto you is born this day in the city of David a savior, who is Christ the Lord. And this shall be a sign unto you: Ye shall find the babe wrapped in swaddling clothes, lying in a manger. And suddenly there was with the angel a multitude of the heavenly host, praising God, and saying, Glory to God in the highest, and on earth peace, good will toward men. (KJV)

This announcement to the shepherds was the first public word from the Lord in four hundred years! Do you suppose the shepherds might have doubted that it really was the voice of God?

Sometimes we have the idea that God speaks only to pastors or to missionaries or to special people who seem to have it all together. Not so! God wants to talk to you, but you've got to meet Him halfway. So open your Bible, open your heart, and let Him speak to you today.

Lord, prepare my heart to hear Your voice and obey it. Amen.

To Ponder: Why does God choose some of the most unlikely people to carry out His purposes?

THE LORD DELIVERS
Read Acts 13–15

They called the apostles in and had them flogged. . . . The apostles left the Sanhedrin, rejoicing because they had been counted worthy of suffering disgrace for the Name.

ACTS 5:40-42

One of the most unusual and possibly confusing statements in the Bible is, "Out of them all the Lord delivered me" (2 Timothy 3:11, KJV). It was written by Paul about the events recorded in Acts 13–15. As Paul and Barnabas preached the gospel in Antioch, they had tremendous results. Acts 13:44 tells us, "Almost the whole city gathered to hear the word of the Lord." But the enemies of Christ stirred up persecution against Paul and Barnabas and finally threw them out of town.

Acts 14:1-6 describes their next stop at Iconium, where they spoke boldly for Christ but were forced to leave when a murder plot was discovered. Paul and Barnabas escaped to Lystra but were followed by men from Antioch and Iconium, who stirred up the crowd against them. Acts 14:19 says, "They stoned Paul and dragged him outside the city, thinking he was dead."

Some years later, when Paul wrote to Timothy about these persecutions, he said this in 2 Timothy 3:11: "But out of them all the Lord delivered me" (KJV). What? He escaped at Antioch and Iconium, but not at Lystra. There his enemies stoned him and left him for dead. But Paul doesn't say he was delivered two out of three times. He says, "Out of them all. . . ."

Christian, if you're feeling a bit bruised and battered right now, remember that God sometimes delivers us through the stones, not from the stones. Our choice is to trust Him in every circumstance so that we can echo the triumphant testimony of the apostle Paul, "Out of them all the Lord delivered me."

Lord, You are my Strong Deliverer. Thank You for Your never-failing presence in my life. Amen.

To Ponder: Paul rejoiced that he was counted worthy of suffering for the Name. Does that sound like something you would say?

WANTED: FRUITFUL LABORERS
Read Romans 12–16

*And the things you have heard me say in the presence
of many witnesses entrust to reliable men who will also
be qualified to teach others.*

2 TIMOTHY 2:2

In Romans 15:14, Paul described a laborer this way: "I myself am convinced, my brothers, that you yourselves are full of goodness, complete in knowledge and competent to instruct one another." He begins with goodness, or Christian character. Back in Romans 13:13-14, Paul spoke of some things that destroy character — drunkenness, immorality, dissension, jealousy. As the antidote to these spiritual poisons, he says simply, "Clothe yourselves with the Lord Jesus Christ."

Then Paul speaks of being filled with knowledge. As laborers, we must saturate our hearts and minds with the Word of God. We must study it, memorize it, and live it. And finally, a laborer must be able to teach another person — to lead that person to Christ and then come alongside and encourage that new believer in the joys and struggles of daily life.

Are you a laborer? Are you developing in Christian character? Are you growing in knowledge of the Word of God? Are you learning to teach others and help them grow in their faith? The crying need today is for people — laborers — who are able and willing to take advantage of the spiritual opportunities all around us.

*Lord, as I abide in Your Word and Your Word abides in me,
make me a fruitful laborer in the spiritual harvest for Your
kingdom. Amen.*

To Ponder: To be clothed with Christ, to follow Christ, to worship Christ are the keys to becoming a fruitful laborer for Christ.

TEMPLE BUILDERS
Read 1 Corinthians 1–6

*I write to you . . . because you are strong, and the word of God
lives in you, and you have overcome the evil one.*

1 JOHN 2:14

You are probably familiar with the teaching in 1 Corinthians 3 that
every Christian is a living temple of God. But did you know you're also
a temple builder?

The apostle Paul saw himself as a wise master builder who had laid
the foundation of Jesus Christ in the lives of the believers in Corinth.
He knew that others would continue the spiritual building process in
the lives of these new converts, and he had a word of warning and
exhortation for them in 1 Corinthians 3:10: "Each one should be careful how he builds." Why the warning?

When the Old Testament people of God set about to build the
temple, did they hurriedly throw something together overnight? Did
they put up a building that resembled a little tool shed? A Quonset
hut? A pup tent? No, they constructed a building according to God's
blueprint and design. The Bible describes it as exceedingly magnificent because it was a place that would be worthy of the name of God.
Paul applies this same divine standard of excellence to what we
build in the lives of others.

When I was a very young Christian, a man named Don
Rosenberger taught me how to study the Bible, encouraged me in the
discipline of Scripture memory, and showed me how to share the
gospel of Christ with others. He prayed with me and helped me learn
how to obey the Lord in everyday life. This didn't happen overnight,
and it didn't happen in Don's free time. He poured the best that he had
into helping me become a disciple of Christ who would, in turn, build
into the lives of others. That's what the Lord wants you and me to be
doing, too.

*Lord, I want to faithfully pour my life into helping others
become Your disciples. Amen.*

To Ponder: Who could benefit from your knowledge of what it means
to follow Christ?

A LIFE THAT COUNTS
Read 1 Corinthians 15–16

"Do not work for food that spoils, but for food that endures to eternal life, which the Son of Man will give you. On him God the Father has placed his seal of approval."

JOHN 6:27

I was watching a television program about one of the battles in the South Pacific during World War II. I had been in that particular battle and fought alongside the men shown in the film. As I watched, it brought to mind an official document I'd read several years before. This document analyzed the battle from the moment we hit the beach until the island was secured. When I got to the last paragraph, I read something that made me ill. In fact, I became so shaky I got out of my chair and sat down on the floor.

The government's conclusion was that the battle had accomplished nothing of strategic importance. It had been a mistake. I could see in my mind those hundreds of slain Marines, as well as hundreds of young Japanese soldiers, who had died in vain in a battle that didn't really matter.

Right then, the Lord brought a verse to my mind: "Therefore, my dear brothers, stand firm. Let nothing move you. Always give yourselves fully to the work of the Lord, because you know that your labor in the Lord is not in vain" (1 Corinthians 15:58).

It may seem to you today that you're banging your head against a brick wall, that nothing is going right in the Sunday school or women's ministry or men's brotherhood. But let me encourage you to stay at it. When you put in your eight hours on the job, having worked as unto the Lord, it is not in vain. When you reach out to your friends and family with the gospel, even if they refuse to listen, it is not in vain. Why? Because the Bible says that whatever you are doing for Christ matters.

Lord, I rejoice that because of my relationship with You, even the most insignificant task has meaning and purpose. Amen.

To Ponder: Our labor in the Lord is not in vain.

MORE THAN LIP SERVICE
Read Revelation 17–19

"Whoever has my commands and obeys them, he is the one who loves me. He who loves me will be loved by my Father, and I too will love him and show myself to him."

JOHN 14:21

The commander of any military base in the United States is given a number of privileges reserved for people of his rank and responsibilities. He and his family are provided with comfortable quarters. There are men assigned to drive his car and cut the grass. He has a reserved parking space, and so on.

Now let's say that one morning he and his family are awakened by the sound of every man and woman on base gathered under his bedroom window to sing a declaration of their undying allegiance and love to him. And what if they did this once a week, yet the commander noticed that although they gathered to sing his praises and declare their love, they didn't carry out his orders?

I'm sure he'd say, "Look, it's nice that you've provided me with a special parking space and people to mow the grass. It's wonderful that you meet once a week to wake me up with your songs of devotion. But what I really want is for you to help me carry out the mission of this base by obeying my orders."

That's what Jesus wants from us — a high degree of fidelity to His mission here on earth. Revelation 17:14 says that Jesus Christ is "Lord of lords and King of kings — and with Him will be His called, chosen and faithful followers."

It isn't wrong to build houses of worship that honor God and to gather to sing songs of devotion to Him. But it grieves the heart of God when we do that and then walk out the door and ignore the commission He has given us. Christian, let's make sure that along with our hymns of devotion, we carry out His orders.

Lord, by Your power, I want to do more than give You lip service. Help me to carry out the work You've assigned me and gifted me to do. Amen.

To Ponder: Jesus said, "If you love me, you will obey what I command" (John 14:15).

GOD'S VESSELS
Read 2 Timothy 2:20-26

Come back to your senses as you ought, and stop
sinning; for there are some who are ignorant of God—
I say this to your shame.

1 CORINTHIANS 15:34

Some time ago I heard of a young man who took a job working in a post office over the Christmas holidays. He was grateful for the work and really gave it his best. During slack times, he would get the broom and clean up around his work area. Did his coworkers commend him for his efforts to give the government an honest day's labor? No, they said, "What are you looking for, a gold star on your paycheck?"

This same sort of thing happened to me when I was a student at the University of Washington in Seattle. Some of my friends got wind of the fact that I didn't cheat on exams. They thought that was silly, because *everybody* did it. When I told them I knew it would displease the Lord, they laughed. But I'd made a commitment to live in such a way that the Lord would be honored. That's a decision every Christian should make.

The person who wants to be used of God will soon discover that a life of holiness is an imperative: "If a man cleanses himself . . . he will be an instrument for noble purposes, made holy, useful to the Master and prepared to do any good work" (2 Timothy 2:21). Christian, do you want to be used of God? Then remember that a pure man is a powerful man.

The apostle John wrote, "Dear friends, if our hearts do not condemn us, we have confidence before God." The boldness we need to serve God is intertwined with a holy life. Remember the Old Testament warning: "The wicked flee when no man pursueth, but the righteous are bold as a lion" (Proverbs 28:1, KJV). Holiness and usability are inseparable.

Lord, by Your Spirit, make my life holy so that I may be used
by You. Amen.

To Ponder: A holy life is a powerful weapon in the hands of a holy God.

WARNING SIGNS
Read 2 Timothy 3

You were bought at a price; do not become slaves of men.

1 CORINTHIANS 7:23

If you heed a warning sign, you can usually save yourself a lot of trouble. For instance, when the little red light flickers on the dashboard of your car, indicating that the engine is low on oil, you can save yourself a lot of trouble if you add some oil.

What are the danger signs that tell you you're not living a holy life and that you're slipping off the straight and narrow path onto the broad road that leads to destruction?

One of these danger signs is set forth by the apostle Paul in 2 Timothy 3, where he speaks of people who are lovers of pleasure more than lovers of God. Now let me state right up front that God does not frown on His people enjoying a little pleasure. Of course not. But here are people who love pleasure more than they love God. You've probably seen them. They're more interested in talking about sports or some motion picture they've seen recently than they are about spiritual things. They may even show signs of boredom when the Word is taught.

The apostle Paul, in that same chapter, gives another sign of moving away from a life of holiness. He speaks of people who are "lovers of self." The burning issue of their lives becomes what is best for them rather than what is best for the work of Christ and His Great Commission. Paul described them as people whose god is their belly and whose glory is in their shame.

Do you recognize any of these warning signs in your own life? If so, you can save yourself some trouble if you face up to it, repent, and get back on track.

Lord, when my thoughts and attitudes would lead me off the track of holy living, lead me back to Your Word and renew my mind. Amen.

To Ponder: "May the words of my mouth and the meditation of my heart be pleasing in your sight, O LORD, my Rock and my Redeemer" (Psalm 19:14).

THE SEPARATED LIFE
Read James 4:4

Do not conform any longer to the pattern of this world, but be transformed by the renewing of your mind.

ROMANS 12:2

If you were to announce a lecture on "The Separated Life" before an average audience in, say, New York City, some might think it had to do with troubled marriages. Even Christians are vague about the biblical teaching on a separated life. It means a life set apart for God, no longer swayed by the pull of worldly attractions and ambitions. In my discussions with Christians across America about the concept of living a separated life, most people have strong opinions on the subject.

I know a man who advocates the idea of having a drink with nonChristians to show them he can be their friend and perhaps to gain an opportunity to witness to them. As a matter of fact, he's had the opportunity to lead people to Christ along the way. He cites the Scripture passage that speaks of becoming all things to all men that by all means we may save some (1 Corinthians 10:22).

The late Paul Little had a different approach. Paul practically lived on the college campus. He was always out there with his shirtsleeves rolled up, mixing in lively discussions with nonChristians. And when one of them would invite him down to the bar to have a drink, he simply thanked them but said he really didn't enjoy that. Would the person like to go to a game the next night—his treat? He kept the lines of communication open, didn't condemn the person, yet didn't participate in something he'd separated himself from.

We don't need to enter into questionable practices with people to show them we're not crazy-headed fanatics. There are many ways to build friendships with nonChristians without doing things we're against.

Lord, show me how to follow Your lead of loving sinners without compromising my walk. Amen.

To Ponder: God wants us to show His love to the ungodly.

OUR CALLING
Read 1 Peter 1:13-16

For God did not call us to be impure, but to live a holy life.

1 THESSALONIANS 4:7

One Sunday evening, our church was giving a special concert, and my wife and I went early. We located a couple of seats in the balcony and settled in for a fifteen-minute wait until the concert began. Right behind us sat two young men engaged in a conversation that it was our unfortunate experience to overhear.

They were discussing the single young ladies in their Sunday school class. There was no mention of the quality of teaching that went on in the class or the worthwhile projects the class sponsored, just the large pool of girls from which to choose. Their interest in these young ladies was less than honorable. Their motives for membership in that class were unholy.

The *Amplified* version of 1 Peter 1:14-16 reads, "Live as children of obedience to God; Do not conform yourselves to the evil desires that governed you in your former ignorance when you did not know the requirements of the Gospel. But as the One Who called you is holy, you yourselves also be holy in all your conduct and manner of living. For it is written, 'You shall be holy, for I am holy.'"

Now just what is a holy life? It is a life that is surrendered to the lordship of Jesus Christ, controlled and empowered by the Holy Spirit, and lived to the glory of God. The apostle Peter referred to people who live that way as "children of obedience."

Lord, I want to be a child of obedience and have my lifestyle reflect Your holiness. Amen.

To Ponder: A holy life boils down to obedience to the Word and will of God.

OVERCOMING THE WORLD
Read 2 Peter 1:3-4

For everyone born of God overcomes the world.
This is the victory that has overcome the world, even our faith.

1 JOHN 5:4

———

Most people have heard about OCD—obsessive compulsive disorder—that can manifest itself in all kinds of phobias. Some people are so afraid of germs and viruses that they can't even shake hands with people for fear of being contaminated. And that's a mild case of OCD.

Friend, I've seen that happen in the spiritual realm. I've seen people get so frightened by the power of the Devil or the dangers all around us in this world that they become immobilized by fear and isolate themselves. Now, it's certainly true this world is a powerful enemy. We don't want to be naïve about that. But sometimes it lures us rather than repels us. Just look what happened to Demas. He was one of Paul's fellow laborers, along with such stalwarts as Mark and Luke. But something happened, and Paul wrote to Timothy, "Demas, because he loved this world, has deserted me" (2 Timothy 4:10). If the pull of the world is powerful enough to cause a colaborer of Paul to leave the cause of Christ and give the rest of his life to living for the world, we'd better watch out!

There are people out there—false prophets—who would lead you astray. But you can overcome them and the lifestyle they propose, not by sealing yourself off from the world, but by staying close to Christ. Remember the words of the apostle John: "The one who is in you is greater than the one who is in the world" (1 John 4:4).

Lord, I praise You for Your victory over sin and death—and the world. Amen.

To Ponder: Although we no longer have to fear what the world can do to us, we do have to remain wise to its lures.

OUT OF THIS WORLD
Read 1 John 2:15-17

For this world in its present form is passing away.

1 CORINTHIANS 7:31

Over the years, I've traveled through numerous countries in Latin America, Asia, Europe, the Middle East, and Africa, preaching the good news of Christ and conducting discipleship and leadership seminars. I don't speak the languages in those countries, and no matter how hard I try to fit in, the fit hasn't been exact. What I've worn and the language I've spoken tell everyone I'm a foreigner.

This is much like our life in Christ. We are foreigners in this world, because our citizenship is in heaven. Although we're instructed by God, "Do not love the world or anything in the world" (1 John 2:15), He also has appointed us ambassadors to carry His message throughout the world. How do we put these two commands together?

The answer is found by studying the life of Jesus Christ. He did not find His identity or purpose in this world. Instead, He carried out His Father's redemptive plan. His pleasure was in doing the will of God. And so it should be for us, Christ's ambassadors. We must see ourselves as pilgrims on a mission. We are to model the life of Christ as we seek to communicate to the unbelieving world around us.

I urge you to pray that God will show you the best way to share Christ with the unbelievers you know, and count on the leading of the Spirit as you live a life of daily discipleship in this world but not of it.

Lord, keep my eyes focused on the mission You've given me—to explain Your saving grace to a world that doesn't speak Your language. Amen.

To Ponder: What would your life look like if you gave top priority to sharing the message of salvation with unbelievers? What would you loosen your grip on, and what would you take hold of?

NO PAIN, NO GAIN
Read Romans 4–5

*Consider it pure joy, my brothers, whenever you face trials of
many kinds, because you know that the testing of your faith
develops perseverance. Perseverance must finish its work so that
you may be mature and complete, not lacking anything.*

JAMES 1:2-4

I have a friend who says that physical conditioning is simply a matter
of how much pain you're willing to endure. And I believe it. But all
those people who voluntarily exercise and abstain from hot fudge sun-
daes are convinced that their ultimate gain is worth their present pain.

I wonder if we have that same attitude toward our life of daily discipleship. Are we willing to endure pain when it comes to growing in
our lives as Christians? In Romans 5:2, the apostle Paul wrote, "And
we rejoice in the hope of the glory of God." But he doesn't stop there.
Notice the next words: "Not only so, but we also rejoice in our sufferings, because we know that suffering produces perseverance; perseverance, character; and character, hope." The hope spoken of in
Romans 5 is much more than keeping our fingers crossed and wish-
ing for the best. It's a confident, joyful expectation.

While all of us want this God-given hope, very few of us get
excited about the process by which it is produced. There is a definite
progression here: suffering, when taken in the right spirit, will produce patient endurance. Over a period of time this persistent obedience to God produces character. And out of integrity of spirit
emerges hope.

We can't skip over any part of the process. One of the clearest
teachings in the New Testament is that God wants His children to grow
up to be strong disciples and not remain spiritual babies. He wants us
to be mature, godly people with staying power in our walk with Him.

*Lord, as You shape me into a fit vessel for Your use, help me
to realize that the pressure You put on me will make me
strong. Amen.*

To Ponder: When a clay pot emerges from the fire, it has beauty,
strength, and color not possible without the heat.

NURTURING YOUR NEW NATURE
Read Romans 6–8

*Therefore, since Christ suffered in his body, arm yourselves
also with the same attitude, because he who has suffered
in his body is done with sin. As a result, he does not live
the rest of his earthly life for evil human desires.*

1 PETER 4:1-2

In the book of Romans, the apostle Paul tells us about our two natures that war within us. And while it is true that the nature we feed will grow strong and dominate the other, we must be very realistic about the power of the old nature and its ability to rebound and gain control. It doesn't take much nourishment for the old nature of sin to revive and flourish again.

Some of the great foundational realities of Christian living are tucked away in Romans 6. In verses 12 and 13 we read: "Therefore do not let sin reign in your mortal body so that you obey its evil desires. Do not offer the parts of your body to sin, as instruments of wickedness, but rather offer yourselves to God, as those who have been brought from death to life."

Paul says that to go forward in spiritual growth, we must deal ruthlessly with sin in our lives. Paul calls us to feed the new nature and starve the old; to be dead to sin and alive to God, walking in newness of life. I know of no better way to do that than to begin each day with a quiet time of personal Bible reading and prayer. Without this time of reading, study, recommitment, and prayer, we cannot hope to provide the nourishment our souls need each day.

Yes, sin will remain with us, but it will no longer make the rules, chair the meetings, and command the army. It will not have its own way. Once we were powerless as the servants of sin, but, thank God, that is no longer the case.

Lord, today I will nourish the life of the Spirit within me by making choices that starve the old nature. Amen.

To Ponder: Which nature are you nourishing today?

MOTIVATING ONE ANOTHER
Read Hebrews 8–10

*I long to see you so that I may impart to you
some spiritual gift to make you strong.*

ROMANS 1:11

From time to time I'm asked what I've found to be the most important principles of Christian living. Of course, the answer could be approached from many angles, but when it comes to our daily walk of discipleship, I usually talk about three principles of living from Hebrews 10 that begin with the two words, "Let us."

First, there is Hebrews 10:22: "Let us draw near to God with a sincere heart in full assurance of faith." This has to do with our fellowship with God. We can call it quiet time, personal devotions, or whatever. The important thing is to set aside time each day to draw near to the Lord.

Verse 23 gives the second "Let us": "Let us hold unswervingly to the hope we profess." This deals with our outreach to the lost through personal witness. We are to hold the confession of our faith high like a banner, never growing silent, and never denying the Lord who has bought us for Himself.

Verse 24 gives the third principle: "Let us consider how we may spur one another on toward love and good deeds." We are to encourage and motivate each other in the Christian life. And, of course, one of the best ways to do that is to meet together regularly to worship God and get instruction from His Word.

The Christian life is personal, but it is not private. We are an interdependent body. And this call to be a spiritual motivator is given to all of us, not just the church leadership or full-time Christian worker.

*Lord, thank You for the encouragement You give me through
my brothers and sisters in Christ. Amen.*

To Ponder: Let us draw near to God; let us hold up our witness; let us encourage one another.

BUILDING UP THE CHURCH
Read 1 Corinthians 11–14

*To the church of God in Corinth, to those sanctified in Christ Jesus
and called to be holy, together with all those everywhere
who call on the name of our Lord Jesus Christ.*

1 CORINTHIANS 1:2

I had a friend who decided to paint his car, but about halfway through
he got busy with something else and didn't finish the job. Month after
month, there it stood, half green and half something else, looking terrible. A job half done.

Now, when you and I think of our involvement in the Great
Commission, we need to think of finishing the job. And that involves
two things—winning the lost and building up the saved. We want
those who turn to Christ to become strong, robust, dedicated, mature
disciples. We want to see them built up in the faith, so they can reach
out to others with the gospel and begin to build up those new ones
in the faith.

That is what Paul was pleading for in 1 Corinthians 14:12, where he
told the Christians in Corinth to "try to excel in gifts that build up the
church." It is imperative that you and I know how to help people grow
in their Christian lives. Why? Because if a person comes to Christ and
does not go on to become a mature disciple, the job is half done.

One of the most helpful things anyone ever did for me as a new
Christian was get me started in Scripture memory. It has become a
lifetime habit of memorizing God's Word. Over the years, I've started
scores of other people in Scripture memory. You see, that's how it
works. You take the things others have used to build you up, and you
use them to help others. That's the only way to fulfill the Great
Commission and keep it from being a job half done.

*Lord, show me how I can more effectively use my spiritual
gifts to build up others in the faith. Amen.*

To Ponder: Every Christian should be built up in the faith and
equipped to minister to others. How far are you in the building
process?

A CHEERFUL GIVER
Read 2 Corinthians 6–9

"I tell you the truth," he said, "this poor widow has put in more than all the others. All these people gave their gifts out of their wealth; but she out of her poverty put in all she had to live on."

LUKE 21:3-4

I spent several weeks in the African country of Liberia teaching at a small Bible college. The missionaries who oversaw the college told me of a tragedy several years before, when their house burned down and they lost everything they had. The day after the fire, a little African girl came to them with a pair of well-worn canvas sneakers and gave them to one of their daughters. They were the only shoes the African girl had, and she would likely never get another pair, but she came offering them freely, saying she wanted to help. The missionaries were overwhelmed by her sacrificial giving.

It reminded me of Paul's description of the Macedonian churches' response to the grace of God. Second Corinthians 8:2-4 says, "Out of the most severe trial, their overflowing joy and their extreme poverty welled up in rich generosity. For I testify that they gave as much as they were able, and even beyond their ability. Entirely on their own, they urgently pleaded with us for the privilege of sharing in this service to the saints."

Paul directs our attention to Jesus Christ as the great example of what it means to give: "For you know the grace of our Lord Jesus Christ, that though he was rich, yet for your sakes he became poor, so that you through his poverty might become rich" (verse 9). Paul went on to say that our sacrificial giving should be more than an emotional response on the spur of the moment. It should be thought through and done deliberately. Christian, if you have never done it, sit down and lay out a giving plan that honors the Lord in its sacrificial generosity.

Lord, everything I have comes from You. Guide me as I consider how to give to others out of my abundance. Amen.

To Ponder: If your giving practices were made known to Christians in other lands, would your example be a challenge and encouragement to them?

AFTER SALVATION
Read Philippians 1–4

You know, brothers, that our visit to you was not a failure.

1 THESSALONIANS 2:1

Dawson Trotman used to tell about picking up a hitchhiker who got into his car and promptly used the Lord's name in vain. As Dawson talked to this young man and explained the gospel to him, he felt they had met somewhere before. It turned out that one year before, Daws had led him in prayer to receive Jesus Christ. Here he was, a year later, with no evidence of the new life in Christ within him.

This bothered Dawson, and as he prayed about it and studied the Scriptures, he was convinced of the importance of follow-up in the life of every new believer.

One of the passages underlying Dawson's conviction was Philippians 2:14-16: "Do everything without complaining or arguing, so that you may become blameless and pure, children of God without fault in a crooked and depraved generation, in which you shine like stars in the universe as you hold out the word of life—in order that I may boast on the day of Christ that I did not run or labor for nothing."

How could Paul talk about running and laboring for nothing when, back in 1 Corinthians 15:58, he said that his labor was not in vain in the Lord? These Philippians had been converted to Christ and were part of the local church in Philippi. Then why on earth was Paul talking about laboring for nothing? Because he knew that the Great Commission of Jesus Christ could be fulfilled only if every Philippian believer grew to maturity and did his part.

To see someone come to Christ is only the beginning. Let us take the same attitude of responsibility toward new believers that Paul felt toward the Philippians.

Lord, give me a heart of love and a desire to help new believers to be built up in the faith. Amen.

To Ponder: Is there a younger believer you could help to grow?

295

THE ENEMY OF OUR SOULS
Read the book of Jude

Put on the full armor of God so that you can take your stand
against the devil's schemes.

EPHESIANS 6:11

The city of Colorado Springs, where I live, is the home of the United States Olympic Training Center. Athletes from all over the country come here to train for the Olympic Games. And by the looks on their faces, they're serious about it. They know they'll have to compete against the best athletes in the world.

In the book of Jude, I find a similar sense of reality about the competition. Jude issues a warning to believers that we face a dangerous enemy. And the word pictures Jude paints of Satan's followers are worthy of further study and consideration: He says they have gone the way of Cain and run greedily after the error of Balaam. He calls them clouds without rain; trees whose fruit withers; raging waves of the sea, foaming out their own shame; wandering stars for whom the blackness of darkness is reserved forever.

What does Jude tell us to do to prepare for this battle and gain the victory? "But you, dear friends, build yourselves up in your most holy faith and pray in the Holy Spirit. Keep yourselves in God's love as you wait for the mercy of our Lord Jesus Christ to bring you to eternal life" (Jude 20-21).

Friend, that's exactly what you and I need to do—continually build ourselves in the faith. We must guard our prayer times so that the pressures of daily living don't crowd them out.

As I observe the Olympic athletes running, bicycling, and training around town, I'm reminded of my need to keep myself spiritually fit. It's not a luxury, but a necessity for going head-to-head against a committed foe.

Lord, help me to live each day on the basis of Your Word and
what You've said I need to do to be spiritually fit. Amen.

To Ponder: Our enemy, Satan, is as real as if we could see him or touch him. We need to have a healthy respect for his subtle ways.

THE COST OF COMMITMENT
Read John 13–21

*Jesus took the Twelve aside and told them what was going to
happen to him. "We are going up to Jerusalem," he said, "and the
Son of Man will be betrayed. . . . They will condemn him to death
and will hand him over to the Gentiles, who will mock him and spit
on him, flag him and kill him. Three days later he will rise."*

MARK 10:32-34

A number of years ago, a young farmer in South Dakota felt God's call
to help people in the Third World. He believed his skill in agriculture
could improve their lives and open doors to share his faith in Christ
with them.

So God sent him into a very difficult and dangerous part of the
world. From the time he arrived, he identified himself with the people,
often living among them for months at a time in order to teach them
better techniques of farming and caring for their animals. He would
return from the bush sick and emaciated, but fulfilled in the knowledge
that he was doing what God had called him to do. Over the years, he has
become something of a legend among the people he serves.

I thought of him as I studied the twentieth chapter of John. After
Jesus was raised from the dead, He appeared to His disciples. And on
one occasion, as His disciples were gripped by doubt and fear—the
two great enemies of witness—Jesus did a strange thing. He showed
them His hands and His side, and spoke these words in John 20:21:
"Peace be with you! As the Father has sent me, I am sending you."

What was Jesus trying to get across by showing them His scars
from the cross? In effect, He was saying, "Men, this ministry is no bed
of roses. This is no stroll in the park. Following me may cost you your
life." To the apostles' credit, they did not turn back. They were captured by the vision of taking the good news of Jesus Christ to all the
world. I want to be that kind of person. Do you?

*Lord, free me from my fear and doubt as I see Your vision for
the world, and work with You in fulfilling it. Amen.*

To Ponder: There is personal cost for all who will follow Christ in daily
discipleship.

DOING WHAT COMES NATURALLY
Read Acts 8–9

Yet when I preach the gospel, I cannot boast, for I am compelled to preach. Woe to me if I do not preach the gospel!

1 CORINTHIANS 9:16

There is a saying in management circles that "people do not do what you expect but what you inspect." Today's passage of Scripture indicates this is not true of the personal witness of a motivated Christian. For some Christians, witnessing is reserved for the one night a week when they go out calling in the visitation program. They talk to people about Christ, but that's it for the week.

What a contrast with the report in Acts 8:4-5: "Those who had been scattered preached the word wherever they went. Philip went down to a city in Samaria and proclaimed the Christ there."

We find Philip in the city of Samaria, apparently alone, with no apostle looking over his shoulder, witnessing to the entire city. Later, in Acts 8:26, we find Philip out in the desert, responding to the Lord's prompting to catch up with an Ethiopian man in a chariot. The man was seeking the Lord, and Philip had the wonderful privilege of introducing him to Christ.

I believe the key to this kind of ongoing witness is found in the preceding chapters of Acts, where we see the apostles and other believers filled with the Holy Spirit, being unable to contain themselves when it came to talking about Christ. For them, witnessing was the natural thing to do.

When Christ fills our hearts and minds, we will naturally share Him. We don't need an external manager to inspect us in order to get us to perform. The motivation comes from within, from Jesus.

Lord, give me a vision for the lost so that my witness for You isn't a duty but the natural product of my relationship with You. Amen.

To Ponder: True witness for Christ is not coerced or forced; it is the overflow of a life of fellowship with the Savior.

THE LORD'S WORK
Read Acts 10–12

*We speak as men approved by God to be
entrusted with the gospel. We are not trying
to please men but God, who tests our hearts.*

1 THESSALONIANS 2:4

Can you imagine a farmer "trusting the Lord" for a good corn crop but never bothering to take the seed out of the storage bin and plant it? Although bringing life from the seed is the work of God, He expects the farmer to be involved in the process.

The same principle of cooperation is true of witnessing, and we see it clearly in the book of Acts 2, when thousands responded to his message about salvation.

As I read of Peter's exploits, I say to myself, *What a man! What an outstanding example of Christian witness.* And it's true. Peter was truly a mighty man of God. But the last verse of Acts 2 puts it all back into perspective: "And the Lord added to their number daily those who were being saved." Although the fruit of witness is the result of the Holy Spirit's work, the Lord uses people to accomplish it.

Remember the story of Cornelius the centurion? "One day at about three in the afternoon he had a vision. He distinctly saw an angel of God, who came to him and said, 'Cornelius! . . . Your prayers and gifts to the poor have come up as a memorial offering before God. Now send men to Joppa to bring back a man named Simon who is called Peter'" (Acts 10:3-5).

Why didn't the angel just say, "Believe on the Lord Jesus Christ, and you will be saved?" Why send someone to Joppa to find Simon Peter? Because God uses people, not angels, as His witnesses to Christ.

Christian, what a privilege we have to cooperate with God in telling others of His salvation in Christ.

Lord, thank You for the privilege I have to join You in Your work. Amen.

To Ponder: The *fruit* of our witness is up to the Lord.

THIS ONE THING I DO
Read Colossians 1–4

To this end I labor, struggling with all his energy,
which so powerfully works in me.

COLOSSIANS 1:29

The apostle Paul is remembered for many things: He was a great Bible teacher, a brilliant theologian, and a church planter par excellence. But all these things were an outgrowth of the primary focus of his life: "We proclaim [Christ], admonishing and teaching everyone with all wisdom, so that we may present everyone perfect in Christ. To this end I labor, struggling with all his energy, which so powerfully works in me" (Colossians 1:28-29).

When we observe the life of Paul, we don't see a man who meandered through life saying, "These forty things I dabble at." Instead, we see a man of focus who said, "This one thing I do."

We never see Paul losing his passion and excitement for his goal. Notice how he speaks of his work of bringing people to Christ and building them up in the faith. The word he uses for labor is *kopiao,* which means to work until you are ready to drop. Then he uses the word *agonizomai,* which means to strive, to struggle, to agonize. But he speaks of doing the work through God's energy.

Christian, what about you? Does the prospect of walking with Christ and serving Him start your day with excitement and anticipation? You don't have to be an evangelist or a missionary. All it takes is a clear focus on the person of Jesus Christ and what He has called you to do in your family, your job, your life. Why not give yourself to the task of winning people to Christ and helping them grow to their full maturity in Christ.

Lord, may my walk be consistent through Your energy and power. Amen.

To Ponder: The focus of your life determines how you go through each day.

A BOLD WITNESS
Read 1 Thessalonians 1

I am not ashamed of the gospel, because it is the power of God for the salvation of everyone who believes: first for the Jew, then for the Gentile.

ROMANS 1:16

There is no evidence of timidity on the part of the Christians from Thessalonica. The gospel message did not tiptoe from their lips, nor was it whispered in the hope no one would hear. Having received the gospel, these people entertained no thought of keeping it to themselves. By word and deed they made it known to others. They followed the example of Paul, with a burning zeal that prompted them to proclaim what God had done for them. In 1 Thessalonians 1:5-9, Paul describes his ministry in that city. "Our gospel came to you not simply with words, but also with power, with the Holy Spirit and with deep conviction. You know how we lived among you for your sake. You became imitators of us and of the Lord; in spite of severe suffering, you welcomed the message with the joy given by the Holy Spirit. And so you became a model to all the believers in Macedonia and Achaia . . . your faith in God has become known everywhere. Therefore we do not need to say anything about it."

Paul was speaking of the gospel that came to them, and ultimately sounded out from them to all of Greece. The words *sounded out* are best described as the rumble of a tremendous thunderclap that reverberates long after its initial burst of sound. It pictures a bold, straightforward, continuing witness.

Friend, the message of the gospel of Christ, boldly proclaimed, can burst like thunder from your life today. And by the power of God, it will keep on rolling.

Lord, give me a fresh vision of who I am, and gift me to tell others that You have called me out of darkness into Your marvelous light. Amen.

To Ponder: If God has shed His love abroad in your heart, you will want to proclaim Him to everyone.

REPRODUCING YOURSELF
Read 2 Timothy 2

*Where there is no revelation, the people cast off
restraint; but blessed is he who keeps the law.*

PROVERBS 29:18

There are many meanings of the word *vision*. For instance, vision can
mean the object of imagination. But vision also can mean unusual
discernment or foresight. Based on that, a visionary is a person who
has a picture of what can happen in the future and is working hard to
bring it about.

Dawson Trotman's vision was to see God use the ordinary child of
God to make an impact in the lives of others. What made his vision
powerful was that he was living proof it could be done. He wasn't a
theologian or a scholar; he was a truck driver. And yet he was instrumental in bringing literally thousands of people to Christ and seeing
them grow as disciples.

The heart of Daws' vision came from a man who lived twenty centuries before him—the apostle Paul—and is stated in 2 Timothy 2:2:
"And the things you have heard me say in the presence of many witnesses entrust to reliable men who will also be qualified to teach others." Paul's vision was that every person who knew Christ would tell
others how to come to Christ. And then they would stick with their
new converts to teach them the basics of living the Christian life. The
result was a plan to multiply generations of Christians who would
keep sharing the faith with others.

The Great Commission of Christ is a vision that continues to capture the hearts and lives of men and women around the world. Do you
have the vision? God wants to open your eyes to see the people
around you as they are, and as they can be in Him.

Lord, let me see the world through Your eyes. Amen.

To Ponder: The Great Commission is a purpose big enough to capture your entire life.

TILL ALL HAVE HEARD
Read Revelation 7–9

*Through him and for his name's sake, we received grace
and apostleship to call people from among all the Gentiles
to the obedience that comes from faith. And you also are
among those who are called to belong to Jesus Christ.*

ROMANS 1:5-6

In 1983, I was privileged to attend the International Conference for Itinerant Evangelists in Amsterdam, Holland. That week of study, fellowship, and worship with thousands of traveling evangelists from around the world was an experience I will never forget.

Most of the delegates had been won to Christ by devoted messengers of the Cross, who left their homelands and brought their families to disease-ridden locales among suspicious, even hostile, people throughout Africa, Asia, Latin America, India, and China. Many of their converts became missionaries to their own people and to those in other countries around the world. Seeing those people in Amsterdam, united in Christ, was like a preview of heaven.

In Revelation 7:9-10, the apostle John gives us a glimpse of a magnificent event in the future: "I looked and there before me was a great multitude that no one could count, from every nation, tribe, people and language, standing before the throne and in front of the Lamb. They were wearing white robes and were holding palm branches in their hands. And they cried out in a loud voice: 'Salvation belongs to our God, who sits on the throne, and to the Lamb.'"

What a picture! Here are the fruits of the labors of consecrated men and women of God. But, Christian, the work isn't done. What contribution are you making to world evangelization? Have you prayed about going for a short-term mission or for an extended time? Your skill may open a door to an effective ministry.

Lord, use me in whatever way You choose, to bring people to Yourself. Amen.

To Ponder: The Lord is searching for people who will be willing to do whatever He requires for the Great Commission—to give, to pray, or to go.

UNSELFISH LEADING
Read Judges 9–12

This is how we know what love is: Jesus Christ laid down his life for us. And we ought to lay down our lives for our brothers.

1 JOHN 3:16

I suppose anyone who has read the first eight chapters of the book of Judges could guess what takes place after the death of Gideon. The people turned from following the Lord. But the punishment that followed was not inflicted by some nation who invaded the land from without, but from trouble within caused by a selfish leader.

In Judges 9, we learn of the tyranny of Abimelech, who gained power by committing murder. God had not called him to a position of leadership. His carnal ambition and lust for power were his only call. He surrounded himself with a group of scoundrels who hastened his downfall.

History gives us examples of leaders of nations in our own century who have milked the economy instead of building it, stolen from the people and sent the money to the proverbial Swiss bank account. When things begin to crumble economically and politically, the leader gets in his private jet and flees to another country where he lives in comfort.

The lesson for us is clear. A selfish leader can bring untold grief to people under him. This holds true in a family, a church, an organization, or a nation. What kind of spiritual leadership opportunity is God giving you today? It could be in your family, your church, or with a small group of people hungry to grow in their Christian faith. Whatever the opportunity, accept it as a call from God, step out in faith, and seek His grace to be an unselfish leader. The Lord is waiting to do great things through you.

Lord, help me to focus my leadership energy on goals that benefit Your kingdom. Amen.

To Ponder: Am I guilty of selfish leadership in the responsibilities God has given me?

A UNITED EFFORT
Read Nehemiah 3–4

May the favor of the Lord our God rest upon us; establish the work of our hands for us—yes, establish the work of our hands.

PSALM 90:17

I was sitting aboard a 747 preparing to take off for Seoul, Korea. Out the window I could see mechanics making last-minute inspections. The officers in the cockpit were going through their checklist. The flight attendants were helping everyone get settled. The baggage handlers were getting our suitcases on board. The people in the tower were busy preparing our take-off clearance. It was a huge, unified effort.

That's what we see in Nehemiah, chapters 3 and 4. It took each man doing his own part to build the wall of Jerusalem. But it also took the vision and motivation of leaders throughout the project to stir up the people and help them jump into the job with enthusiasm.

Nehemiah 3:1 says that "the high priest and his fellow priests went to work and rebuilt the Sheep Gate." Imagine that! Holy priests doing common labor! But verse 5 mentions a section of the wall repaired by the men of Tekoa, whose nobles "would not put their shoulders to the work under their supervisors."

My wife and I were having dinner with some long-time friends of ours, along with two young men. Just before dessert, one young man excused himself and went to the kitchen to help clean up. The other young man just sat there. He was a graduate of one of our service academies, but he had flunked the test of true leadership.

Even the King of kings, Jesus Christ, did not come to be served, but to serve (Matthew 20:28). Service takes many forms, some highly visible and some behind the scenes. But each type is essential for the work of God.

Lord, keep me from thinking I'm above the lowly tasks that come my way. Amen.

To Ponder: There is multiplicity in Christ's kingdom; to promote someone else's welfare is to be a good leader.

A LEADER'S CHARACTER
Read Isaiah 31–35

Be shepherds of God's flock that is under your care,
serving as overseers—not because you must, but because
you are willing, as God wants you to be; not greedy
for money, but eager to serve; not lording it over
those entrusted to you, but being examples to the flock.

1 PETER 5:2-3

Books and articles about leadership written by secular writers often differ from biblical principles. All too often, those who teach leadership are concerned primarily with style. Should the leader simply make the decisions and carry them out, or should he consult with the people to get their input before he acts?

The most important issue in leadership is character. It has always seemed to me that leadership style depends on the circumstances. For instance, I like the idea of consulting with people and receiving their wisdom on the subject. Why do solo thinking when one has a whole group of skilled people to draw from? On the other hand, if I'm in an airplane and the cockpit is filling with smoke, the landing gear is stuck, and an engine is out, I don't want the captain coming back to the passenger section and asking my opinion about what to do. I want him to muster all his expertise, to recall all his training, and to get that airplane safely on the ground. I want him in total control and not asking advice from anybody.

So when the Bible deals with the subject of leadership, it doesn't dwell on the style of the leader, but on the character of the leader. Notice the words of the prophet in Isaiah 32:1: "See, a king will reign in righteousness and rulers will rule with justice." The leader's daily walk of righteousness is fundamental. Now look at Isaiah 32:17: "The fruit of righteousness will be peace; the effect of righteousness will be quietness and confidence forever."

Lord, help me to walk in Your righteousness, so that when I
lead, I can do it with quietness and confidence.

To Ponder: In leadership, character is the bottom line.

LOVE MEANS LISTENING
Read Jeremiah 33:1-11

After the reading from the Law and the Prophets, the synagogue rulers sent word to them, saying, "Brothers, if you have a message of encouragement for the people, please speak." Standing up, Paul motioned with his hand and said: "Men of Israel and you Gentiles who worship God, listen to me!"

ACTS 13:15-16

How do you feel when you make a phone call, and a recorded voice answers and asks you to leave a message at the sound of the beep? Or when your phone conversation is interrupted by call waiting, and your party asks you to hold while he sees if this call is more important than yours?

What we really want is to have someone listen to us as if they care. You know what I mean. You call long-distance to the Apex Washer, Dryer, and Ironing Board Company. You call and call, and finally get through. An operator says, "Hold, please." After a long wait, the operator comes on the line again and says, "May I help you?" So you tell the person you'd like to speak to Mr. Green. "Who's calling?" You give your name. "Hold, please." Finally you get Mr. Green's office. "May I speak to Mr. Green?"

"I'm sorry, he's away from his desk. May I take a message?"

Sound familiar? Think about that in light of God's remarkable promise in Jeremiah 33:3: "Call to me and I will answer you." No hold buttons. No busy signals. Never an interruption by someone more important than you. You have His attention every day, all day, day and night. Because God loves you, He pays attention to you. He listens when you talk to Him.

Friend, that's the example for us with our families. When your child calls, answer. When your spouse wants to talk after you're home from work, talk. And listen! It takes such little effort, and it pays such big dividends.

Lord, thank You for inviting me to talk to You about everything. Give me keen ears to hear Your response. Amen.

To Ponder: God's ear is always open to the person who seeks Him.

OPEN TERRITORY
Read Ezekiel 16–19

He said to them, "Go into all the world and
preach the good news to all creation."

MARK 16:15

Do you have anyone in your church who seems territorial about his or her ministry? This person may be in charge of the kitchen or the choir robes or the nursery or the Sunday school. If someone comes along with a suggestion for improvement, the person in charge blows up. It reminds me of the poster of the great big gorilla who says, "If I want any advice from you, I'll beat it out of you."

In light of that, consider Ezekiel 16:1-3: "The word of the LORD came to me: Son of man, confront Jerusalem with her detestable practices and say, 'This is what the Sovereign LORD says to Jerusalem. . . .'" Ezekiel had been called by God to minister among the captives in Babylon. His older contemporary, the prophet Jeremiah, was left to preach to those in Jerusalem. Was Ezekiel trying to move in on Jeremiah's territory here? No. God was using His messengers among His scattered people, wherever they were.

In the New Testament, we find Paul, the apostle to the Gentiles, winning people to Christ in a synagogue in Greece. We find Peter, the apostle to the Jews, sharing Christ with a Roman centurion named Cornelius.

In the task of proclaiming God's message, there are no territorial lines, and all of us need all the help we can get. I was speaking in a church where the pastor is a godly man with a very successful long-term ministry. His only territory was the harvest field of God, and he was open to everything he could learn from others. Christian, let's labor together, because we can't do it alone!

Lord, keep me from staking out my "turf" at church, and
strengthen me in my desire to quietly serve others. Amen.

To Ponder: Our service in the church is to build up the believers, to the glory of God. Our ministry to the world is to cooperate with our fellow believers in spreading the gospel, to the glory of God.

LOVE WITHOUT LIMIT
Read Jonah 3–4

*"This is to my Father's glory, that you bear much fruit,
showing yourselves to be my disciples."*

JOHN 15:8

I know a man who was the pastor of a church in the South when he and his wife began to feel that God was calling them to Africa. They came up with the usual reasons why they shouldn't go: They were too old—he was forty-five; they had too many children—seven. And yet, two facts kept coming back to their hearts: Those without Christ were really lost, and the Great Commission still stands. So they went, and faced some rather tough years.

They left their beautiful home for a bamboo hut in the jungle. Their health and the health of their children were threatened by parasites and tropical diseases. They found themselves walking for miles through steaming heat, crossing treacherous rivers in dugout canoes, sleeping in rat-infested native huts. They watched in helplessness as a young mother brought her newborn baby, convulsing in the early stages of tetanus, because an old grandmother had rubbed country medicine—a mixture of dirt, leaves, and cow manure—into the baby's navel. They had to stand by and watch as a young girl drank the deadly poison of sassa wood to prove she was not a witch.

As this family stayed on and related in love to their lost and ignorant world, they began to see fruit. The lostness of these people had brought them to Africa, and Christ's love sustained them through the hard times.

This is not a love that casually says, "Be ye warmed and filled," but a love characterized by sacrifice—a Christ-inspired and God-given love that knows no limits.

*Lord, increase my faith and strengthen my discipleship.
Amen.*

To Ponder: If Christ has called us to a labor, it is of eternal consequence.

COMING IN GLORY
Read Zechariah 9–11

God exalted him . . . that at the name of Jesus every knee
should bow, in heaven and on earth and under the earth,
and every tongue confess that Jesus Christ is Lord,
to the glory of God the Father.

PHILIPPIANS 2:9,10-11

Zechariah gives us two starkly contrasting pictures of the Lord Jesus Christ. The first comes from Zechariah 9:9: "Rejoice greatly, O Daughter of Zion! Shout, Daughter of Jerusalem! See, your king comes to you, righteous and having salvation, gentle and riding on a donkey, on a colt, the foal of a donkey."

When I was a kid, I read Flash Gordon comic books. His archenemy was Ming the merciless. Ming had piercing eyes, lips that curled in a sneer, a coat that sparkled, and shoulders that stuck way out. He was the picture of power and authority.

One would think God would look something like Ming the merciless—dazzling clothing, huge shoulders, piercing eyes, an imposing, frightening figure. But no! God lay in a manger, wrapped in swaddling clothes. And when He entered Jerusalem at the height of His public ministry, He entered on a donkey, the animal symbolizing servanthood.

On the heels of this picture in Zechariah, we have the second portrait in chapter 9, verses 10-11: "He will proclaim peace to the nations. His rule will extend from sea to sea and from the River to the ends of the earth. As for you, because of the blood of my covenant with you, I will free your prisoners from the waterless pit."

Here we see the King of kings and Lord of lords making His entrance into this world as its deliverer and ruler. He is the absolute ruler of the kingdom of God.

Two beautiful pictures of the same wonderful Lord.

Lord, I can't comprehend the vastness of Your love, but I bow before You in gratitude to be the recipient of it. Amen.

To Ponder: Jesus is the King to whom all power has been given in heaven and on earth.

IN THE LIGHT
Read Acts 24–26

For God, who said, "Let light shine out of darkness,"
made his light shine in our hearts to give us the light of the
knowledge of the glory of God in the face of Christ.

2 CORINTHIANS 4:6

I heard about an automobile dealer who attended a weekend Christian conference for men. Even though the man was a church member, he wasn't particularly interested in the things of the Lord. He came as a favor to the friend who invited him.

During the weekend, something happened to this man. He had never heard the message of Christ explained in such a clear way before, and somewhere during that weekend—to put it in his own words—"The light went on." He went away from the conference a changed man. He has a hunger for the Word now and has begun to memorize key portions. He's studying the Bible with a group of other men, and he has begun to witness to his business associates and friends.

His story reminds me of the testimony of Paul as he stood before King Agrippa. On the road to Damascus, the light went on for Paul, and he was never the same. The Lord gave him a mission to help others see the light as well. Christ had appeared to him for a purpose: to go to the Gentiles and pass along the message that would open their eyes and turn them from the power of Satan to God.

In Acts 26:19, Paul said, "So then, King Agrippa, I was not disobedient to the vision from heaven." Paul's words carry the sense of a continuing change—"not once have I been disobedient to the heavenly vision." For Paul, that day marked a change in lifestyle, a change of purpose, and a divine call.

Lord, I love Your light. Help me to continue to walk with You today. Amen.

To Ponder: Once you have seen the light, you can never be content unless you are walking in daily fellowship with Christ and sharing His love with others.

311

PREPARED TO TESTIFY
Read Acts 27–28

*"Repentance and forgiveness of sins will be preached
in his name to all nations, beginning at Jerusalem.
You are witnesses of these things."*

LUKE 24:47-48

I remember when someone first taught me how to prepare my Christian testimony. I was told to sit down with a sheet of paper and a pen, and write my recollections from three areas of my life: my lifestyle before I came to Christ; how I came to Christ; and something of my life after I came to Christ.

I began to think and write, and finally I was ready to boil it down to three minutes, giving equal time to each part. Ever since then, I've had many fascinating opportunities to share my testimony.

In Acts 28, we find Paul giving his testimony over and over again while he is under house arrest, awaiting trial before Caesar in Rome: "They . . . came in even larger numbers to the place where he was staying. From morning till evening he explained and declared to them the kingdom of God and tried to convince them about Jesus from the law of Moses and from the Prophets" (Acts 28:23). No doubt, as Paul reasoned with them from the Law, he gave them his personal testimony as well, trying to persuade them to turn to Christ in repentance and faith.

One of the things that made the apostle Paul so powerful was the fact that his life had a focus, like an arrow heading straight for the center of the target. His mission in life was to be a messenger of the gospel, and he gave himself to it.

Christian, are you prepared to witness for Christ?

Lord, by your Spirit, may I always be able to tell how grateful I am to be saved by Your grace. Amen.

To Ponder: If someone gave you three minutes to tell them about your Christian faith, could you present the whole gospel in a clear, cohesive way in that amount of time?

GOD'S GREAT MERCY
Read Jonah 1–4

*The Pharisee stood up and prayed about himself: "God, I
thank you that I am not like other men—robbers,
evildoers, adulterers—or even like this tax collector."*

LUKE 18:11

When God told Jonah to go to the great and wicked city of Nineveh
and preach to the people, Jonah headed in the opposite direction. Why
did he do that? Jonah 4:2 says, "That is why I was so quick to flee to
Tarshish. I knew that you are a gracious and compassionate God, slow
to anger and abounding in love, a God who relents from sending
calamity."

It seems that if Jonah had believed God was going to be harsh and
unmerciful, he would have been delighted to go to Nineveh and
preach. Jonah wanted this bloodthirsty nation to get what he thought
it deserved. But God's mercy extended far beyond the borders of Israel,
and Jonah knew it!

I was in a church once where all the people had a similar heritage
and shared the same theological persuasion. They had a very comfortable fellowship, a good preacher, and everything was great. Then
their pastor heard Dawson Trotman speak on the need to reach out
to the lost. He began urging people to invite nonChristians into their
homes and into the church to win them to Christ, but they were too
wrapped up with "enjoying the Lord" inside their own congregation.

Christian, are you afraid God wants to use you in the lives of
people you think deserve judgment? Afraid God wants you to show
kindness where you would rather show resentment and spite? As we
have received forgiveness in Christ, let us become His messengers of
mercy to others.

Lord, keep me from being self-centered. Amen.

To Ponder: Our resistance to being equipped to witness grieves the
Holy Spirit.

THE REFLECTION OF YOUR SOUL
Read Mark 10:17-31

"No one can serve two masters. Either he will hate the one and love the other, or he will be devoted to the one and despise the other. You cannot serve both God and Money."

MATTHEW 6:24

My wife, Virginia, and I were in southern California, where I had been asked to speak at a military base. We were housed in a building overlooking the Pacific Ocean, and Virginia was sitting in front of the large bay window, watching the breakers roll in. "LeRoy," she called, "look at this! When the sky is blue, the water is blue. And when the sky is gray, the water is gray." I watched the water for a while and saw the same thing.

It was a good example of what happens in our lives, that is, *whatever dominates our thoughts will be reflected in our lives.*

A classic example of this is found in the story of the rich young ruler in Mark 10. We are told that Jesus loved him, but said, "One thing you lack. Go, sell everything you have and give to the poor, and you will have treasure in heaven. Then come, follow me" (10:21).

That young man took a careful look at Jesus, a careful look at his large pile of trinkets, and he turned his back on Jesus. He went over to his stock of baubles, sat down in the middle of them, and played with them for the rest of his life! Like the cloud over the ocean, his riches dominated him, so his life simply reflected what was on his mind.

Christian, follow Christ, and His beauty—not the things of this world—will be reflected in your life.

Lord, I want to live with eternity in view. Help me to seek only You and give the things of this world their proper place in my life. Amen.

To Ponder: What would people say dominates your mind, based on observation of your life?

A BURNING MESSAGE
Read Romans 1–3

But now a righteousness from God, apart from law,
has been made known. . . . This righteousness from
God comes through faith in Jesus Christ to all who believe.
There is no difference, for all have sinned and fall short
of the glory of God, and are justified freely by his grace
through the redemption that came by Christ Jesus.

ROMANS 3:21-24

To find the secret behind the dynamic quality of the apostle Paul's life, look at Romans 1. Here we find three "I am" statements that reveal the heart of this man of God.

In Romans 1:14, Paul says, "I am obligated both to Greeks and nonGreeks, both to the wise and the foolish." Paul felt he had a debt to the world, not just to a select few, to tell them about the saving grace of Jesus Christ.

In verse 15, the apostle says, "I am so eager to preach the gospel also to you who are at Rome." The Greek word translated here as *eager* has the idea of "burning up." This is a strange thing when you consider that Paul was a Jew, and Romans hated Jews. He was small and frail, and Romans admired strength. He was not a powerful orator, and Rome was full of them.

The third "I am" is in verse 16: "I am not ashamed of the gospel, because it is the power of God for the salvation of everyone who believes: first for the Jew, then for the Gentile." Paul had a burning desire to share the gospel, because he was not trusting in his natural abilities nor was he deterred by the lack of them. His confidence was in God and in the message of the gospel.

If you can say from your heart, like Paul, "I am a debtor; I am eager; I am not ashamed," the Lord will use you in a remarkable way.

Lord, I am willing to be molded into a workman who need not be ashamed. Amen.

To Ponder: The most important factor in being used by God is not our natural abilities, but our desire.

I'VE GOT GREAT NEWS!
Read Romans 5:1-11

They preached the good news in that city
and won a large number of disciples.

ACTS 14:21

I have seen men and women who are normally the life of the party—able to hold their own and discuss practically anything—clam up and hide quietly in the corner when an opportunity to present the gospel came along.

Maybe you're like that. If so, let me ask you a question. Has hearing the gospel ever turned a person into a drunk or gotten him on drugs? Has the gospel turned good people bad? Has the gospel turned people from love to hate? Take a few minutes and make a list of all the good things the gospel does, and in another column list all the bad things the gospel does. I guarantee you'll find one of your lists quite long and the other list nonexistent.

The word *gospel* means good news. But the way we hesitate to share the message of the gospel would make a person think it was bad news. Consider the words of the announcement made by the angel to the shepherds, regarding the coming of Christ into the world: "Fear not: for, behold, I bring you good tidings of great joy, which shall be to all people."

Did you catch those words? The angels spoke of good tidings of great joy. That's why the message must be proclaimed among all nations, to every creature—especially to those who live in your neighborhood, work with you in the same office, play racquetball with you, sit beside you in a college classroom.

Wherever you live, work, or play, people need to hear the "good tidings of great joy." A Savior is born! The gospel of Christ is good news!

Lord, You are my light and my salvation, and I will express to others my joy in You. Amen.

To Ponder: Failure to speak words that edify grieves the Holy Spirit.

WE ARE VICTORS
Read Revelation 10–13

But thanks be to God, who always leads us in triumphal procession in Christ and through us spreads everywhere the fragrance of the knowledge of him.

2 CORINTHIANS 2:14

Throughout the book of Revelation, the apostle John reminds us that, spiritually, we face a real and powerful enemy. Satan is called by a number of different names: the beast, the dragon, and Apollyon, which means destroyer. As we think about the fact of a supernatural enemy bent on our destruction, trying every means at his disposal to destroy our lives and witness, it could cause us to live in fear and admit defeat. But the overwhelming tone of Scripture is one of victory.

In Revelation 12:10-11, we read: "Now have come the salvation and the power and the kingdom of our God, and the authority of his Christ. For the accuser of our brothers, who accuses them before our God day and night, has been hurled down. They overcame him by the blood of the Lamb and by the word of their testimony."

Is it possible for us to overcome the enemy on a daily basis? The ministry of Dr. Bob Cook, past president of the National Religious Broadcasters, has always been one filled with new insights from Scripture. When I asked him how he managed to remain vital for so many years, he told me he tries to keep on the offensive, to keep digging in the Word. When the Lord reveals something to him, he freely shares it with someone who needs a word of encouragement. "It's like shooting a shotgun," he said. "When you pull the trigger, there's a kick that comes your way as well."

To overcome the enemy, we trust in the blood of Christ and share our testimony with others. God will use it to help others and to strengthen us.

Lord, I rejoice in Your victory over Satan that not only has defeated him for eternity in the heavenly realms, but also defeats him in my daily life. Amen.

To Ponder: Every time I share the love and faithfulness of God with someone, I affirm His love and mercy in my own life as well.

SALT-BLOCK CHRISTIANS
Read Revelation 20–22

*"In the same way, let your light shine before men, that they may
see your good deeds and praise your Father in heaven."*

MATTHEW 5:16

In the final paragraph of Revelation, John records these words of Jesus
Christ: "The Spirit and the bride say, 'Come!' And let him who hears
say, 'Come!' Whoever is thirsty, let him come; and whoever wishes,
let him take the free gift of the water of life" (22:17). Here is a three-
fold invitation given by the Holy Spirit speaking through the Word of
God; by the bride of Christ, His church; and by those who have
already responded to Christ. To whom is this invitation given? To all
who are thirsty.

When I was a kid growing up in Iowa, my dad would scatter large
blocks of salt in the pasture where the milk cows grazed. Apparently,
these cows needed salt that was not in their grain and hay. Shortly
after the cow went to the salt lick, she would head for the water tank.
And that is exactly what Jesus Christ wants for His people. If we are
salt in the world, the way we live and the words we say should make
the nonChristians around us thirsty for God.

I recall a family who wanted to lead one of their friends to Christ.
They did all the usual things, even taking him to hear the gospel
preached. One week they invited the guy over for dinner. The family
did nothing special, just went about as they normally did. The kids
were friendly and talkative at the meal, the father led in a prayer of
thanksgiving for the food, the kids helped with the dishes, did their
homework, and scurried off to bed.

Later that week, the man called and said he had become a
Christian. The way the family lived had convinced him of his need for
Christ.

*Lord, help me to be salt in the world, creating thirst for the
Living Water. Amen.*

To Ponder: My home, my lifestyle, and my responses to the difficulties of life affect how nonChristians perceive their need for Christ.

AUTHOR

LeRoy Eims is director of Public Ministry for The Navigators. Over the years, LeRoy has served The Navigators in a variety of positions, including deputy president, director of U.S. Ministries, U.S. director of Western Division, and International Ministry representative.

LeRoy travels widely in the United States and in many foreign countries. He is in demand as a conference speaker in seminaries and churches, as well as for Christian Life conferences and denominational groups.

For many years LeRoy has had a vital interest in winning people to Christ and teaching others how to evangelize and make disciples. His books reflect this commitment: *Be the Leader You Were Meant to Be, Be a Motivational Leader,* and *The Lost Art of Disciplemaking.*